ALASKA
Travel Guide

2025

Step-By-Step Road Trips, Cruise Stop Recommendations, and Adventure Planning for Every Explorer

SOPHIA GLACIER

DISCLAIMER

This book is provided for informational and entertainment purposes only. While every effort has been made to ensure the accuracy of the information presented, the author, publisher, and distributors make no guarantees or warranties, express or implied, regarding the completeness, reliability, or accuracy of the content. Information may become outdated, change without notice, or vary based on circumstances, local regulations, and environmental conditions.

Travel at Your Own Risk: The recommendations, travel tips, itineraries, and activities described in this guide involve inherent risks, including but not limited to weather conditions, wildlife encounters, road and trail conditions, transportation disruptions, natural hazards, personal safety concerns, and physical exertion. The author and publisher are not responsible for any injuries, losses, damages, accidents, legal issues, or other consequences that may arise from following any information or suggestions contained in this book. Travelers should use their own judgment, conduct independent research, and follow all local laws, guidelines, and safety advisories before engaging in any travel activities.

No Professional Advice: This guide does not provide medical, legal, financial, or safety advice. It is not a substitute for professional guidance from trained experts, including tour operators, government agencies, health professionals, or law enforcement authorities. Travelers should consult with appropriate professionals before making decisions related to health, travel insurance, visa requirements, emergency preparedness, or adventure activities.

Third-Party Services and External Links: This book may reference third-party businesses, tour operators, accommodations, transportation services, websites, and government agencies for convenience. The author and publisher do not own, operate, endorse, or control any of these entities and are not liable for their actions, policies, reliability, service quality, pricing, safety standards, or availability. Any transactions, bookings, or interactions with these third parties are made at the reader's own risk, and readers are encouraged to conduct their own due diligence.

Environmental and Cultural Responsibility: Travelers are encouraged to respect the environment, wildlife, and local cultures by following responsible travel practices, local regulations, and ethical guidelines. The author and publisher do not take responsibility for any reader's actions that may violate environmental laws, cultural sensitivities, or ethical considerations.

Copyright Notice: All content in this book, including text, layout, and design, is protected by copyright law. No part of this publication may be reproduced, stored, or transmitted in any form, including digital, print, or audio, without prior written permission from the author or publisher. Unauthorized reproduction or distribution may result in legal action.

Final Acknowledgment: By reading this book and using its information, you acknowledge that you assume full responsibility for your travel choices, personal safety, and any risks associated with your trip. The author, publisher, and affiliates cannot be held liable for any outcomes related to the use of this guide.

If you require official travel advice, legal guidance, or safety information, consult with the appropriate government agencies, embassies, licensed tour operators, and professional advisors before planning your trip.

Contents

INTRODUCTION	10
PLANNING	13
2.1 Geography and Climate	13
2.2 When to Visit	15
2.3 Travel Documents and Requirements	16
2.4 Budgeting	17
2.5 What to Pack	18
GETTING AROUND	21
3.1 Transportation	21
3.2 The Alaska Marine Highway System	22
3.3 The Alaska Railroad	23
3.4 Driving in Alaska	24
ANCHORAGE	27
4.1 Visit Anchorage	27
4.1.1 Downtown Anchorage	28
4.1.2 Anchorage Museum at Rasmuson Center	29
4.1.3 Tony Knowles Coastal Trail	31
4.1.4 Alaska Native Heritage Center	32
4.2 Food and Dining in Anchorage	33
4.2.1 Seafood Specialties	34
4.2.2 Local Breweries and Pubs	35
4.2.3 International Cuisine	36
4.3 Accommodation in Anchorage	37
4.4 Getting Around Anchorage	38
4.5 Day Trips from Anchorage	40
4.5.1 Girdwood and Alyeska Resort	41
4.5.2 Portage Glacier	43
4.5.3 Wildlife Conservation Center	44
5.1 Discover Fairbanks	46
5.2 Key Attractions in Fairbanks	47
5.2.1 Chena Hot Springs Resort	47
5.2.2 Aurora Borealis Viewing	48
5.2.3 Morris Thompson Cultural and Visitors Center	50
5.2.4 University of Alaska Museum of the North	51
5.3 Dining in Fairbanks	52
5.4 Accommodation in Fairbanks	53
5.5 Getting Around	54
5.6 Adventures Beyond Fairbanks	56
5.6.1 Dalton Highway to the Arctic Circle	56

5.6.2 Riverboat Discovery Cruise 57
5.6.3 Pioneer Park 58
JUNEAU **61**
6.1 Why Visit Juneau? 61
6.2 Key Attractions 62
6.2.1 Mendenhall Glacier and Ice Caves 62
6.2.2 Mount Roberts Tramway 63
6.2.3 Whale Watching Tours 65
6.3 Exploring Downtown Juneau 66
6.4 Dining in Juneau 68
6.5 Accommodation 69
6.6 Getting Around 70
6.7 Outdoor Activities in Juneau 71
6.7.1 Hiking Trails 71
6.7.2 Kayaking and Canoeing 73
6.7.3 Glacier Gardens Rainforest Adventure 74
7.1 Introduction 77
7.2 Getting to the city 78
7.3 National Park 79
7.3.1 Park Road and Shuttle Buses 79
7.3.2 Wildlife Viewing 81
7.3.3 Visitor Centers 83
7.3.4 Sled Dog Kennels 84
7.4 Hiking 85
7.4.1 Easy Trails 85
7.4.2 Moderate to Challenging Hikes 87
7.4.3 Backcountry Camping 88
7.5 Accommodation near Denali 89
7.5.1 Campgrounds 89
7.5.2 Lodges and Hotels 91
7.6 Dining 92
Seward **95**
8.1 Introduction 95
8.2 Getting to Seward 96
8.3 Visiting 97
8.3.1 Alaska SeaLife Center 97
8.3.2 Downtown Seward 98
8.3.3 Seward Boat Harbor 99
8.4 Outdoor Adventures in Seward 100
8.4.1 Kenai Fjords National Park 100
8.4.2 Exit Glacier and Harding Icefield Trail 102
8.4.3 Boat Tours and Cruises 103

8.4.4 Kayaking and Fishing 104
8.5 Dining in Seward 105
8.6 Accommodation in Seward 106
8.7 The Scenic Seward Highway 107
   8.7.1 Points of Interest Along the Way 107
   8.7.2 Driving Tips and Recommendations 108
   8.7.3 Wildlife Viewing Opportunities 109

Homer 111
9.1 Discover Homer 111
9.2 Getting to Homer 112
9.3 Exploring Homer 113
   9.3.1 Homer Spit 113
   9.3.2 Pratt Museum 115
   9.3.3 Art Galleries and Local Crafts 116
   9.3.4 Alaska Islands and Ocean Visitor Center 117
9.4 Outdoor Activities in Homer 118
   9.4.1 Fishing Charters 118
   9.4.2 Kachemak Bay State Park 120
   9.4.3 Bear Viewing Tours 122
9.5 Dining in Homer 123
9.6 Accommodation in Homer 124

Ketchikan 127
10.1 Discover Homer 127
10.2 Getting to Ketchikan 128
10.3 Exploring 129
   10.3.2 Totem Heritage Center 130
   10.3.3 Southeast Alaska Discovery Center 131
   10.3.4 Saxman Native Village 133
10.4 Outdoor Activities in Ketchikan 134
   10.4.1 Fishing 134
   10.4.2 Hiking Trails 135
   10.4.3 Misty Fjords National Monument 136
10.5 Dining in Ketchikan 138
10.6 Accommodation in Ketchikan 139

Sitka 141
11.1 Unique Heritage 141
11.2 Getting to Sitka 142
   11.3.2 National Historical Park 143
   11.3.2.1 St. Michael's Cathedral 144
   11.3.3 Russian Bishop's House 145
   11.3.4 Sheldon Jackson Museum 147
11.4 Outdoor Activities in Sitka 148

11.4.1 Whale Watching Tours 148
11.4.2 Hiking on Baranof Island 149
11.4.3 Kayaking and Wildlife Viewing 150
11.5 Dining in Sitka 151
11.6 Accommodation 152

Valdez 155

12.1 Introduction 155
12.2 Getting to Valdez 156
12.3 What to visit 157
12.3.1 Valdez Museum and Historical Archive 157
12.3.2 Old Town Valdez 158
12.3.3 Maxine & Jesse Whitney Museum 159
12.4 Outdoor Adventures 160
12.4.1 Prince William Sound 160
12.4.2 Worthington Glacier 161
12.4.3 Keystone Canyon 162
12.5 Dining 163
12.6 Accommodation 165

Skagway 167

13.1 Historical Overview 167
13.2 Getting to Skagway 168
13.3 Exploring 169
13.3.1 White Pass & Yukon Route Railway 169
13.3.2 Klondike Gold Rush National Historical Park 170
13.3.3 Historic Downtown 171
13.3.4 Red Onion Saloon Brothel Museum 172
13.4 Outdoor Activities 174
13.4.1 Hiking Trails 174
13.4.2 Dog Sledding Tours 175
13.4.3 Glacier Tours 176
13.5 Dining 177
13.6 Accommodation 178

Haines 181

14.1 Introduction 181
14.2 Getting to Haines 182
14.3 Exploring Haines 183
14.3.1 American Bald Eagle Foundation Museum 183
14.3.2 Sheldon Museum and Cultural Center 184
14.3.3 Hammer Museum 185
14.4 Outdoor Activities in Haines 187
14.4.1 Chilkoot Lake State Recreation Site 187
14.4.2 Hiking and Biking Trails 188

14.4.3 River Rafting and Kayaking..........189
14.5 Dining in Haines..........190
14.6 Accommodation in Haines..........192
Kodiak – The Emerald Isle..........194
15.1 Introduction to Kodiak..........194
15.2 Flying – The Fastest Option..........195
Taking the Ferry..........196
Getting In and Best Ways to Travel..........197
Best Times to Visit..........198
15.3.1 Fort Abercrombie State Historical Park..........199
15.3.2 Alutiiq Museum..........200
15.4 Outdoor Activities in Kodiak..........201
15.4.1 Fishing and Hunting..........201
15.4.2 Kayaking and Boating..........202
15.5 Dining in Kodiak..........203
15.6 Accommodation..........204
Wrangell-St. Elias National Park and Nearby Towns..........206
16.1 Overview of Wrangell-St. Elias National Park..........206
16.2 Getting to the Park..........206
16.2.1 Kennecott Mines National Historic Landmark..........207
16.2.2 Hiking and Backpacking..........209
16.2.3 Glacier Tours..........210
16.3 Nearby Towns..........211
16.3.1 McCarthy..........211
16.3.2 Chitina..........212
Nome – On the Edge of the Bering Sea..........214
17.1 Discovering Nome..........214
17.2 Getting to Nome..........215
17.3 Exploring Nome..........216
17.3.1 Gold Rush History..........216
17.3.2 Bering Land Bridge National Preserve..........217
17.3.3 Iditarod Trail Sled Dog Race Finish..........218
17.4 Outdoor Activities in Nome..........219
17.4.1 Bird Watching..........219
17.4.2 Dog Sledding..........220
17.4.3 Beachcombing for Gold..........221
17.5 Dining and Accommodation in Nome..........222
Bethel and the Yukon-Kuskokwim Delta..........224
18.1 Introduction to Bethel..........224
18.2 Getting to Bethel..........224
18.3.1 Cultural Centers..........225
18.3.2 Kuskokwim River..........226

18.4.1 Wildlife Viewing ... 227
18.4.2 Fishing and Boating ... 228
18.4.3 Birding in the Delta ... 229

The Arctic Circle and Northern Alaska ... 230

19.1 Utqiagvik (Barrow) ... 230
19.1.1 Introduction to Utqiagvik ... 230
19.1.2 Getting There ... 230
19.1.3 Exploring Utqiagvik ... 231
19.1.4 Arctic Ocean Access ... 233
19.2.1 Oil Fields and Tundra Tours ... 234
19.2.2 Dalton Highway Adventure ... 235
19.2.3 Wildlife Viewing ... 236

Practical Travel Tips ... 238

20.1 Wildlife Safety ... 238
20.2 Health and Safety ... 239
Cold, Wind, and Hypothermia ... 239
Heat and Dehydration ... 240
Altitude Sickness ... 240
First Aid and Medical Help ... 240
Travel Insurance and Evacuation ... 240
Medications and Prescriptions ... 241

20.3 Communication and Connectivity ... 241
Cell Service and Where It Works ... 241
Wi-Fi and Internet Reality ... 242
Navigation and Battery Life ... 242
Satellite Phones and Emergency Devices ... 242
Plan for No Service ... 243

20.4 Local Customs and Etiquette ... 243
20.5 Responsible Travel ... 244
20.6 Emergency Preparedness ... 245

Sample Itineraries ... 248

21.1 3-Day Itineraries ... 248
21.1.1 Anchorage and Surroundings ... 248
Day 2: Scenic Drive to Girdwood and Outdoor Adventure ... 249
Day 3: Hiking and Glacier Views ... 249
21.1.2 Juneau Explorer ... 250
Day 1: Glaciers, Scenic Views, and Local Flavor ... 250
Day 2: Whale Watching and Gold Rush History ... 250
Day 3: Outdoor Adventure and Hidden Gems ... 251

21.2 7-Day Itineraries ... 252
21.2.1 Southcentral Alaska Highlights ... 252
Day 1: Arrive in Anchorage and Explore the City ... 252
Day 2: Drive to Seward (125 miles, 2.5 hours) ... 253

Day 3: Kenai Fjords National Park – Glacier and Wildlife Boat Tour 253
Day 4: Drive to Homer (170 miles, 4 hours) 254
Day 5: Homer – Fishing or Bear Viewing 254
Day 6: Drive Back North to Girdwood (225 miles, 4.5 hours) 254
Day 7: Return to Anchorage (40 miles, 45 minutes) 254
21.2.2 Inside Passage Adventure 255
Day 1: Arrive in Juneau and Explore the Capital 255
Day 2: Mendenhall Glacier and Whale Watching 255
Day 3: Ferry to Sitka (4.5-hour ride, Alaska Marine Highway System) 256
Day 4: Explore Sitka – Wildlife and Russian Heritage 256
Day 5: Ferry to Ketchikan (11-hour overnight ferry ride) 257
Day 6: Explore Ketchikan – Totem Poles and Rainforest Walks 257
Day 7: Fly Home from Ketchikan 257

Faq 259
1. General Questions 259
Why should I visit Alaska in 2025? 259
How do I use this travel guide? 259
2. Planning Your Trip 259
What's the best time to visit Alaska? 259
Do I need a passport or visa to visit Alaska? 259
How much does a trip to Alaska cost? 260
What should I pack? 260
3. Transportation in Alaska 260
What's the best way to get around Alaska? 260
Can I drive in Alaska? 261
How do I take the Alaska Marine Highway ferry? 261
4. Wildlife and Safety 261
Is Alaska safe for travelers? 261
Can I see the northern lights? 261
5. Destinations & Experiences 262
What are the top must-visit places in Alaska? 262
What are the best hiking trails in Alaska? 262
Where can I go for the best fishing? 262
6. Practical Tips 263
Will I have cell service and internet in Alaska? 263
What's the best way to book tours and excursions? 263
Is tipping expected in Alaska? 263
What's the best way to budget for an Alaskan trip? 263

Conclusion 264

INTRODUCTION

Alaska is the biggest state in the U.S., covering **663,268 square miles**, which is more than **Texas, California, and Montana combined**. Even though it's massive, not many people live here—just about **730,000 people**, mostly in **Anchorage, Fairbanks, and Juneau**, while the rest are spread across small towns and villages, some of which you can only reach by **boat or plane**.

Alaska got its name from the **Aleut word "Alyeska"**, meaning **"great land"**, and that's exactly what it is—a place of **huge mountains, giant glaciers, and wide-open spaces**. For thousands of years, **Indigenous peoples** like the **Iñupiat, Yup'ik, Athabaskans, and Tlingit** have lived here, surviving off the land and the sea. The **Russians came in the 1700s for fur trading**, but the U.S. bought the land in **1867 for $7.2 million**—which seemed like a bad deal at the time. That changed when **gold was discovered in the late 1800s**, bringing thousands of prospectors and settlers who built some of the towns and roads that still exist today.

The weather here is **extreme**. Winters can be **brutal**, with **months of darkness, freezing temperatures, and heavy snow**, especially in the **far north**. Summers are the opposite—**long, sunny days** where the sun barely sets. In some places, it shines **24 hours a day** for weeks. The best time to visit depends on what you want to do—**summer is great for hiking, fishing, and wildlife, while winter is best for Northern Lights, dog sledding, and snow sports.**

Every year, more than **2 million people visit Alaska**, and most come between **May and September**. Many arrive on **cruise ships**, stopping in places like **Juneau, Ketchikan, and Skagway**, while others **fly into Anchorage or Fairbanks** to explore on their own. Visitors spend an average of **$1,700 per trip**, but it depends on the kind of trip—**some people camp and explore on a budget, while others book luxury lodges, helicopter tours, and high-end fishing trips.**

If you've seen photos of **bears catching salmon, glaciers crashing into the ocean, and the Northern Lights filling the sky**, you might wonder if Alaska is really like that. The answer is **yes**, but only if you go to the **right places at the right times**. Summers bring **wildflowers, whales, and endless daylight**, while winters bring **snow-covered landscapes and the magic of the Aurora Borealis**. Some areas are remote and untouched, while others have **modern cities, restaurants, and shopping centers**.

This guide will help you figure out **where to go, how to get there, and what to expect**, so you can plan an **unforgettable trip without stress or confusion**. Whether you're here for **a quick cruise stop, a road trip, or a full adventure into the wild**, this book gives you all the important details—**transportation, accommodations, food, must-see attractions, hidden gems, and budget tips**—so you don't waste time or money.

Let's get started.

EVERYTHING YOU NEED. NOTHING YOU DON'T

CHAPTER ONE
PLANNING

2.1 Geography and Climate

This place is huge, and it feels like five different worlds. Each region is so different that where you go really depends on what you want to do. Let me break it down so it's simple.

The **Southeast**, or Inside Passage, is all about rain, green forests,

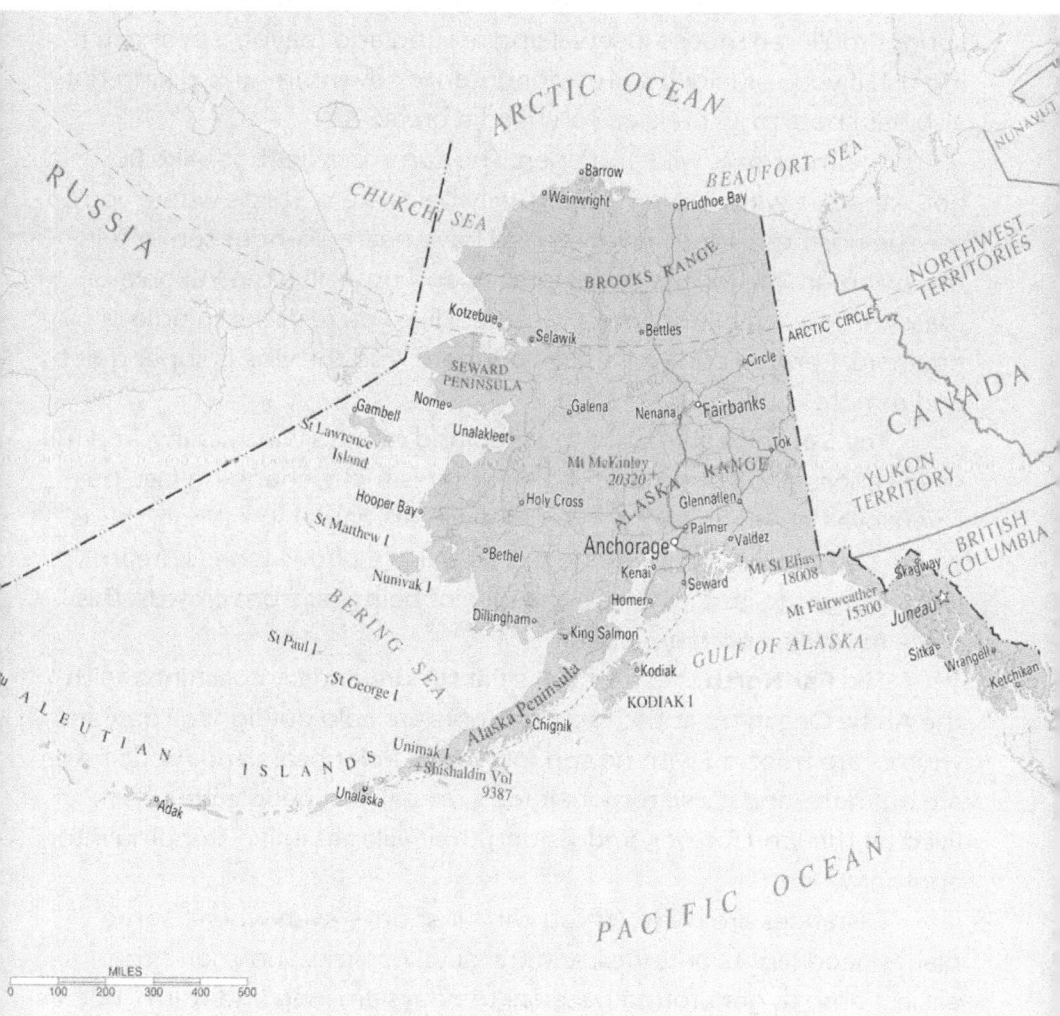

ALASKA ACTION PLAN

and water. It's cool in the summer, doesn't get super cold in the winter, but it rains a lot. This is where you'll see whales, sea lions, and otters everywhere. It's perfect if you want to kayak, hike in lush forests, or see those giant glaciers that drop into the ocean. The land shoots straight up into steep mountains, so it feels dramatic and wild, but it's also full of Native culture, like totem poles and small villages.

The **Southcentral area** is like a mix of everything. There are mountains, valleys, and a ton of glaciers. Summers are nice and mild, maybe around 60°F, but it can rain on the coast. This is where people come to fish for salmon and halibut or just sit back and soak in a hot spring. You'll see moose just walking around and maybe a bear catching fish if you're lucky. It's great for outdoor adventures like hiking but also has spots to just relax if you need a break.

The **Interior** is wild and open. The summers get hot—like 80°F hot—and the winters are freezing, way below zero. This is where you'll see the northern lights in winter and have nearly 24-hour sunlight in the summer. The forests go on forever, and rivers like the Yukon are massive. You can hike, camp, or just feel like you're in the middle of nowhere. Caribou and wolves live out here, and the vibe is super quiet and remote.

The **Southwest** feels untouched and raw. It's windy, rainy, and full of volcanoes and flat tundra. The weather is tricky, changing fast, but if you love fishing or want to see grizzly bears catching salmon, this is where you go. Birds migrate here, so it's also a birdwatcher's dream. It's harder to get to, but if you like the idea of being far from crowds, this place feels like another planet.

The **Far North** is extreme. It's flat tundra and icy coastlines, with the Arctic Ocean up at the top. Summers are cold but light all day, and winters are freezing with no sun for weeks. Polar bears and Arctic foxes are out here, and it's so remote it feels unreal. The people here have lived off the land forever, and visiting their villages is like stepping into another world.

Distances are huge, so you can't just drive everywhere. Some places need flights or ferries, and travel takes time. Summer is the easiest time to get around because the days are long and warm, but it's also crowded.

2.2 When to Visit

Summer (June to August) is the easiest time to visit because the days are long, with sunlight lasting almost 20 hours in most places. The weather is warm, around 60–70°F, but mornings and nights can still feel cold, so bring layers. This is the best time for hiking because trails are clear of snow, and everything is green with blooming flowers. Wildlife is everywhere—bears fish by the rivers, moose wander in open areas, and salmon fill the streams. You can also see whales on boat tours or go fishing for salmon and halibut. Summer is crowded, so book your flights, hotels, and tours early.

Fall (September to October) is quieter because there are fewer tourists. The weather is cooler, with highs of 40–50°F and frosty nights. Trees turn red and yellow, making the views incredible, especially for photos. Bears are still active, feeding near rivers, and this is one of the best times to see the northern lights because the skies are darker. Daylight hours get shorter as it gets closer to winter, so start your hikes and outdoor activities earlier in the day. Pack warm clothes because it feels much colder than summer, especially at night.

Winter (November to March) is cold and snowy, but it's the best time to see the northern lights if you're in a dark, remote area. Days are short, with only 4-6 hours of light, but the nights are long and great for aurora viewing. The cold is serious—temperatures in the Interior drop to -40°F, while coastal areas are around 20-30°F. This is the season for dog sledding, snowmobiling, ice fishing, and skiing. You'll need proper winter clothes like insulated boots, thick jackets, gloves, and hats. Roads can be icy, so plan ahead if you're driving.

Spring (April to May) feels like a mix of winter and summer. Snow starts melting, rivers swell, and wildlife wakes up—bears come out of hibernation, and birds return. Temperatures range from 30°F in the morning to 50°F during the day, so pack for all kinds of weather. There are fewer people around, which makes it a good time for a quieter visit. Trails might still have snow or mud, so hiking can be tricky in some places. You'll get a mix of peaceful landscapes and changing weather.

For **hiking**, summer is the best. For **wildlife**, come in spring or early summer when animals are active. To see **northern lights**, visit from late fall through winter when the skies are dark. Each season has something unique, but the right time depends on what you want to do.

2.3 Travel Documents and Requirements

You need a **valid photo ID** if you're a U.S. citizen traveling to Alaska, like a state driver's license or a passport. If you're flying, make sure your ID is TSA-approved, especially if your state requires REAL ID compliance. If you're not from the U.S., you'll need a **passport** to enter, and depending on where you're from, you might also need a **visa or an ESTA** (Electronic System for Travel Authorization) if you're from a visa-waiver country.

For people visiting from Canada and planning to drive, you'll need your **passport** to cross the border, and you might need a visa or eTA (Electronic Travel Authorization) depending on your nationality. If you're renting a car, bring your **driver's license**, and it's a good idea to carry an International Driving Permit if your license isn't in English.

Some areas, especially national parks or private lands, require **permits** for specific activities. For example, if you're planning to camp in remote areas or do backcountry hiking, you'll often need a special permit, which you can apply for through the park's website or visitor center. Always check these rules ahead of time because some permits are limited and must be reserved in advance. If you're visiting lands managed by Alaska Native corporations, you may need permission to access those areas.

Carry proof of any **medical insurance or travel insurance**, especially if you plan to visit remote areas where medical services are limited. Some remote tours or lodges may ask for proof of coverage in case of emergencies.

2.4 Budgeting

Staying here costs money, but you can plan smart and save. Hotels and lodges are expensive in summer because everyone comes here. If you want to spend less, stay in motels, hostels, or campgrounds. Camping is cheap and gives you the best views, with tent spots and even basic cabins. Book your room or site early because things fill up fast, especially when it's busy.

Food can be pricey too, especially in smaller towns where everything has to be shipped in. Eating out every day at seafood places or restaurants gets expensive quickly, so if your place has a kitchen, buy groceries and cook for yourself. Local stores have snacks, fresh fish, and basic supplies, and it's way cheaper than eating out all the time. Bring snacks with you if you're driving long distances—gas station food costs more and doesn't taste great.

Getting around isn't cheap either. Flights between towns cost a lot, and renting a car can be pricey, especially for big SUVs or 4x4s. Gas costs more than what you're probably used to, especially in smaller places. Stick to one area if you want to save, or split rental and gas costs with friends. Ferries are a good option for getting between coastal spots, but they add up too, so plan carefully. Public buses are rare, so renting or driving is your best bet.

Activities like tours and cruises are the most expensive things. Whale watching, glacier tours, and fishing charters are amazing but cost a lot, so pick the ones you care about most. If you're on a tight budget, do free stuff like hiking trails, wildlife watching, or visiting state parks, which usually cost little or nothing. You can spend hours hiking trails with incredible views for no extra cost.

2.5 What to Pack

You need to pack the right stuff because the weather here changes fast. **Bring layers you can add or take off easily.** For summer, wear a t-shirt as your base, add a warm sweater or fleece for mornings and evenings, and always carry a waterproof jacket. Rain shows up even on sunny days, so don't skip the jacket. If it's winter, pack thick thermal underwear, a heavy jacket with good insulation, gloves, a hat, and a scarf to keep warm. **Windproof clothes are key** because even if it's not too cold, the wind makes it feel worse.

Shoes matter a lot. Hiking boots with good grip and ankle support are necessary if you're hitting the trails—mud, rocks, and slippery spots are everywhere. If you're kayaking or walking near water, get water-resistant shoes that stay on your feet. For winter, insulated snow boots will keep your feet warm and dry, and they work well on icy paths too.

Keep your feet and hands warm no matter what. Wool socks are the best because they stay warm even if they get wet, unlike cotton. Always bring gloves, even in summer, because cold mornings or handling wet gear can freeze your fingers. A warm hat that covers your ears is a must because it makes a big difference when it's windy or cold.

You'll need some extras to stay comfortable. A small backpack is great for carrying water, snacks, and extra layers while you're out. Bring sunscreen because the sun reflects off snow and water, and it can burn you even on cold days. For bug-heavy areas in summer, don't forget bug spray. Sunglasses help with glare, especially near glaciers or water.

If you're doing activities like hiking or kayaking, pack the right gear. For hikes, trekking poles help with balance on tough trails, and a rain cover for your backpack keeps everything dry. For kayaking, wear quick-drying clothes and pack a waterproof bag for your phone or camera. Fishing? You'll need gloves and polarized sunglasses to see better in the water.

Safety stuff is simple but important. A flashlight or headlamp is smart for dark mornings or evenings, especially in winter. A first-aid kit with band-aids and blister pads is helpful, and a portable charger keeps your phone working, which is important in case of emergencies. If you're going somewhere remote, a water bottle with a filter and a map or GPS is always a good idea.

Bring practical clothes that dry fast and are easy to layer. Don't pack heavy or bulky stuff you don't need. Stick to things that keep you warm, dry, and ready for anything, and you'll have a much better trip.

ALASKA ACTION PLAN

EVERYTHING YOU NEED. NOTHING YOU DON'T

CHAPTER THREE
GETTING AROUND

3.1 Transportation

If you want to get around fast, **flights are your best option**. Many towns don't even have roads connecting them, so planes are used like buses here. You'll probably fly out of Anchorage or Juneau, but smaller airlines use tiny planes to reach other places. **Book early because flights fill up fast, especially in summer,** and check baggage rules—these small planes have strict limits. Be ready for delays, though, because bad weather can mess with flight schedules.

Ferries are slower but really beautiful. They run along the coast and connect towns and islands. You can even take your car on most of them, which makes it easier to keep exploring when you arrive. The schedules are not super frequent, so you'll need to plan ahead. Some trips can take all day, so **pack snacks, water, and something to do.** The views are incredible, with mountains and water all around, and sometimes you'll spot whales or sea lions.

Trains only run on a few routes, but they're all about enjoying the views. They're not fast, but **if you want to sit back and see rivers, mountains, and wildlife through huge windows, this is a great choice.** Tickets sell out fast in summer, so book early. Trains work better for relaxing journeys than for getting somewhere quickly, so use them if you have time to enjoy the ride.

If you're driving, **rent a car as early as possible, especially in summer,** because cars sell out fast, and prices can get high. A 4x4 is a good idea if you're planning to drive on rough or gravel roads. Gas stations can be really far apart, so fill up whenever you can, especially before heading into remote areas. In winter, roads can get icy or snowy, so make sure your car has winter tires, and always check conditions before heading out. Keep a paper map with you because cell service doesn't work everywhere.

ALASKA ACTION PLAN

3.2 The Alaska Marine Highway System

The ferry system connects towns and islands along the coast and is one of the easiest ways to get around when there are no roads. It runs routes between places like Ketchikan, Juneau, Sitka, and even as far as Kodiak. If you're starting from the lower 48 states, you can board at Bellingham, Washington. **Book your tickets as early as possible, especially in summer,** because ferries get busy, and space for cars fills up fast. If you're bringing a car or RV, you need to include its size when you book. Prices depend on how far you're going and whether you're adding extras like cabins.

The terminals are easy to find. In Juneau, it's at Auke Bay, about 12 miles from downtown. You can take a taxi or a bus there, and buses stop near Main Street downtown. Ketchikan's terminal is just a short drive from its downtown too, and taxis or shuttles are available. If you're starting in Bellingham, the terminal is on Harris Avenue, and it's well-marked with signs.

On the ferry, the best spot is the observation deck. **You'll see mountains, forests, and sometimes whales or eagles while you're sailing.** Inside, there are big windows and plenty of seats, so you can relax and enjoy the views. There's usually a small cafeteria where you can buy simple meals like soup or sandwiches. Prices are fair, but if you want something specific, it's better to pack your own food because the options are limited.

EVERYTHING YOU NEED. NOTHING YOU DON'T

If your trip is long, there are cabins with beds and private bathrooms. Cabins cost extra and sell out fast, so book early if you want one. If you don't want to spend more, you can sleep in a reclining chair, pitch a tent on the deck if the weather's good, or even sleep in your car on some routes. Public showers are available on most ferries, which is great for overnight trips.

Ferry schedules depend on the route. Some run daily in summer, while others only go a few times a week, especially to less-visited places like Kodiak. Trips can take anywhere from a couple of hours to a full day. A trip from Juneau to Sitka takes around 10 hours, but a longer ride, like from Whittier to Kodiak, can take over 24 hours. Always check the schedule and plan ahead because missing your ferry can mean waiting days for the next one.

Before boarding, you'll often find places nearby to grab food or coffee. In Ketchikan, you can eat at The Alaska Fish House, about 10 minutes from the terminal, for fresh seafood. In Juneau, Tracy's King Crab Shack is a great spot downtown for crab legs and bisque before heading to the ferry terminal.

3.3 The Alaska Railroad

The Alaska Railroad gives you big windows, comfy seats, and some of the best views you'll ever see while traveling. The main trains run from Anchorage to Fairbanks and Seward. The Anchorage station is downtown on West 1st Avenue, easy to get to by bus, taxi, or a short walk if you're staying nearby. Trains usually leave in the morning and get you to your destination by late afternoon or evening, depending on the route. Schedules are set, so check ahead to plan your timing.

Booking tickets is simple. You can do it online, by phone, or at the station. **Buy your tickets early, especially in summer,** because seats sell out fast. You can choose basic tickets with big seats and great views or upgrade to dome cars for seats with panoramic glass roofs. Dome cars cost more, but they're worth it for the full experience.

Onboard, the train is super comfortable. Seats are wide with lots of legroom, and the windows are huge so you can see everything—mountains, rivers, forests, and maybe even wildlife like moose or bears.

Some trains have outdoor viewing platforms where you can step out for fresh air and take pictures. There's also a dining car that serves hot meals, snacks, and drinks. Food prices are reasonable, but if you want to save money or prefer your own food, you can bring snacks or meals onboard.

The trains are heated in winter and air-conditioned in summer, but it's smart to **bring layers like a jacket or sweater** because sitting near the windows can feel cool. Pack a camera or keep your phone charged because the views are amazing, and you'll want to take pictures. If your trip is long, bring headphones, a book, or something to keep you entertained.

3.4 Driving in Alaska

Driving here is the best way to visit because you can stop when you want and take in the views, but you need to be prepared. **The highways, like the George Parks Highway between Anchorage and Fairbanks or the Seward Highway to the coast, are easy to drive, smooth, and well-maintained.** But once you leave the main roads, you'll find gravel roads, bumpy patches, and places where you'll need to drive slower. As i told you before, If you're heading somewhere remote, rent a car that can handle tough roads—a 4x4 or an SUV is worth it for safety and comfort.

Rent your car early, especially in summer, because they sell out fast, and prices go up the longer you wait. Most rental spots are in Anchorage, Fairbanks, or at airports, which makes it easy to grab a car when you land. Check your rental before leaving—make sure it has a spare tire, a jack, and emergency tools. In winter, make sure the car has snow tires or chains, especially if you're driving on icy roads or through mountain passes.

Gas stations are far apart once you leave towns, so don't take chances. Fill up every time you see a station, even if your tank isn't empty, because the next one might not be for 100 miles or more. Some smaller stations only take cash, so have some with you just in case. Towns like Anchorage and Fairbanks have gas stations on main streets, like Northern Lights Boulevard in Anchorage or Cushman Street in Fairbanks, but once you head out, services get sparse.

You won't have cell service in many remote areas, so don't count on GPS to guide you. **Download maps before you leave or carry a paper map in case your phone loses signal.** It's smart to plan your route ahead of time and stick to it, especially in places where roads split off into gravel paths that can be confusing.

The scenery is incredible, but you need to pay attention. Wildlife is common near the roads, especially moose, which are huge and can be dangerous if they wander onto the road. Slow down if you see one and give it space. Night driving can be tricky because there aren't streetlights, and it's pitch black in rural areas, so take it slow and use high beams when it's safe.

CHAPTER FOUR
ANCHORAGE

4.1 Visit Anchorage

Anchorage has so much to do, and it's all close by, whether you want to check out cool museums, walk scenic trails, or learn about local culture. **Start with the Anchorage Museum at Rasmuson Center.** It's on 6th Avenue downtown and has a mix of history, art, and hands-on science exhibits. You'll see stuff like Alaska Native art and tools, plus modern displays about life here. There's also a planetarium where you can watch shows about the stars and northern lights. It's big, so plan a couple of hours if you want to explore it all.

If you like being outdoors, the **Tony Knowles Coastal Trail** is perfect. It starts near downtown and goes for 11 miles along the coast. You don't have to do the whole thing—just pick a section and enjoy the views. You'll see mountains, water, and maybe even a moose or bald eagle. The trail is great for walking, biking, or even skiing in the winter. The part near Kincaid Park has some of the best views and feels like you're far from the city.

Another great spot is the **Alaska Native Heritage Center**, a short drive from downtown. You'll see traditional houses built around a lake, and inside, there are displays about Native cultures. They have live performances like dancing and storytelling, and you can watch artists making crafts like beadwork and carvings. It's hands-on and really helps you understand the people who've lived here for thousands of years.

For wildlife, go to **Potter Marsh**, just south of the city along the Seward Highway. There's a long boardwalk where you can walk right into the marsh without disturbing it. It's quiet and beautiful, with birds, salmon in the water, and maybe even a moose nearby. It's free, easy to find, and a quick stop if you're heading out of town.

Don't miss **Earthquake Park**, a peaceful spot west of downtown where you can see what happened during the massive 1964 earthquake. There are trails and signs that explain how the land shifted, and you also get awesome views of the inlet. It's a quick visit but interesting and a nice mix of history and nature.

For food and local shops, head to **Fourth Avenue downtown.** Try a reindeer sausage from a street vendor or grab breakfast at **Snow City Café,** which is famous for dishes like salmon benedict. If you're visiting in the summer, the Anchorage Market is worth checking out. It has handmade crafts, snacks, and live music, all in one spot.

4.1.1 Downtown Anchorage

Downtown Anchorage is where everything feels close, simple, and lively, especially around **Fourth Avenue**, which is the main street where you'll find cool shops, good food, and interesting things to see. If you're staying nearby, you can just walk there. If not, the **People Mover buses** stop at the **Downtown Transit Center on 6th Avenue**, which is only a few minutes away from Fourth Avenue.

When you walk along Fourth Avenue, start with shopping because there are some fun spots. **Alaska Wild Berry Products**, right on the street, has awesome chocolates and jams that are locally made. Their chocolate-covered blueberries are really popular and cost about $10–$15, so they're great to snack on or take home. A little further down, you'll see **Once in a Blue Moose**, which is full of cute souvenirs, like T-shirts, mugs, and ornaments. Prices are usually between $10 and $50, depending on what you pick. For more options, check out **Grizzly's Gifts**—it's bigger and has everything from keychains to jackets with an Alaskan twist.

When you get hungry, you'll find plenty of spots close by. Try **Humpy's Great Alaskan Alehouse**, which is just off Fourth on 6th Avenue. It's famous for seafood dishes like halibut tacos or salmon chowder, and meals cost around $15–$25. If you're in the mood for something quick and local, grab a reindeer sausage from a street vendor near F Street. It's delicious, filling, and costs about $6–$8. You can eat it while you walk around and explore more.

If you like art, there's **Sevigny Studio** nearby on 5th Avenue, where you can check out local paintings and unique pieces inspired by Alaska's nature. For something even more special, stop at **Oomingmak Musk Ox Producers Co-op** on 6th Avenue and H Street, a short walk from Fourth. They sell handmade scarves and hats made from musk ox wool, which is super soft and warm. These are expensive—starting at $200—but they're one-of-a-kind and help support Native communities.

As you walk along, you'll notice small plaques and murals that tell stories about the area, especially how the city was rebuilt after the 1964 earthquake. If you need a break, head over to **Town Square Park** on 5th Avenue and E Street. It's a small park where you might catch local events or just relax, especially in summer when the weather is nice.

For coffee or a snack, go to **Dark Horse Coffee** on G Street, which is cozy and a few blocks from Fourth Avenue. Their coffee is locally roasted, and a cup costs around $5. Grab a pastry if you're hungry—they're fresh and perfect for an energy boost while you explore.

Downtown is super easy to walk around, and everything you need.

4.1.2 Anchorage Museum at Rasmuson Center

The **Anchorage Museum at Rasmuson Center**, located at **625 C Street** in downtown Anchorage, is a hub for art, history, and culture, offering an immersive look at the North. It's easily reachable by car or the **People Mover bus system**, with stops like the **Downtown Transit Center** nearby, just a short walk from the museum. If you're driving, parking is available on surrounding streets or in nearby public parking lots, making it convenient no matter where you're coming from.

The museum's **Alaska Exhibition** is a highlight, showcasing artifacts, photography, and stories that capture the state's history, diverse communities, and natural environment. You'll see everything from Native Alaskan tools and traditional clothing to pieces that reflect the state's role in modern history. The exhibition connects you to Alaska's past and present in a way that feels personal and engaging.

For a more interactive experience, the **Discovery Center** is packed with hands-on science exhibits that are perfect for visitors of all ages. You can explore topics like the northern lights, the Arctic ecosystem, and how science shapes daily life in the region. It's especially popular with families because the exhibits are both fun and educational.

The museum also features changing exhibits that bring something fresh to every visit. For example, large-scale art installations inspired by winter landscapes and an exhibit on humor and identity in Alaskan culture add layers to what you can experience. It's worth checking the museum's website before you go to see what's currently on display.

The museum's location in downtown Anchorage means you're surrounded by great spots to eat and explore before or after your visit. **Snow City Café**, just a few blocks away on L Street, is a local favorite for breakfast or lunch, offering dishes like salmon benedict or fluffy pancakes for around $15–$20. For something quicker, you can grab coffee and pastries at **Dark Horse Coffee** on G Street, just a short walk away, with most items under $10.

The museum's hours vary by season, with winter hours (October–April) running Tuesday to Saturday from 10 a.m. to 6 p.m., and Sunday from 12 p.m. to 6 p.m. On the first Friday of each month, it stays open until 9 p.m. Admission costs $25 for adults, $18 for seniors, students, and military personnel, and $12 for kids aged 6–12, while kids under 6 get in free. **If you're an Alaska resident, you'll pay $20, and if you visit on the third Thursday of the month between October and April, admission is just $5.**

The museum is built on the traditional homeland of the Dena'ina people, and this is acknowledged through exhibits and events that honor their culture and contributions. Walking through, you'll feel a deep connection to the history and resilience of the region.

When you leave, the area around the museum offers plenty to do, with local shops and small galleries nearby.

4.1.3 Tony Knowles Coastal Trail

The **Tony Knowles Coastal Trail** is one of the best ways to enjoy the outdoors here. It starts downtown near **Second Avenue and H Street** by Elderberry Park and stretches 11 miles all the way to **Kincaid Park**. The trail is smooth and paved, so you can walk, bike, run, or even rollerblade. It's easy to get to if you're downtown, but if you're not, you'll

need to drive or walk, as buses don't stop directly at the trailhead. If you have a car, parking is available at spots like **Westchester Lagoon**, about a mile into the trail.

The first part of the trail gives you incredible views of **Cook Inlet**, with mountains in the background. If it's a clear day, you might even see Denali far off in the distance. Along the way, keep an eye out for wildlife. Moose sometimes wander onto the trail, especially in the quieter sections, and if you're by the water, you might spot beluga whales during migration season.

About three miles in, you'll reach **Earthquake Park**, a really cool spot where you can learn about the 1964 earthquake that reshaped the land. There are signs explaining what happened and benches where you can take a break and look out at the coast. It's a peaceful place with a mix of history and nature.

Further along, around mile eight, you'll get to **Point Woronzof**, which is a must-stop for photos. The views here are wide open, with the inlet, mountains, and planes taking off and landing at the airport in the distance. It's especially beautiful at sunset, so if you're there later in the day, take some time to enjoy it.

The trail ends at **Kincaid Park**, where the path gets a bit steeper with slight hills. If you're biking, it's a fun workout, but it's also a good place to stop, rest, and take in the views. If you started downtown and don't want to bike or walk back, plan for someone to pick you up because it's a long way back—22 miles round trip.

If you didn't bring a bike, you can rent one at **Westchester Lagoon** for about $20–$40, depending on how long you need it. Bring water, snacks, and a jacket because the coastal breeze can get chilly, even on sunny days. If you get hungry after your trip, you're close to downtown, where you can grab something hearty, like pancakes or salmon benedict at **Snow City Café** on L Street for around $15–$20.

The trail is simple to follow, with plenty of benches and spots to stop along the way.

4.1.4 Alaska Native Heritage Center

The **Alaska Native Heritage Center**, at **8800 Heritage Center Drive**, is a short 15-minute drive from downtown, and it's where you can really learn about the cultures of Alaska's Native peoples. To get there, you'll need a car or a rideshare, since buses don't stop right at the center. There's lots of parking, so that's easy, and once you're there, everything is set up to explore at your own pace.

Inside the main building, you'll see exhibits filled with Native art, tools, and traditional clothing. **Workshops happen throughout the day**, where you can watch people make things like beadwork and carvings, and sometimes you can even join in. There are live performances, too—dances, drumming, and storytelling that show you the traditions passed down over generations. Check the schedule when you get there, so you don't miss any of these.

Outside, there's a big lake surrounded by full-size traditional houses from different Native groups like the Yupik and Inupiat. These aren't just models—they're real examples of how people lived, and there are guides at each one to explain everything. Walking around the lake feels peaceful, and it's cool to see how different groups adapted to Alaska's tough environment.

The best time to visit is in summer when all the activities and performances are running daily, but even in winter, there's plenty to see inside. Admission costs **$29 for adults**, **$25 for seniors**, and **$19 for kids**. If you're an Alaska resident, you'll pay less—**$14 for adults** and **$12 for kids**. After 4 p.m., tickets are half price, so that's a great option if you're looking to save some money.

There's no cafe at the center, but there are vending machines for quick snacks. If you're hungry after, head back downtown for a meal. **Snow City Café** on L Street has big, tasty meals like salmon benedict or pancakes, with dishes around $15–$20.

Plan to spend at least two hours here, maybe three if you want to see everything.

4.2 Food and Dining in Anchorage

The food scene here is all about fresh flavors and a mix of local and international choices. **Seafood is the star,** and it's super fresh because it's caught right nearby. You'll find wild salmon, halibut, shrimp, and king crab on menus everywhere. Salmon might be grilled, smoked, or in a creamy chowder that warms you up, and halibut is often served as crispy fish-and-chips or in soft tacos. King crab legs are served with melted butter and feel like a fancy treat, but they're so worth it. If you want something quick, grab a **reindeer sausage** from a food cart downtown—Fourth Avenue is a great place to find one.

If you're staying downtown, you can walk to most places. **Public buses stop near Town Square Park and Fifth Avenue Mall**, which are good starting points for exploring the food spots. Food trucks park near popular areas like **Town Square Park**, especially in summer, and they serve everything from tacos to Asian noodles. The trucks are casual and fast, making them perfect if you're out exploring and need a quick bite.

For something international, you've got a ton of choices. **Sushi spots often use local fish, like fresh salmon or halibut, in their rolls. Thai and Indian places sometimes include locally grown vegetables, and there's plenty of Italian and Mexican food scattered around town. These places are affordable, and meals usually cost about $15–$25. Check around Northern Lights Boulevard or Spenard Road if you're up for a bit of a food adventure.

If you like sweets, find a bakery or coffee shop offering **wild berry pies** made with blueberries, lingonberries, or salmonberries. These berries are picked locally, so they're super fresh and delicious. Pair a slice of pie with a locally roasted coffee at one of the shops near G Street downtown. Most drinks and pastries are around $5–$10, and it's a cozy way to take a break.

4.2.1 Seafood Specialties

If you're into seafood, this city is full of places serving some of the freshest dishes you'll ever eat. **Glacier Brewhouse**, right downtown at **737 West 5th Avenue**, is famous for its **Alder Grilled Salmon** that's smoky and tender, and their **Herb Crusted Halibut**, which has this perfect crunch on the outside and soft, flaky fish inside. Meals here cost about **$30 to $40**, and it's a spot where you know every bite will be worth it. You can walk there easily if you're staying downtown, or take the **People Mover bus to the Transit Center on 6th Avenue**, just a short walk away.

For a fancy night out with great views, head to **Crow's Nest** on the top floor of the Hotel Captain Cook at **939 West 5th Avenue**. Their **Resurrection Bay Black Cod** is buttery and flavorful, cooked to perfection, and they always have seasonal seafood specials that highlight local catches. It's pricey—expect to spend **$40 to $70 per dish**—but the combination of high-quality food and stunning views makes it a special experience.

If you want something more relaxed, check out **Humpy's Great Alaskan Alehouse** at **610 West 6th Avenue**, a short walk from anywhere downtown. Their **Halibut Fish and Chips** are crispy and golden, served with fries and tartar sauce, while their **Smoked Salmon Chowder** is creamy and full of flavor. Prices here are around **$15 to $25**, and the atmosphere is lively and fun, especially in the evenings.

For a quieter dining spot, **Kincaid Grill** on **6700 Jewel Lake Road** offers incredible seafood dishes in a more intimate setting. Their **Troll-Caught King Salmon** is rich, flaky, and paired with sides that perfectly complement the fish. It's a bit further from downtown, so you'll need to drive or take a cab, but the food is totally worth it. Expect to pay around **$35 to $50** per dish.

One place you shouldn't miss is **Bridge Seafood Restaurant** at **221 West Ship Creek Avenue**. The restaurant is literally built over a creek, so you can enjoy the view while you eat. They serve fresh dishes like **Tiger Prawns and Reindeer Sausage Skewers**, and their salmon and halibut plates let the natural flavors shine. Meals here cost **$25 to $40**, and the location near the **Ship Creek fishing area** adds to the charm.

4.2.2 Local Breweries and Pubs

If you love beer, the local breweries here are incredible. **Midnight Sun Brewing Company**, at **8111 Dimond Hook Drive**, is the oldest brewery in town and super popular for good reason. You'll want to drive or grab a rideshare since public buses don't stop close by, but there's plenty of parking when you get there. Their taproom is cozy, and you can see where all the beer magic happens while you enjoy a pint. Try their **Arctic Devil Barleywine**, which is rich and smooth, or the **Panty Peeler Tripel**, which has a light fruity and spicy kick. Pints cost about **$7 to $9**, and if you can't decide, order a flight to taste a few.

At **Anchorage Brewing Company**, located at **148 West 91st Avenue**, you'll find some of the most creative beers in town. They specialize in sours and barrel-aged beers that are bold and different. Their **A Deal With The Devil Barleywine** is strong, sweet, and unforgettable, while their sour beers, like the **Galaxy White IPA**, are tart and refreshing. It's sleek and modern inside, with a chill vibe that's great for focusing on the beer. Pours are a bit pricier at **$8 to $12**, but these beers are truly next-level. You'll need a car or rideshare to get here, but it's totally worth the trip.

If you're downtown, **49th State Brewing Company** at **717 West**

3rd Avenue is super easy to find. You can walk there from most hotels, or take the **People Mover bus** to a stop nearby. Their rooftop deck is awesome, with views of the mountains and water. The beer? Even better. Their **Solstice IPA** is crisp and refreshing without being too bitter, and their **Prospector's Gold Lager** is light and smooth. Pints run around **$6 to $9**, and the place is always lively, especially in the summer.

For a more modern vibe, **King Street Brewing Company** at **9050 King Street** is a fantastic spot. The taproom is bright and open, with big windows looking into the brewing area. Their **King Street Pilsner** is clean and crisp, great if you like something light, while their **Imperial Stout** is rich and chocolatey for when you're in the mood for something heavier. Pints cost **$7 to $10**, and there's usually a new experimental brew to try if you're feeling adventurous. Driving is the best way to get here, and parking is easy.

If you want a smaller, relaxed spot, head to **Turnagain Brewing** at **7920 King Street**, just down the road from King Street Brewing. They focus on sours and Belgian-style beers, so it's a little different from the others. Try the **Fjord Sour Ale**, which is tangy and fruity, or the **Dubbel Vision**, which is smooth with a touch of spice. Pints are affordable at **$6 to $8**, and the place feels friendly and chill, perfect for taking it easy.

4.2.3 International Cuisine

If you're looking for food that feels like traveling the world, there are some awesome spots here that serve international dishes packed with flavor. At **Queen of Sheba** on **2813 Dawson Street**, you can try Ethiopian food that's bold and unique. The **doro wat**, a spicy chicken stew, is amazing, and it comes with **injera**, this soft, tangy bread you use instead of a fork. They also have big vegetarian plates with lentils, greens, and spiced veggies. Meals are around **$12 to $20**, and it's easy to get there by car since parking is nearby. If you don't drive, just hop on the **People Mover Route 20**, which stops a short walk away.

For Indian and Nepalese dishes, **Yak & Yeti Himalayan Restaurant** at **3301 Spenard Road** is perfect. Their **butter chicken** is creamy and comforting, and the **momo dumplings** are full of flavor and come with a tasty dipping sauce. Everything is super filling, and prices are around **$10 to $18**, so it won't break the bank. Parking is easy if you're driving, or you can use the **People Mover Route 40**, which gets you close enough to walk in a few minutes.

If you're in the mood for Thai food, head to **Thai Orchid Restaurant** at **360 Boniface Parkway**. The **pad Thai** is sweet, savory, and has just the right amount of peanuts on top, while the **green curry** is creamy and has a nice spicy kick. Most dishes cost about **$11 to $16**, and the portions are big enough to share. There's parking if you're driving, or you can take the **People Mover Route 31**, which stops nearby.

If you want something modern and fancy, try **Crush Bistro**, which is right downtown at **343 West 6th Avenue**. They do fusion dishes, mixing flavors from all over the world. You might find **Korean tacos**, Mediterranean-inspired flatbreads, or even creative pasta dishes. It's a bit more expensive, with meals costing **$15 to $30**, but the food is always plated beautifully, and it's perfect for a special night out. You can walk there easily if you're staying downtown, or park in nearby lots, with the **Downtown Transit Center** just a block away.

4.3 Accommodation in Anchorage

There are plenty of places to stay here, and you'll definitely find something that works for you, whether you want luxury, something comfortable, or just a simple and cheap spot to crash.

If you're looking for a fancy place, **The Hotel Captain Cook** at **939 West 5th Avenue** is a top choice. The rooms are big, with amazing views of the mountains or the Cook Inlet. You've got restaurants inside, a pool, a spa, and even a fitness center. It's right downtown, so you can walk to the Anchorage Museum or other attractions in minutes. Rooms usually cost around **$300 per night**, and if you're driving, they've got parking. You can also use the **People Mover bus**, which stops nearby.

Another great luxury pick is **Sheraton Anchorage Hotel & Spa** at **401 East 6th Avenue**. It's quieter but still close to downtown. The rooms are modern, and they've got a spa where you can relax. Prices are a bit lower, around **$200 to $250 per night**, and you can walk to most places or grab a quick cab ride. There's parking if you're driving, and public buses stop nearby, too.

If you don't want to spend too much but still want something comfortable, **Hilton Anchorage** at **500 West 3rd Avenue** is a solid choice. It's right in the middle of downtown, so you can walk to shops, restaurants, or the museum. They've got a pool and a gym, and the rooms are clean and modern. Prices start at around **$200 to $250 per night**, and if you're not driving, the **People Mover bus stops** are really close.

For something a bit different, try **Marriott Anchorage Downtown** at **820 West 7th Avenue**. The rooms are nice, and the views are great, either of the city or the mountains. It costs about **$220 to $270 per night**, and it's perfect if you're walking around downtown. Parking is easy, too, if you've got a car.

If you're on a budget, **Base Camp Anchorage** at **1037 West 26th Avenue** is a cool, friendly hostel. You can stay in a dorm for about **$40** or get a private room for around **$70**. It's a little out of downtown, so you'll need a car or rideshare, but parking is free, and the vibe is super chill. They've even got a kitchen you can use.

Another cheap option is **Ingra House Hotel** at **641 Ingra Street**. It's simple, but it's clean, and it's good if you just need a place to sleep. Rooms are around **$60 to $80**, and there's a shared kitchen if you want to cook. You can drive there or take a bus—it's close to stops.

If you want something cozier, there are small lodges like **Copper Whale Inn** at **440 L Street**. It feels more like staying at someone's home, with cool touches like fireplaces and comfy rooms. It's close to the Tony Knowles Coastal Trail, and rooms cost around **$120 to $150**. It's easy to walk to nearby cafes or use a rideshare if you're heading further out.

Most of these places are near restaurants and shops, so it's easy to grab food or visit without going far.

4.4 Getting Around Anchorage

Getting around here is pretty easy once you figure out what works best for you. If you're going for something affordable and straightforward, the **People Mover buses** are your best bet. They run **from 6 AM to 10 PM**, and they cover all the main parts of the city like downtown, midtown, and shopping spots like **Dimond Center**. If you're heading to the airport, take **Route 40**, which follows **Spenard Road** straight there. For getting around downtown, **Route 10** is super handy—it stops at places like the **5th Avenue Mall**, the **Anchorage Museum**, and other central spots. A ride costs just **$2**, but if you're planning to hop on and off a lot, get a **day pass for $5**. Most bus stops are easy to spot, especially downtown, like at the **Downtown Transit Center on 6th Avenue**. Plus, the buses have racks if you're bringing a bike along.

If you need to get somewhere faster, taxis and rideshares like **Uber and Lyft** are everywhere. A quick ride downtown will cost you around **$10 to $15**, and a trip to the airport will usually run between **$20 and $30**. You can grab a taxi outside most big hotels, like **The Hotel Captain Cook** on **939 West 5th Avenue**, or near busy areas like **Town Square Park**. But honestly, using a rideshare app on your phone is quicker, and it's usually a bit cheaper too.

If you're staying for a few days or want to explore at your own pace, renting a car is the way to go. You'll find rental agencies like **Enterprise, Hertz, and Avis** at **Ted Stevens Anchorage International Airport** and downtown on streets like **5th Avenue**. Daily rates usually start around **$50 to $70**, but book early if you're visiting during a busy time since prices can jump. Driving here is super easy because the streets are wide and well-marked. Parking downtown isn't a problem, with metered spots costing **$1 to $2 per hour** and lots near major attractions like the **Anchorage Museum** and **Delaney Park Strip**. If you're here in winter, make sure your rental car has snow tires—this is really important if the roads are icy.

For shorter trips, walking works perfectly if you're downtown. Everything is close, and the streets are easy to navigate. You can walk between places like **4th Avenue**, full of shops and restaurants, and the start of the **Tony Knowles Coastal Trail**, which is near the **Alaska Center for the Performing Arts** on **6th Avenue**. The trail is a must-do if you like scenic views of the water and mountains—it's a peaceful way to explore and see some wildlife too.

If biking sounds more your style, the city has great trails. The **Tony Knowles Coastal Trail** is super popular, running about 11 miles with stops at cool spots like **Earthquake Park** and **Westchester Lagoon**. You can rent bikes from shops like **Pablo's Bicycle Rentals** on **4th Avenue**, with prices starting around **$20 per day**. Just stick to bike-friendly paths since some streets aren't the best for cyclists.

4.5 Day Trips from Anchorage

Girdwood and Alyeska Resort

Drive about **45 minutes south** along the **Seward Highway**, which has some of the most jaw-dropping views you'll ever see. You might even spot beluga whales along Turnagain Arm if you're lucky. Once you get to Girdwood, head straight to **Alyeska Resort** at **1000 Arlberg Avenue**. Take the **Alyeska Aerial Tram** to the top of the mountain, where you'll see glaciers, forests, and the coastline—it's seriously breathtaking. Tram tickets cost around **$35 per adult**, and it runs daily during the summer and winter. At the top, you can eat at **Seven Glaciers Restaurant**, where the food is fancy but totally worth it. If you're not into fancy dining, check out **The Bake Shop** in town for some killer sweet rolls or soup. You can also hike the **Winner Creek Trail**, which is easy and has fun wooden bridges. In the winter, it's a top spot for skiing.

Portage Glacier

Take the **Seward Highway south** for about an hour until you reach **Portage Lake Road**. This place is all about seeing the glacier up close. Hop on the **Portage Glacier Cruise**, which costs around **$30–$50 per person**, depending on the season. The boat takes you right up to the face of the glacier, and it's unforgettable. If you don't want to do a boat ride, visit the **Begich, Boggs Visitor Center** nearby, which has cool exhibits about the glacier and how it's changed over time. There's also the **Portage Pass Trail**, which is a short hike with awesome views. Parking is free at the visitor center, and there are bathrooms and picnic spots if you want to hang out for a bit.

Alaska Wildlife Conservation Center

About **45 minutes south** of the city on the Seward Highway, you'll find this wildlife sanctuary at **Mile 79**. It's a place where rescued animals live, and you'll see bears, moose, musk oxen, and more. Admission costs **$17 per adult**, and you can either walk around or drive through the park. The bear feeding times are super fun to watch. Plan to spend at least an hour here—it's perfect for families or anyone who loves animals. There's a small gift shop for snacks and souvenirs, and parking is free.

Whittier and Prince William Sound

Drive an hour south and pass through the **Anton Anderson Memorial Tunnel**—a super long, one-lane tunnel that costs **$13 per car**. Whittier is tiny, but it's the gateway to **Prince William Sound**, where you can take a glacier cruise. These tours cost around **$150–$200 per person** and last a few hours. You'll see glaciers, waterfalls, and maybe even seals or otters. After the cruise, grab some fresh fish and chips at **Swiftwater Seafood Cafe**, located at **144 Blackstone Road**. It's a small spot, but the food is fresh and delicious.

Eklutna Lake

Head **45 minutes north** on the Glenn Highway to this peaceful lake surrounded by mountains. You can rent kayaks or bikes from **Lifetime Adventures**, which is near the parking area. Rentals cost about **$50 for a kayak** or **$35 for a bike**, and the lake is perfect for exploring. The water is super blue, and there are trails around the lake if you'd rather hike. Parking is just **$5**, and there are picnic tables, so bring some snacks or lunch to enjoy the view.

Hatcher Pass and Independence Mine

Drive about **1.5 hours north** along the Glenn Highway, then take the scenic **Hatcher Pass Road**. The **Independence Mine State Historical Park** is the main attraction. You can wander through old mining buildings and learn about the gold rush days. Parking costs **$5 per car**, and the trails nearby are amazing for hiking in the summer or snowshoeing in the winter. Pack some snacks because there aren't a lot of food options around here, but the views alone are worth the trip.

4.5.1 Girdwood and Alyeska Resort

Girdwood is super easy to get to and feels like a whole different world. It's about **45 minutes south of Anchorage** along the **Seward Highway**, which has some of the best views you'll ever see. You might even spot beluga whales along Turnagain Arm while you drive. If you're not driving, you can take the **Alaska Railroad** during the summer—it leaves Anchorage in the morning and comes back in the evening.

Tickets for the train are around **$80 round trip**, but driving is faster and gives you more freedom. Once you're there, parking is free, especially at **Alyeska Resort** and the nearby trailheads.

Start your day at **Alyeska Resort**, which is at **1000 Arlberg Avenue**. The big draw here is the **Alyeska Aerial Tram**, which runs daily during the summer and winter. The tram costs **$35 per adult** and takes you to the top of Mount Alyeska. From up there, you'll see glaciers, mountains, and Turnagain Arm spread out below you—it's like standing inside a postcard. At the top, you can check out **Seven Glaciers Restaurant** if you want something fancy. The food is amazing, but it's not cheap; expect to spend about **$40 per plate**. If that's too much, no worries—there are other places to eat in town.

If you like hiking, the **Winner Creek Trail** is perfect. It's an easy **3-mile round trip**, so you don't need to be a pro to enjoy it. The trail is super pretty, with thick forests, little waterfalls, and a fun wooden bridge. If you're feeling adventurous, you can check out the **Hand Tram**, which is this cool cable basket that lets you cross the creek. It's a bit of a thrill, but sometimes it's closed, so check ahead. Wear sturdy shoes because it can get muddy, especially if it's rained recently.

If you're visiting in winter, the resort is all about skiing. They have runs for everyone, from total beginners to pros. Ski lift tickets start at **$89 a day**, and you can rent all your gear right there. If you've never skied before, they've got lessons, so don't worry—you can still give it a shot.

For food, you've got to stop by **The Bake Shop** at **194 Olympic Mountain Loop**. They're famous for their massive cinnamon rolls, and the soups and sandwiches are really good too. It's affordable, with most meals costing around **$10–$15**, and it's a cozy place to sit and relax. If you're into craft beer, check out **Girdwood Brewing Company** at **2700 Alyeska Highway**. They've got great beers, and their outdoor seating is perfect if the weather's nice.

If you've got time for one more quick stop, check out **Virgin Creek Falls**, which is at the end of Timberline Drive. It's a short hike, but the waterfall at the end is beautiful and not too crowded.

4.5.2 Portage Glacier

Getting to Portage Glacier is super simple and totally worth it. It's just **50 miles south of Anchorage**, and the drive along the **Seward Highway** takes about **an hour**. You'll pass mountains, water, and maybe even see beluga whales if you're lucky. When you get close, follow the signs to **Portage Lake Road**, where there's plenty of free parking near the lake and visitor center. If you're not driving, you can book a shuttle or guided tour from Anchorage, but driving is the best way since you can stop for pictures along the way.

Once you're at **Portage Lake**, the best thing to do is the **Portage Glacier Cruise**. The boat, called the **M/V Ptarmigan**, runs every day from mid-May to late September and takes you right up to the glacier. Tickets cost around **$35 for adults and $20 for kids**, and the ride lasts about an hour. The boat has a warm cabin, but you'll want to head outside to really see the glacier up close. Sometimes, big chunks of ice fall into the water, which is awesome to watch. Make sure to book your ticket early during the summer because it can get busy, especially on weekends.

If you don't want to do the boat, you should check out the **Begich, Boggs Visitor Center**, which is right by the lake. It's open seasonally and costs **$5 per person**. Inside, you'll find exhibits about the glacier's history and how it's changed over time. There's also a short movie you can watch that explains the glacier and its environment—it's actually pretty interesting. The big windows in the center give you a good view of the lake if you don't feel like going outside. They also have a small cafe for snacks and drinks and a gift shop where you can grab some cool souvenirs.

If hiking is your thing, the **Portage Pass Trail** is amazing. It's about a **4-mile round trip**, and it's considered a medium-level hike because there's an uphill section at the start. Once you get to the top, the views of the glacier and the lake are insane. The trail is rocky and can get muddy, so wear good shoes and bring a jacket because it gets windy at the top. The trailhead is near **Whittier Tunnel Road**, and there's free parking nearby. This hike is perfect if you want to see the glacier without taking the boat.

For food, you can stop at the **Portage Cafe**, which is along the Seward Highway close to the lake. They have sandwiches, soups, and hot drinks, and most meals cost between **$10 and $15**. If you'd rather bring your own food, there are picnic spots by the lake where you can sit and enjoy the view. It's super relaxing and a nice way to soak in the scenery.

Portage Glacier is one of those places that looks like it's straight out of a movie.

4.5.3 Wildlife Conservation Center

The **Alaska Wildlife Conservation Center** is just **45 minutes south of Anchorage**, right off the **Seward Highway at Mile 79**, and it's super easy to get to. If you're driving, the road is smooth, and the views along the way are incredible. You'll see mountains, water, and maybe even wildlife like beluga whales or sheep along Turnagain Arm. When you arrive, there's **free parking** right at the entrance. If you don't have a car, you can book a tour from Anchorage, but driving yourself gives you more time to explore at your own pace.

When you get there, you'll pay **$17 for adults**, **$13 for teens**, and **$10 for kids aged 6 to 12**, while little ones under 6 are free. The center is open year-round, but summer is the best time to visit since the animals are more active, and the weather is nicer for walking around. In summer, hours are usually **9 AM to 6 PM**, but check their website before you go.

Inside, you can either walk or drive through the **1.5-mile loop** that takes you past all the animal enclosures. Walking is great because the paths are wide and easy to follow, but if you've got little kids or the weather's not great, driving is a good option too. You'll see tons of cool animals like **grizzly bears, moose, caribou, bison**, and even wolves. The bear enclosure is one of the best spots—they're super active, and if you time it right, you can watch them being fed, which is amazing to see up close. Feeding times are posted near the enclosure, so be sure to check when you arrive.

The **musk oxen** are another favorite. They look like something out of the Ice Age with their thick, shaggy coats. These animals were brought back to Alaska after almost disappearing, and the center plays a big role in keeping their population healthy. You'll also see wood bison, which were extinct in the wild until places like this helped reintroduce them. It's really cool to learn about their stories while seeing them up close.

If you're visiting with kids, they'll love the hands-on activities. During the summer, there are fun programs where they can see animal artifacts like antlers and skulls or even interact with smaller animals during special presentations. The signs around the enclosures explain everything about the animals, like what they eat, how they live, and why they needed rescuing, so you'll learn a lot as you walk around.

If you get hungry, there's a **Snack Shack** near the entrance that sells hot dogs, sandwiches, chips, and drinks. Most items are around **$5 to $10**, and it's perfect for a quick bite. There are also picnic tables scattered throughout the park, so you can bring your own food and enjoy lunch while looking out at the mountains. The vibe is super relaxed, and it's a nice way to take a break during your visit.

Plan to spend about **1 to 2 hours** here, but you could easily stay longer if you want to see everything and take your time. Bring a jacket, even in the summer, because the area can get breezy. In winter, dress warm since it's all outdoors, but the snow-covered scenery makes it just as beautiful.

CHAPTER FIVE
FAIRBANKS

5.1 Discover Fairbanks

Fairbanks feels like the kind of place that's different from anywhere you've ever been. It's like stepping into a quiet town surrounded by endless wilderness, where everything is open, calm, and peaceful. People call it the **gateway to the Arctic** because it's where many adventures start, but it's also a town with its own special vibe. One of the coolest things about Fairbanks is the **northern lights**. If you're here between **late August and mid-April**, you've got a great chance of seeing them. They don't just sit in the sky—they move, they glow, and they make everything around you feel magical. You'll stand there with your head tilted back, just watching green, pink, and purple lights dance above you.

Summers here are wild because of the **midnight sun**. You'll get almost 24 hours of daylight, which feels totally weird but in a fun way. You can go hiking, fishing, or even golfing late at night, and it still feels like the middle of the afternoon. People love being outside during summer because the weather is warmer, and there's so much to do. The rivers are perfect for kayaking, the trails are great for biking or walking, and there's this laid-back energy that makes everything feel chill and happy.

Winter is completely different. It's freezing cold, no doubt, but the snow makes everything look like a winter wonderland. The days are short, but that's when people do some of the coolest stuff, like **dog sledding**. Imagine riding across snowy trails with a team of huskies pulling you—it's something you'll never forget. There's also **ice fishing** if you're up for a little adventure or soaking in **hot springs** while it's freezing outside. You'll feel the cold on your face, but the hot water keeps you warm, and it's such a cool experience. Even just walking around in the snow feels special here because it's so quiet and beautiful.

Fairbanks has a lot of history, especially from the **gold rush days**. You'll hear stories about miners who came here hoping to strike it rich, and you'll see parts of the town that still look like they did back then. There's also a big connection to **Native Alaskan culture**, with traditions and art that people still celebrate and share. The mix of history and culture gives the town a unique feel, like it's a small place with a big story to tell.

It's not just a town you visit; it's a place where you feel like part of something bigger.

5.2 Key Attractions in Fairbanks

5.2.1 Chena Hot Springs Resort

Chena Hot Springs Resort is a relaxing place about **60 miles northeast of Fairbanks**, at the very end of **Chena Hot Springs Road**. The drive takes about **1.5 hours**, and it's pretty easy to get there since you're just following one road the whole way. The scenery is nice too, with forests and rivers along the way. If you're driving in the winter, make sure your car has good snow tires because the road can get icy. If you don't have a car, there are shuttles from Fairbanks you can book ahead, usually costing about **$30–$50 round trip**.

The big thing here is the **hot springs**, and they're amazing. It's an outdoor pool with natural hot water that stays warm no matter how cold it is outside. Imagine sitting in steaming water while it's snowing around you—it's like being in another world. The springs are open year-round, but winter is extra special because you might see the **northern lights** while you soak. Admission costs around **$15 for adults** and **$12 for kids aged 6–17**, and kids under 6 get in free. Don't forget to bring your swimsuit and a towel, but if you forget, you can rent them there for a small fee.

Another really cool thing at the resort is the **Ice Museum**. It's kept cold all year, and everything inside is made of ice—there are sculptures, an ice bar, and even ice beds. You can take a tour, which costs **$15 per person**, and for a little extra, you can try an appletini served in a martini glass made of ice. The tours run every day and are a fun way to see some amazing ice art. Just remember to dress warm—it's freezing inside!

If you're staying for a while, there are other fun activities to try. In winter, you can go **dog sledding**, which costs around **$100 per person**, or hop on a snowmobile to zoom through the snowy trails. They also have aurora tours to help you find the best spots to see the northern lights. In the summer, there are hiking trails around the resort where you might see wildlife like moose or foxes, and it's a great time to enjoy the long daylight hours.

For food, the resort has a restaurant that serves hearty meals, including dishes made with vegetables from their **geothermal greenhouse**. You can get things like burgers, soups, or grilled salmon, with prices between **$15 and $30 per dish**. There's also a little cafe near the lobby if you just want a snack or coffee, which costs less than **$10**.

If you want to stay overnight, they have rooms and cabins starting at **$200 per night**. It's a good option if you want to do multiple activities or just relax without rushing back to Fairbanks. Staying overnight is also great for seeing the northern lights since you'll be far from city lights.

Chena Hot Springs has a cool history too. Gold miners discovered it over 100 years ago and used the hot water to relax after long days of work.

5.2.2 Aurora Borealis Viewing

Fairbanks is one of the best places in the world to see the **northern lights**, and it's all about finding the right spot and being prepared.

ALASKA ACTION PLAN

The aurora is strongest from **late August to mid-April**, usually between **10 PM and 2 AM**, but it can show up earlier or later, so don't be discouraged if it doesn't appear right away. The key is getting away from city lights. Check an **aurora forecast app** or website before heading out—this helps you know how active the lights might be and if the sky will be clear.

The best spots to watch are places where the sky is wide open and dark. **Murphy Dome**, about a **30-minute drive northwest of Fairbanks**, is a favorite because it's high up and gives you a clear view of the sky. You'll drive along **Elliott Highway**, then turn onto **Murphy Dome Road** to get there. The road is usually fine, but in winter, make sure your car has snow tires or chains since it can get icy. There are no lights or services at the top, so bring everything you need, like warm clothes, snacks, and hot drinks.

If you want to stay closer to the city, **Creamer's Field** on **College Road** is a good spot. It's quieter at night and has enough distance from the bright city lights to see the aurora clearly. Another simple option is pulling off along **Chena Hot Springs Road**. The drive out of town only takes about **15–20 minutes**, and there are lots of places to stop and watch the sky.

If you'd rather not figure it all out on your own, book a **guided aurora tour**. These tours usually pick you up from your hotel and take you to remote, dark spots like a cabin or yurt where you can stay warm while waiting. Guides know the best areas for clear skies and strong aurora activity. Many tours include hot drinks and snacks, which make the wait more comfortable. These tours usually cost between **$100 and $150 per person**, but they save you the hassle of driving and setting everything up yourself.

Taking pictures of the aurora is exciting but takes a little preparation. You'll need a **tripod** to keep your camera steady since long exposures are a must. Set your camera to manual mode, with a wide aperture (like f/2.8), an ISO around **800–1600**, and an exposure time of about **10–30 seconds** to capture the colors and movement. Keep extra batteries in a warm pocket because the cold drains them fast. If you're not into photography, just bring binoculars—they give you a closer look at the way the lights shimmer and shift.

EVERYTHING YOU NEED, NOTHING YOU DON'T

Staying warm is super important because nights here can drop to **-20°F** or even lower. Wear several layers: thermal underwear, a fleece or wool layer, and a thick winter jacket. Insulated boots with warm socks are a must, and gloves, a hat, and a scarf will keep your hands and face protected. Bring hand warmers too—they're cheap and make a huge difference if you're standing still for a long time.

If you need a bite to eat before heading out, grab dinner at a local spot like **The Cookie Jar Restaurant** on **Danby Street**, where meals like hearty soups or burgers cost around **$15–$25**. It's cozy and fills you up before a cold night outside. Pack some snacks or a thermos with hot cocoa to keep warm while you wait.

5.2.3 Morris Thompson Cultural and Visitors Center

The **Morris Thompson Cultural and Visitors Center** is right at **101 Dunkel Street**, near the Chena River in Fairbanks. It's one of the easiest places to find and is perfect if you want to really get what makes this part of Alaska special. Inside, there are **free exhibits** that feel like they're showing you the real story of the region—how the seasons change everything, what life is like for the animals and people, and how the Alaska Native communities have lived here for centuries. You'll see **life-sized displays** of wildlife, tools, and even scenes that make you feel like you're stepping into another time.

One of the coolest parts is the **"Seasons of Alaska" exhibit**, which shows you how everything—people, animals, and the land—shifts with the seasons. The **Alaska Native section** is just as amazing, with art, clothing, and tools made by local communities that tell their stories. If you're into bringing something unique home, the **gift shop** inside sells handmade stuff like moose-hide slippers, baskets made from birch, and intricate beadwork. These aren't just souvenirs—they're authentic pieces made by local artists, and buying them supports their work.

For practical help, the **Explore Fairbanks Visitor Center** inside is where you can grab maps, brochures, and advice from locals who really know the area. They'll give you tips on what to see, where to eat, and how to make the most of your time. It's super helpful if you're not sure what to do next or if you need guidance on nearby attractions.

The center is open every day, with hours depending on the season. From **January to May** and **September to December**, it's open from **8 AM to 5 PM**. In the summer, it stays open a bit later, closing at **6 PM**. They're closed on big holidays like Christmas and Thanksgiving, so double-check if you're visiting around those dates.

Getting there is easy if you're driving—there's plenty of parking around. If you're using public transport, the **MACS Transit Blue Line** has a stop close to the center, and it's just a short walk from there. Once you're done exploring, grab some food nearby. **Big Daddy's BBQ** is a short walk away and has ribs, pulled pork, and other barbecue dishes for around **$10–$20**. It's hearty and filling, just what you need after taking in all the exhibits.

The Morris Thompson Center isn't just a quick stop—it's a place that helps you connect to the history, the culture, and the people of this area.

5.2.4 University of Alaska Museum of the North

The **University of Alaska Museum of the North** is at **1962 Yukon Drive** on the University of Alaska Fairbanks campus. You can't miss it—the building's curved, modern design is inspired by the aurora borealis and stands out as you get close. Inside, it's packed with exhibits about the wildlife, art, history, and science of the region, and it's perfect for understanding what makes this area so unique.

One of the first things you'll see is the **Gallery of Alaska**, where they've got life-sized displays of animals, tools, and even a **steppe bison fossil** that's over 36,000 years old. The huge bowhead whale skull is a real show-stopper and gives you a sense of just how massive these creatures are. You'll also see displays about Alaska Native cultures, with traditional clothing, tools, and art that help you understand the way people have lived and thrived in this environment for centuries.

Another highlight is the **Rose Berry Alaska Art Gallery**, which features modern and historical art inspired by the landscapes and wildlife. It's not just paintings—there are sculptures, carvings, beadwork, and more. It all shows how deeply connected the artists are to the land. One piece that really stands out is a driftwood sculpture that feels like it belongs out in the wilderness.

For something completely unique, there's the **Place Where You Go to Listen**, an installation that turns natural events like auroras, earthquakes, and the sun's movement into sound and light. It's like listening to the Earth itself, and it's peaceful and mesmerizing in a way you have to experience to understand.

The museum is open **daily year-round**, but hours change depending on the season. In summer, from **mid-May to mid-September**, it's open from **9 AM to 7 PM**. During the rest of the year, it's open Monday to Saturday from **10 AM to 5:30 PM**. Tickets cost **$16 for adults**, **$9 for kids aged 5–13**, and are free for kids under 5. Students with ID get in for about **$14**. Parking is available right outside the building, and it's free after 5 PM or on weekends. If you're coming during the day, parking costs **$1.25 per hour** or **$5 per day**. If you're not driving, you can take the **MACS Blue Line bus** from downtown Fairbanks, which stops near the museum, and it's a quick and easy ride.

If you get hungry, there's a small **cafe** inside for snacks and drinks. Before you leave, check out the **gift shop**, where you can buy locally made jewelry, art, and books—great for souvenirs or gifts. If you want something more filling, head to **Lemon Grass Thai Cuisine**, which is about a mile away on **Old Chena Pump Road**. They've got amazing Thai dishes, with prices between **$12 and $20**, and it's a favorite among locals.

5.3 Dining in Fairbanks

Fairbanks has some of the best places to eat, where the food feels real and connected to the land around you. If you want something special, try the local dishes like **wild salmon, reindeer sausage**, or **king crab**. These are the kind of meals that make you feel like you're tasting the area, not just eating out.

There's this place called **The Pump House Restaurant & Saloon** at **796 Chena Pump Road**. It's got a cool old-time vibe, like you're stepping back into the gold rush days, and they serve food that's fresh and full of flavor. Think **grilled salmon, halibut, and elk sausage**. It's a little more on the fancy side, with meals costing about **$20 to $40**, but the portions are great, and you get to sit by the river. It's super close—just about a **10-minute drive from downtown**, and parking is easy.

If you want something totally different, head over to **Lemongrass Thai Cuisine** at **388 Old Chena Pump Road**. They make food that's bold and spicy, like **green curry or pad thai**, and it's perfect if you're in the mood for something warm and hearty. Most dishes cost between **$12 and $20**, and it's cozy enough to feel like home but still exciting because of the flavors.

For a more laid-back vibe, **Big Daddy's BBQ & Banquet Hall** at **107 Wickersham Street** is where you need to go. They've got that real barbecue feel with dishes like **pulled pork sandwiches and smoked ribs**. Meals are affordable, around **$10 to $20**, and it's right in the center of town, so you can walk there easily if you're staying nearby. It's the kind of place where you eat big and leave happy.

When you're just looking for a snack or a coffee, stop by **McCafferty's Coffee House** at **408 Cushman Street**. Their coffee is amazing—freshly brewed and perfect to warm you up if it's chilly outside. Grab a pastry or a latte and chill for a bit before heading back out to explore.

If you're here in the summer, check out the **Tanana Valley Farmers Market** on **2600 College Road**. It's open from May to September and has all kinds of local goodies like **grilled salmon skewers, fresh berries, and handmade pies**. Prices are super reasonable, and it's not just about the food—you'll find crafts and souvenirs, too. It's fun to walk around and see what the locals are making and selling.

5.4 Accommodation in Fairbanks

Fairbanks has plenty of places to stay, and you can find something perfect no matter what you're looking for. If you want a once-in-a-lifetime experience, **Borealis Basecamp** is about **25 miles north of the city**, at **2640 Himalaya Road**. You'll sleep in these cool **geodesic domes with clear ceilings**, so if you're lucky, you can watch the **northern lights** right from bed. It's quiet, surrounded by trees, and super cozy inside with heat and private bathrooms. It costs around **$400 to $600 per night**, depending on the season, and you'll need a car to get there since buses don't go that far. It's the kind of place you book if you want your stay to be an adventure in itself.

If you need something central and easy to get around, check out **SpringHill Suites by Marriott** in downtown Fairbanks, at **575 1st Avenue**. It's close to restaurants, shops, and even the Chena River for a nice walk. The rooms are spacious and have everything you need, and there's even an on-site restaurant if you don't feel like going out. Prices start at about **$220 per night**, and if you're using public buses, you'll be within walking distance of some key stops, which makes getting around easy.

For something less expensive but still comfy, **La Quinta by Wyndham** is close to the airport, at **4920 Dale Road**. It's only a **5-minute drive from the terminal**, so it's great if you're flying in late or leaving early. The rooms are clean, breakfast is free, and it's nice and quiet. Rooms here start at about **$160 per night**, and while it's not downtown, it's easy to drive into the city in under 10 minutes.

If you like meeting other people while traveling, **Sven's Basecamp Hostel** at **301 Nordale Road** is a fun option. You can stay in a shared dorm for about **$30 per night** or get your own cabin for around **$80**. It's a laid-back spot with a friendly vibe, plus they have fire pits and picnic tables if you want to hang out outside. You'll probably need a car or a taxi to get there since public transport doesn't stop nearby, but it's great if you're on a budget.

For something peaceful and a little more homey, **A Taste of Alaska Lodge** is perfect. It's about **15 minutes from downtown**, on **551 Eberhardt Road**, and it's set on a huge property surrounded by nature. The rooms are cozy and have a rustic vibe, and it's a great spot if you want to relax after a day out exploring. Prices are usually between **$150 and $250 per night**, and the views of the land around you make it feel like a proper escape.

5.5 Getting Around

Getting around Fairbanks isn't hard, and you've got a few good options depending on what you need. The **MACS Transit buses** are the cheapest way to travel if you're staying in town. They run between places like **downtown**, the **University of Alaska Fairbanks**, and the **airport**, and tickets are just **$2 for one ride** or **$5 for a day pass**. You can catch the **Blue Line** if you're heading to spots like the **Morris Thompson Cultural and Visitors Center** at **101 Dunkel Street**. Just check the schedules ahead of time since the buses run about once an hour, and you don't want to wait too long. The main bus hub is on **Cushman Street**, where you can connect to most routes easily.

If you need to get somewhere fast, **taxis and rideshares like Uber and Lyft** are easy to use. They're great for short trips, like getting from **downtown to the University of Alaska Museum of the North**, which is at **1962 Yukon Drive**. A ride usually costs around **$10 to $20**, depending on the distance. You can call local taxis like **Arctic Taxi** or just grab a rideshare through the app. These are perfect if you're traveling late or don't want to deal with bus schedules.

For total flexibility, renting a car is the way to go. Most car rental places like **Hertz, Avis**, and **Budget** are right at the **Fairbanks International Airport**, so you can grab a car as soon as you land. Prices are usually between **$50 and $100 per day**, depending on the type of car and the time of year. Driving is easy since the roads are in good shape and parking is free in most places, like downtown or at attractions like the **Tanana Valley Farmers Market** on **2600 College Road**. If you're planning to visit places outside the main town or don't want to rely on buses, a rental car makes everything a lot simpler.

For something more active, biking can be a fun way to get around in the summer. **Beaver Sports**, located at **3480 College Road**, rents bikes starting at **$20 a day**. You can ride along trails by the **Chena River**, which is a nice way to see the town and enjoy some fresh air. Just keep in mind that biking isn't really an option in the winter unless you've got the right gear for the ice and snow.

Walking works well if you're staying downtown since most shops, restaurants, and attractions are close by. For example, you can easily walk from **Golden Heart Plaza** to places like **Lavelle's Bistro** on **575 1st Avenue**, where you can grab a bite to eat. But during the winter, walking isn't always the best idea because of icy sidewalks, so make sure to wear boots with good grip and bundle up if it's cold.

If you're heading out early in the morning or planning late-night activities, buses might not run at those times, so having a taxi or a rental car is more reliable. For spots like the **Fairbanks Curling Club** at **1962 2nd Avenue**, which opens early for events, driving yourself or booking a ride is the easiest way to get there.

5.6 Adventures Beyond Fairbanks

5.6.1 Dalton Highway to the Arctic Circle

Driving the **Dalton Highway** is one of those trips where preparation makes all the difference. This legendary road starts just outside of Fairbanks at the **Elliot Highway junction**, about **84 miles north of the city**. Known as the "Haul Road," it stretches over **400 miles** to the oil fields of Prudhoe Bay, cutting through the wilderness and offering access to the **Arctic Circle**, one of its most iconic stops.

The road itself is challenging. Most of it is **unpaved gravel**, with stretches of dirt and asphalt in varying conditions. It's rough, with sharp rocks, potholes, and even muddy patches if it's been raining. In the winter, the road can be icy and treacherous, so snow tires or chains are a must. **A 4x4 or all-wheel drive vehicle** is essential, and many rental companies in Fairbanks either prohibit or heavily restrict taking their vehicles on the Dalton. If you're renting, check with local providers like **GoNorth**

or **Arctic Outfitters**, who specialize in vehicles equipped for this route. Costs typically start around **$100 per day**, but it's worth it to have a car suited for these conditions.

Fuel is your lifeline on the Dalton, and there are only two places to fill up: **Yukon River Camp** at **Mile 56** and **Coldfoot Camp** at **Mile 175**. It's vital to fill up at both because the stretches between stops are long and isolated. Yukon River Camp also has a small café and convenience store. A basic meal like a burger or soup will cost around **$12 to $20**, making it a good spot for a quick break.

The **Yukon River Bridge** is a major highlight early in the journey. This impressive structure spans one of the most significant rivers in North America. There's a pullout where you can stop, stretch your legs, and take in the view. From here, the road starts to climb into higher terrain, and the scenery becomes more dramatic, with rolling hills giving way to tundra landscapes as you approach the Arctic.

The **Arctic Circle sign** is at **Mile 115**, marked by a simple wooden sign in a gravel lot. This spot is a rite of passage for Dalton travelers, where you can officially say you've entered the Arctic region. There's a picnic area here, but no facilities, so plan accordingly. It's the perfect place for a photo and to soak in the sense of adventure.

Wildlife is abundant along the highway, and the further north you go, the more likely you are to spot **caribou, moose, musk oxen, and even grizzly bears**. The tundra is alive with animals, especially in the summer, but remember to keep a safe distance. If you stop for photos, stay in your car or keep your movements quiet and slow.

Further along, **Coldfoot Camp**, at **Mile 175**, is one of the only places to stay overnight. It was originally a mining camp and is now a basic yet welcoming stop for travelers. Cabins cost around **$200 per night**, and the on-site restaurant serves hearty meals like beef stew and chili for **$15 to $25**. Coldfoot is also home to the **Arctic Interagency Visitor Center**, where you can learn about the region's ecology and history.

5.6.2 Riverboat Discovery Cruise

The **Riverboat Discovery Cruise** is a great way to see what life along the **Chena River** is all about. The boat leaves from **1975 Discovery Drive, not far from downtown Fairbanks, about **10 minutes by car**. If you're driving, there's free parking right next to the dock. If you don't have a car, taxis or Uber are the easiest ways to get there. Public buses don't stop directly at the dock, so plan ahead if you're using them.

The cruise runs from **May to mid-September**, with departures in the morning and early afternoon. Tickets cost about **$70 for adults** and **$40 for kids**, and it's smart to book early because spots fill up fast, especially in summer. The whole trip takes about **3 hours**, and you'll be on a paddlewheel boat called the **Discovery III**. It's got both indoor and outdoor seating, so you can move around and enjoy the views no matter the weather.

Once the boat starts, you'll cruise down the **Chena River**, passing forested riverbanks, floatplanes landing right on the water, and homes tucked along the shore. There's live narration the whole time, so you'll hear stories about the people and history of the area as you go.

One of the highlights is stopping by the **Susan Butcher Kennels**, where you'll watch a live sled dog demonstration. These dogs are strong, fast, and trained to handle the toughest winter races. The trainers show you how they prepare for events like the Iditarod, and it's amazing to see these animals in action.

The cruise also stops at a recreated **Athabascan village**. You'll get off the boat and walk through the village with guides who explain how their ancestors survived and thrived in this environment. They show you things like **how they prepare salmon**, tan animal hides, and build log cabins. It's hands-on, and you get to see how people adapted to the land here for generations.

There's also a snack bar on the boat where you can grab sandwiches, chips, or drinks, with prices around **$5 to $10**. It's perfect for a quick bite while you enjoy the ride. When you get back to the dock, there's a gift shop where you can pick up locally made items like jewelry, art, and books about the area.

5.6.3 Pioneer Park

Pioneer Park is the perfect place to relax, have fun, and learn some cool stuff about Fairbanks' history. You'll find it at **2300 Airport**

ALASKA ACTION PLAN

Way, super close to downtown—it's just a quick **5-minute drive**. Parking here is free and super easy, right by the main entrance. If you're not driving, taxis or Uber will get you there fast. There's also the **MACS Transit Yellow Line**, which stops nearby, but double-check the schedule so you don't miss it.

The park is open **all year**, but the best time to visit is between **late May and early September**, when everything inside is open. You don't have to pay to get into the park, which is great if you're on a budget, but some attractions like the **Pioneer Air Museum** or the **mini train ride** cost a little extra.

Once you step inside, it feels like you've gone back in time. The first thing you'll want to check out is **Gold Rush Town**, a little street lined with historic log cabins that were moved here from different spots in Fairbanks. Each cabin has something unique, like a mini-museum or a shop where you can pick up handmade souvenirs. Walking down the wooden paths feels like exploring what Fairbanks might've been like in the old days.

If you're into planes or history, head to the **Pioneer Air Museum**. It's packed with cool stuff, like old bush planes and pictures that show how aviation helped connect this huge state. It costs about **$5** to get in, and it's small enough to explore without feeling overwhelmed but packed with enough to keep you interested.

For kids—or anyone who likes a bit of fun—the **playground** is awesome, and the **miniature train ride** is a must. It's a short loop around the park, and tickets are just **$2 or $3 per person**. You'll get to see the park from a different angle while relaxing on the ride. It's a win for families who want to keep the little ones entertained.

One of the coolest things here is the **SS Nenana**, this massive old riverboat parked right in the middle of the park. It's a reminder of how people used to get around before there were proper roads. While you can't always go inside, it's an impressive sight and makes for a great photo stop.

If you get hungry, you've got options. The **Alaska Salmon Bake** is a popular spot inside the park, serving grilled salmon, cod, and prime rib in an outdoor buffet setup. It costs about **$35 per person**, but it's all-you-can-eat, so you can really fill up. There's also an ice cream shop and some snack stands if you just want something light, like a hot dog or popcorn, for around **$5–$10**.

There's even a **theater** where you can catch fun shows during the summer. They usually feature stories about life in Alaska, and tickets cost about **$10–$20**, depending on the performance. It's a fun way to end your visit if you're there in the evening.

The park also has plenty of green space and picnic tables if you'd rather bring your own food and just chill out. Bathrooms are easy to find, clean, and close to all the main attractions, which makes spending the day here comfortable.

If you've got time after exploring the park, the **Chena Riverwalk** is just a few minutes away, and it's a great spot for a peaceful walk along the water. Or, if you're still hungry, head to **Big Daddy's BBQ** at **107 Wickersham Street**, where you can grab a big plate of BBQ for around **$15–$25**.

CHAPTER SIX
JUNEAU

6.1 Why Visit Juneau?

Juneau is a small city with a big personality, sitting between tall mountains and the calm waters of the **Gastineau Channel**. You can't drive here—there are no roads connecting it to the rest of the state—so you'll need to fly or take a ferry. If you're flying, you'll land at **Juneau International Airport**, which is just **8 miles from downtown**. Getting to the city is easy—grab a taxi or rideshare, or hop on the **Capital Transit Bus** for about **$2**, which will take you straight to the center of town. If you're coming by ferry on the **Alaska Marine Highway**, you'll arrive at the terminal about **14 miles north of downtown**, so plan for a shuttle or taxi to finish the trip.

Juneau feels cozy and easy to explore, especially downtown, where most things are within walking distance. The main streets, like **Franklin Street**, are lined with old buildings from the gold rush days, giving everything a historic vibe. You can walk past shops selling local crafts, seafood restaurants, and small museums that tell the story of how Juneau grew from a mining town into the state's capital.

This city is full of history, but it's not stuck in the past. The culture of the **Tlingit people**, who've lived here for thousands of years, is a big part of everyday life. You'll see totem poles carved with stories of their ancestors and might even hear traditional songs or see dances if there's an event happening in town. Their connection to the land is everywhere, and it gives the city a special sense of identity.

What really makes Juneau stand out is the nature that surrounds it. Huge mountains rise up on one side, and forests stretch out for miles, with glaciers not far away. Even in the city, you'll see bald eagles flying overhead, and if you're lucky, you might spot a whale or a seal along the shore. It's the kind of place where nature feels right next to you all the time, and even a short walk can lead to an amazing view.

When you're ready to eat, you'll find plenty of places serving fresh seafood. If you want a great meal, try **Twisted Fish Company** on **Ma-**

rine Way, where you can enjoy dishes like crab legs or salmon for about **$25–$40**. For something quick but still delicious, head to **Sandpiper Café** on **Willoughby Avenue**, where you can grab breakfast or lunch for **$10–$15**. The food here is fresh and full of flavor, and there's always something that fits your budget.

6.2 Key Attractions

6.2.1 Mendenhall Glacier and Ice Caves

The **Mendenhall Glacier** is one of the coolest places you'll ever see. It's huge, bright blue, and sits at the edge of **Mendenhall Lake**, just **12 miles from downtown Juneau**. You can get there super easily. If you're driving, take **Egan Drive** for about **20 minutes**, and you'll see signs pointing you to the **Mendenhall Glacier Visitor Center**, which has plenty of parking. If you're using the bus, take the **Capital Transit Route 3**, which drops you about a mile away. From there, you can walk or grab a quick taxi.

When you arrive, the **Mendenhall Glacier Visitor Center** is the first stop. It's at **6000 Glacier Spur Road**, and it's the perfect spot to see the glacier up close without hiking. You'll pay about **$5 per person** to enter, and inside you'll find big windows that give you the perfect view, plus cool exhibits that explain how glaciers form and why they're so important. The rangers here are super helpful—they'll tell you the best trails to take, where you might

spot animals, and what's safe for the day.

If you like walking, you should check out the **Nugget Falls Trail**. It's an easy **2-mile round trip** trail that takes you right up to this amazing waterfall near the glacier. The sound of the water and the icy view behind it is something you won't forget. If you're feeling adventurous, the **West Glacier Trail** is a tougher hike that gets you to higher spots with incredible views. If conditions are good, you can even explore the famous **ice caves**, which look like glowing blue tunnels. You'll definitely want to go with a guide for this—it's safer, and they'll make sure you see the best spots. Guided hikes usually cost around **$150–$200 per person**, and they're worth it for the experience.

If hiking isn't your thing, you can still get close to the glacier by joining a **kayaking tour** on **Mendenhall Lake**. You'll paddle past floating ice and get amazing views of the glacier's face. These tours cost about **$100–$150 per person** and include all the gear you need.

While you're there, keep your eyes open for wildlife. You might see bald eagles flying overhead, mountain goats on the rocky slopes, or even black bears near the streams during salmon season. Early mornings and late afternoons are the best times for spotting animals because it's quieter then.

If you get hungry, there's a small café near the visitor center where you can grab sandwiches, hot drinks, or snacks for **$5–$10**. It's perfect for a quick break before you head back to town. Or, you can drive back to downtown Juneau, where there are plenty of places to sit down and enjoy a full meal.

The whole area around the glacier is peaceful and stunning.

6.2.2 Mount Roberts Tramway

The **Mount Roberts Tramway** is one of the easiest and coolest ways to see all of Juneau from way up high. It's right in **downtown Juneau** at **490 S Franklin Street**, super close to the cruise ship docks, so you can't miss it. The tram takes you straight up the side of **Mount Roberts** to about **1,800 feet** in just a few minutes, and the whole ride is in a glass cabin, so you get amazing views the entire time. You'll see the **Gastineau Channel**, the forest, and even islands in the distance if the

EVERYTHING YOU NEED, NOTHING YOU DON'T

weather is clear.

Tickets cost around **$45 for adults**, and the tram runs every day from **mid-May to early September**, starting at **8 AM** and going until about **9 PM**, depending on the season. The best times to ride are early in the morning or later in the evening because it's less crowded, and the light makes everything look even more magical. If the weather's foggy, you might want to wait for a better day since the view is a big part of the experience.

When you get to the top, there's plenty to do. First, you've got the **Timberline Bar & Grill**, where you can sit down and enjoy a meal with one of the best views you'll ever have. They serve dishes like fresh salmon and halibut, and prices range from about **$15–$30** depending on what you order. It's a great spot to relax, and even just grabbing a coffee or dessert to enjoy on the deck feels special with the mountain air and the view.

There's also the **Chilkat Theater**, which shows short films and has live presentations about the **Tlingit people**, the Native group from this area. These are free and give you a cool way to learn about the history and traditions of the region. Right outside, you'll see beautifully carved **totem poles** and other pieces of Tlingit art that make the top of the tramway feel even more special.

If you want to stretch your legs, there are several hiking trails that start right from the tram station. Even the shorter trails, like the **Mountain House Loop**, give you awesome views and let you explore the alpine scenery. If you're feeling adventurous, you can hike farther into the forest for even more peace and quiet and a chance to spot wildlife like **marmots**, **mountain goats**, and **eagles**. It's cooler up there, so bring a jacket and wear good shoes if you plan to hike.

For souvenirs, the **Raven Eagle Gift Shop** has some of the best locally made items, like jewelry, Native art, and unique keepsakes. It's a great place to find something special to bring home or give as a gift.

6.2.3 Whale Watching Tours

The **Alaska State Museum**, found at **395 Whittier Street**, sits right in the heart of Juneau, making it easy to include in your plans whether you're exploring the downtown area or heading to other attractions. Its central location means it's just a **10-minute walk** from the cruise ship docks or downtown hotels. If you're coming from farther out, public transportation via the **Capital Transit Bus** will drop you nearby on **Egan Drive**, and from there, it's a short walk to the museum's entrance. If you're driving, the museum has ample parking nearby, making it convenient for those renting a car. It's open **Tuesday to Saturday from 9 AM to 5 PM**, and admission is **$14 for adults**, with free entry for children under 18, making it a budget-friendly yet incredibly enriching activity for families.

As soon as you step inside, you're surrounded by a thoughtfully designed space that takes you through Alaska's history, culture, and natural wonders. One of the museum's biggest highlights is its **Native Alaskan exhibits**, which display intricately carved **totem poles**, woven baskets, and ceremonial robes from communities like the Tlingit, Haida, and Yup'ik. Each item tells a story, whether it's about daily life, spiritual beliefs, or the relationship between the people and their environment. The **Smithsonian Arctic Studies Center**, a permanent feature, brings in rare and fascinating objects from the Smithsonian's collection, giving you a close look at tools, clothing, and ceremonial items that played vital roles in Native traditions.

The museum doesn't stop there—it also dives into Alaska's **Russian colonial history** with artifacts like religious icons, fur trade tools, and maps from the time when the land was part of the Russian Empire.

Another area captures the excitement of the **Gold Rush era**, showing mining tools, personal letters, and vivid photographs of the rugged individuals who ventured here seeking their fortunes. It's a window into a time of incredible hardship and opportunity.

If you're more interested in Alaska's wildlife and natural beauty, the museum has an entire section dedicated to its unique ecosystems. Life-sized displays of **grizzly bears, caribou, and marine life** give you a close look at the state's diverse species, while exhibits about fisheries and forests show how these resources have shaped life here for centuries. Many of these displays are interactive, making them engaging for visitors of all ages.

Art lovers will be thrilled by the museum's collection of **contemporary Alaskan art**, which includes paintings, carvings, and multimedia pieces that reflect both traditional influences and modern interpretations. These exhibits rotate regularly, so even if you've been before, there's likely something new to see.

For those who enjoy shopping for meaningful souvenirs, the **museum's gift shop** is a must-visit. It features locally made jewelry, prints, and books that connect to the exhibits, allowing you to take a piece of your experience home. Items range from affordable keepsakes under **$20** to unique handcrafted pieces that make for great gifts.

The area surrounding the museum is equally worth exploring. Just a short walk away, you'll find **restaurants and cafes** where you can grab a bite after your visit. For something quick, head to **Sandpiper Cafe on Willoughby Avenue**, where you can enjoy hearty breakfasts and lunches for around **$10–$15 per meal**. If you're looking for something more refined, **Salt, located on Seward Street**, offers upscale dishes like fresh seafood for **$25–$40 per entrée**.

6.3 Exploring Downtown Juneau

Downtown Juneau is small and super easy to explore on foot, with most of the action happening along **South Franklin Street**. If you're coming from the cruise ship docks, you're basically right there already. If you're staying farther out, you can take the **Capital Transit Bus**, which has stops close to everything, or grab a taxi—it's quick and convenient either way. Parking is available too if you're driving, but honestly, you won't need a car to enjoy this part of town.

Walking down South Franklin feels alive, with colorful shops, great restaurants, and little pieces of history everywhere you look. For shopping, stop at **Trickster Company**, which is on South Franklin and full of cool, modern Native art. They sell stuff like prints, jewelry, and even skateboards with Native designs, and prices start at around **$15–$20** for smaller items. If you want local snacks or souvenirs, check out **Alaska Knifeworks**, where you can find smoked salmon, berry jams, and handmade knives that are both useful and beautiful. There's something here for every budget, from $10 keepsakes to premium crafted items.

When it's time to eat, you've got plenty of choices. If you want something fast and super tasty, head to **Deckhand Dave's Fish Tacos** at the **Food Truck Lot on South Franklin Street**. Their fish tacos are amazing, and they cost about **$5–$10** each. If you want a full meal with a view, go to **The Hangar on the Wharf** at **2 Marine Way**, where you can sit right by the water and enjoy dishes like crab-stuffed halibut. Meals here are a bit pricier, usually around **$20–$35**, but the portions are big, and the food is fresh.

You can't miss the **Red Dog Saloon** on South Franklin—it's got this old-timey vibe with sawdust on the floor and live music. Grab a beer for about **$7**, and soak up the history of the place. Nearby, the **Alaska State Capitol Building** on **Main Street** is another must-see. You can walk there in just a few minutes, and they offer free self-guided tours where you can check out the unique architecture and learn about the state's history.

If you want to take a break, head to **Marine Park**, which is right by the water. It's a quiet spot where you can sit on a bench and watch boats come and go while taking in the fresh air. For something a bit different, walk up to **Calhoun Avenue**, where the streets are lined with historic houses that show off what life was like here decades ago.

Make sure you wear comfy shoes because even though most of downtown is flat, some areas like the Capitol Building have small hills. Bring a light jacket too, because the weather can change quickly, even on sunny days. If you need a caffeine fix or a snack, stop at **Heritage Coffee Roasting Co.**, where a cup of coffee costs around **$5**, and you can relax in a cozy spot.

6.4 Dining in Juneau

Most of the restaurants are downtown, which makes it really easy to walk from one place to another. If you're not staying in the middle of town, you can just hop on a **Capital Transit Bus**—they have stops near the main food spots, especially on **South Franklin Street**, so you don't have to worry about finding a car or parking.

Start with **Twisted Fish Company Alaskan Grill**, right at **550 South Franklin Street**, super close to the cruise docks. It's all about seafood here. You can try their grilled salmon, buttery Dungeness crab, or halibut tacos—they're all amazing. Meals start at about **$20**, but for the bigger dishes like the crab legs, it's around **$35–$40**. The restaurant's got big windows that look out over the harbor, which makes everything taste even better.

If you want a more laid-back spot, check out **The Hangar on the Wharf** at **2 Marine Way**. This place is in an old airplane hangar, which is kind of cool, and they do things like seafood chowder that's loaded with fresh clams and halibut, or their famous crab-stuffed halibut. Meals cost around **$25–$40**, and the portions are really big, so you'll definitely leave full. After you eat, you can walk by the docks—it's right there.

For something quick, head to **Deckhand Dave's Fish Tacos** at the **Food Truck Lot on South Franklin Street**. This is probably the best spot for crispy halibut or rockfish tacos, and they cost about **$5–$10 each**, so it's super affordable. You'll sit outside on picnic tables, and it's a great spot if you're in the middle of exploring downtown. Plus, the whole area feels really lively with people coming and going.

Not everything in Juneau is seafood—**Salt** on **Seward Street** is perfect if you're in the mood for something a little more creative. They mix local ingredients with global flavors, so you might find dishes like scallops with wild berries or short ribs with unique sauces. It's more upscale, so expect to pay around **$30–$45 per meal**, but it's great if you're looking for a place to celebrate or just want a fancy night out.

For breakfast or brunch, go to **Sandpiper Cafe** on **Willoughby Avenue**. They do things like smoked salmon eggs Benedict or sourdough pancakes, and it's all super filling. Meals cost around **$12–$18**, and it's one of those cozy places where the staff are really friendly and make you feel at home.

And if you're craving something sweet, stop by **Coppa** on **Glacier Avenue**. They make their ice cream with local flavors like spruce tips or rhubarb, which you probably won't find anywhere else. A scoop costs about **$5**, and it's perfect to grab and eat while you walk around.

6.5 Accommodation

If you want something small and charming, go to **Silverbow Inn & Suites** on **120 Second Street**. It's right downtown, so you can walk to almost everything. The best part? They've got a rooftop hot tub where you can relax and look at the mountains after a long day. Rooms here cost around **$150–$200 per night**, and they include breakfast with fresh bagels and coffee that's really good. Plus, the bus stops nearby, so it's easy to get around if you don't have a car.

For families or if you like a little more space, **Four Points by Sheraton Juneau** is a solid choice. It's on **51 Ferdinand Street**, really close to the water and just a block from South Franklin Street. The rooms are clean, big, and some have amazing views of the harbor or mountains. Rates usually go from **$200–$250 per night**, and they have a restaurant in the hotel, so you don't always have to head out for meals. If you're driving, there's parking, and if you're not, the bus stops are right nearby.

If you want to save some money, the **Juneau Hotel** on **1200 West 10th Street** is a great pick. It's about a 10-minute walk or a short bus ride from downtown, and they have suites with kitchens, which means you can cook your meals and save even more. Rooms start at **$120 per night**, and they also have a free shuttle to and from the airport, which makes things really easy if you're flying in.

For something historic, try the **Alaskan Hotel & Bar** on **167 South Franklin Street**. This hotel has been around since 1913, and it's got a really cool vintage vibe. The rooms are simple, but they're clean and full of character. It's one of the cheapest options downtown, with prices starting at **$80 per night**. There's also a bar downstairs that's super popular with locals, so it's a fun place to hang out. You can easily walk to all the best spots from here, and public transport is just steps away.

If you love nature and want a quieter place, check out **Amalga Cabin** near the **Mendenhall Glacier area**, about 20 minutes from downtown. It's peaceful, surrounded by trees, and has everything you need, like a small kitchen and a cozy bedroom. It's great for couples or anyone who wants to relax. Rates are around **$200 per night**, and you'll need a car to get there, but it's worth it for the quiet vibes and the easy access to hiking trails and outdoor activities.

Most of these spots are close to bus stops or easy to drive to, so getting around isn't a problem at all. Juneau's hotels and inns are all about making your stay comfortable and convenient, with great locations and friendly staff.

6.6 Getting Around

Getting around is really simple because the city is small, and everything you need is pretty close. If you're staying downtown, you can walk almost everywhere. The streets like **South Franklin Street** and **Willoughby Avenue** are full of shops, restaurants, and things to see, so walking is a great way to get around. Just wear good shoes since a few parts of the city are hilly, especially near the waterfront and the Capitol.

If you need to go farther, the **Capital Transit Bus** is super affordable and really easy to use. A single ride costs just **$2**, and if you plan to take the bus more than twice in a day, get a **$5 day pass**, so you can ride as much as you want. The buses cover most of the city, and the main stops downtown are near **Willoughby Avenue**. If you're heading to the **Mendenhall Glacier**, you'll take the **Route 3 bus**, which drops you off close to the visitor center. Buses run about every 30 minutes during the day, but they don't go late at night, so make sure you plan your return trip.

Taxis are another easy option if you don't want to deal with schedules or if you're out after the buses stop running. Companies like **Evergreen Taxi** and **Juneau Taxi and Tours** can pick you up from downtown, the airport, or even the ferry terminal. A short ride downtown usually costs around **$10–$15**, and a trip to something like the glacier area might be about **$25–$30**. It's a good idea to call ahead because you won't find taxis just driving around waiting to be hailed like in bigger cities.

If you want more freedom, renting a car could work, especially if you're staying outside downtown or want to explore beyond the bus routes. You can rent from places like **Hertz** or **Avis** at the airport. It'll cost about **$50–$80 per day**, depending on the time of year. Parking downtown can be tricky during summer because it gets busy, but there are metered spots on streets like **Franklin Street**, and some hotels have parking lots for guests.

For something more active, you could rent a bike from **Cycle Alaska**, which is on **Willoughby Avenue**. A bike rental costs around **$20–$30 a day**, and riding around Juneau is a lot of fun, especially along the harbor or the paths going toward the valley. It's a great way to see more while still keeping things easy.

6.7 Outdoor Activities in Juneau

6.7.1 Hiking Trails

The **Mendenhall Glacier Trail** is super easy and perfect if you just want to enjoy the views without too much effort. It starts at the **Mendenhall Glacier Visitor Center**, which is on **Glacier Spur Road** about 20 minutes by car from downtown. If you don't have a car, you can take the **Route 3 bus**, which gets you close enough to walk the rest. Parking at the visitor center is **$5**, and the trail itself is free to use. The trail is only **0.8 miles one way** and is flat, so it's great if you're with kids or don't want a tough hike. If you keep going on the **Nugget Falls Trail**, you'll walk about **2 miles round trip**, and it takes you right up to a massive waterfall near the glacier. You don't need special gear, just comfy shoes and maybe a light jacket if it's windy near the glacier.

Now, if you're ready to sweat a little, the **Mount Roberts Trail** is where you'll get those jaw-dropping views of the city and the mountains. The trailhead is downtown near the **Mount Roberts Tramway** on **6th Street**, so you can just walk there if you're staying in the area. The full trail is **4.5 miles one way**, and it's steep, especially in the beginning, but totally worth it once you get above the trees. If you don't want to hike the whole thing, you can take the tram halfway up for about **$35 round trip** and start hiking from there. Just remember, the higher you go, the rockier it gets, so wear good hiking boots. Also, pack water and snacks because you won't find anything up there until you hit the tram station, where there's a small cafe.

The **Perseverance Trail** is another favorite, and it's pretty easy to get to since the trailhead is at the end of **Gold Street**, just a short walk from downtown. This trail is about **3 miles round trip**, with a steady incline, so it's not too hard but not completely flat either. The cool thing about this trail is the history—you'll see old mining stuff along the way, and the waterfalls and wildflowers make it super pretty. If you want to extend the hike, you can take a side trail to **Ebner Falls**, which adds about **1 mile**, and it's worth it if you love waterfalls. Bring a small picnic or grab a snack in town before you go because there's nowhere to buy food on the trail.

For a serious adventure, the **West Glacier Trail** is a bit harder but totally awesome. You'll find it off **Skaters Cabin Road**, about a 20-minute drive from downtown. If you're using public transport, take the **Route 3 bus**, but you'll have to walk about a mile to the trailhead from the stop. The trail is **4 miles one way** and takes you through forests, over rocks, and close to Mendenhall Glacier. If the conditions are safe, you might even see the famous ice caves, but be really careful because they're only accessible during certain times of the year. You'll need solid hiking boots and maybe trekking poles for this one. Pack extra water and food because this trail is no joke.

For all these hikes, make sure to bring the right stuff—water, snacks, and layers because the weather can flip from sunny to rainy fast. If you're heading out to more rugged trails like Mount Roberts or West Glacier, bear spray is a good idea because wildlife, like bears, can pop up. Also, always pack out your trash so the trails stay nice for everyone else.

After your hike, you're probably going to be hungry. If you're near downtown, grab some fish tacos at **Deckhand Dave's** on **South Franklin Street**—they're around **$12**, and they're super good. If you're by Mendenhall Glacier, stop at **Herbert Glacier Cafe** for a coffee or sandwich before heading back.

6.7.2 Kayaking and Canoeing

Start with **Mendenhall Lake**. It's super easy to find—just go to the **Mendenhall Glacier Recreation Area** on **Glacier Spur Road**, about 12 miles from downtown. If you're driving, park at the visitor center for **$5**, or if you're using the **Route 3 bus**, it drops you close, and you can walk from there. This is a great place to paddle because you'll be surrounded by incredible views of icebergs floating in the water and the glacier right in front of you. Most people go with a guided tour, which costs about **$150–$200 per person**, including everything you need, like the kayak, safety gear, and a guide who knows the area. The tours usually last a few hours, so bring a light jacket and maybe a snack since there's nothing to buy once you're on the water. If you're hungry afterward, head to **Herbert Glacier Cafe** nearby for a sandwich or something warm.

Another great spot is **Auke Bay**, about a 20-minute drive from downtown Juneau. You can rent a kayak from **Alaska Boat & Kayak Rentals** at the harbor for about **$50–$75 per day**. If you don't have a car, the **Route 4 bus** can take you close to the harbor. This area is calm and perfect for paddling, and you'll likely see sea lions, otters, and maybe even a humpback whale if you're lucky. Paddle around the small islands, and you'll feel like you're in your own little world. When you're done, stop by **The Hot Bite** near the harbor for a casual meal—their fish tacos are awesome and cost about **$12**.

If you're short on time and want to stay near downtown, the **Gastineau Channel** is a solid choice. You can rent a kayak or join a short guided tour with **Alaska Kayak Adventures**, which costs around **$30 per hour** for rentals or **$75–$100** for a guided paddle. The best part about this area is how easy it is to access—you can walk to the launch point from downtown. It's also a great spot to get views of the city from the water. Afterward, grab some food at **Deckhand Dave's Fish Tacos** on **South Franklin Street**. It's nearby and super affordable, with meals starting around **$12**.

For something more remote, check out the **Channel Islands State Marine Park**. This place is about a 30-minute boat ride from

Juneau, and it's perfect if you want to get away from everything and paddle in peace. Tours to this area usually cost **$200–$300 per person**, including the boat ride, kayak, and a guide. You'll paddle around quiet inlets, see puffins and maybe orcas, and feel like you're in untouched wilderness. Bring layers and a dry bag for your stuff because it can get windy and splashy.

6.7.3 Glacier Gardens Rainforest Adventure

It's located on **7600 Glacier Highway**, about 6 miles from downtown Juneau, and getting there is simple. If you're driving, just follow **Egan Drive**, and you'll find parking right on site. Don't drive? No problem. The **Route 4 bus** stops close, and taxis or ride-shares are always an option from downtown or the cruise ship terminal.

Once you get there, you'll start a **guided tour** that's already included in your **ticket**, which costs about **$25–$30 for adults** and **$15 for kids**. The guide takes you through the gardens on an **electric cart**, so you don't have to worry about walking up hills. You'll hear all about how this place was created after a landslide left the area barren. Instead of letting it go to waste, the owners turned it into this one-of-a-kind mix of rainforest and carefully designed gardens.

The highlight of the tour is when the cart takes you up to a lookout point. The view there is incredible—think wide-open views of the **Gastineau Channel**, **Douglas Island**, and the forest stretching as far as you can see. Whether the sun's out or it's a bit cloudy, the view is stunning, so make sure your camera is ready.

Walking through the gardens, you'll see those famous **flower towers**, where old trees have been flipped upside down and transformed into giant flower pots. Every turn you take, there's another spot that'll make you stop and go, "Wow." If you come between **May and August**, the flowers will be in full bloom, and everything will be super vibrant. If you're visiting during other times, don't worry—the rainforest itself is gorgeous year-round, with its mossy trees and quiet paths.

After your tour, you can grab a coffee or a snack at the **cafe near the entrance**. Prices are pretty reasonable, around **$3–$10**, and it's a good spot to relax before heading back. The **gift shop** next to it has

ALASKA ACTION PLAN

some cool local souvenirs and even small plants you can take home as a reminder of your visit.

Make sure to wear **comfortable shoes** since you'll be walking a bit, even though the cart covers the main route. Bring a **light jacket** because it can get cool or damp, even if it's sunny downtown. If you're using the bus, double-check the **Route 4 schedule**, especially in the afternoon, so you're not stuck waiting too long.

ALASKA ACTION PLAN

CHAPTER SEVEN
DENALI NATIONAL PARK AND PRESERVE

7.1 Introduction

Denali National Park is huge, wild, and amazing, with over six million acres of land. It's about **240 miles north of Anchorage** and **120 miles south of Fairbanks**, so you can drive there on the **George Parks Highway (AK-3)**. If you don't have a car, you can take the **Alaska Railroad**, which stops near the entrance, or hop on a bus or shuttle from Anchorage or Fairbanks, especially during the summer when more options are available.

When you arrive, the first place to go is the **Denali Visitor Center**, which is close to the park entrance. Here's where you'll find maps, get information about the park, and learn about shuttle buses. The entrance fee is around **$15 per person for a seven-day pass**, and kids under 16 don't pay anything. If you plan to camp or go deeper into the park, this is where you get permits or book buses that take you further inside.

The park is famous for **Denali**, North America's tallest mountain, standing at **20,310 feet**. It's massive, and on clear days it looks like something out of a movie. But don't be surprised if you don't see it right away—it's often covered by clouds, and only about **30% of visitors get a good look at it.** The best time to catch a view of the mountain is early in the morning or late at night, when the skies are clearer.

Denali is all about wildlife. You'll see **grizzly bears**, **moose**, **wolves**, **caribou**, and **Dall sheep**, especially if you stick to early morning or evening hours when the animals are most active. There are also tons of birds, like golden eagles, and in summer, the tundra comes alive with colorful flowers that make the whole place look magical.

The landscape here changes a lot, from wide-open tundra where you can see for miles to thick spruce forests that feel like they're from another time. Rivers like the **Teklanika and Savage** run through the valleys, and the snow-covered **Alaska Range** creates a dramatic backdrop no matter where you are. Most people stick to the **Park Road**, which is 92 miles long and offers stunning views. If you take a shuttle bus, you can stop at places like **Eielson Visitor Center** or **Wonder Lake**, which are great for taking pictures or just soaking in the beauty.

If you get hungry, there aren't many food options inside the park, so it's smart to bring snacks or meals. Near the entrance, there's a place called **Denali Park Village**, where you can grab something quick for **$10–$20**. If you're heading to **Healy**, about 11 miles away, you'll find spots like **49th State Brewing Co.**, where meals start at **$15**. It's a good place to relax after a day of exploring.

For staying overnight, there are a few choices depending on your budget. Close to the entrance, you'll find **Denali Bluffs Hotel** with rooms starting at around **$200**, or you can choose something more affordable like **Denali Hostel & Cabins** for **$50–$100 per night**. If you love camping, check out **Riley Creek Campground**, which costs about **$30 per night** and has basic facilities like bathrooms and picnic tables.

7.2 Getting to the city

Getting to Denali is pretty straightforward, but you have a few choices depending on how you want to travel. If you're driving, the park entrance is at **Mile 237 on the George Parks Highway (AK-3)**. It's about a **4 to 5-hour drive from Anchorage** or around **2 hours from Fairbanks**. The road is smooth and easy to follow, but don't forget to fill up on gas because once you're closer to the park, gas stations become rare. Good places to stop for gas or snacks are **Wasilla** if you're coming from Anchorage and **Healy** if you're coming from Fairbanks. Along the way, you can pull over at **Talkeetna**, a cute little town with shops, restaurants, and even some scenic spots where you can stretch your legs.

If you're not into driving, you can take the **Alaska Railroad**, which is super relaxing and gives you incredible views of mountains, forests, and maybe even some wildlife along the way. The train ride from Anchorage takes about **7.5 hours**, while from Fairbanks it's about **4 hours**, so it's slower than driving, but it's a whole experience. The train stops at the **Denali Depot**, which is close to the park entrance, and there are shuttles or short walks to get you where you need to go. Tickets start at about **$100 one-way**, but if you want fancier seats with meals and better views, it'll cost more. Book early if you're traveling in the summer since it gets busy.

There are also bus and shuttle options if you're coming from Anchorage or Fairbanks. These are good if you don't want to drive or don't have a car. The ride takes about the same amount of time as driving, but buses often make stops along the way, so you can grab a snack or just enjoy the views. Buses usually cost around **$50 to $100**, and most will drop you off right near the **Visitor Center**, which is super convenient.

Timing is really important. If you're visiting between **May and September**, all the transportation options will be running, and the roads will be in great shape. If you're planning to come earlier or later in the year, check schedules because buses and trains don't always run outside of summer. Winter roads can get icy, so be extra careful if you're driving. Always check the weather before heading out.

7.3 National Park

7.3.1 Park Road and Shuttle Buses

The Park Road is the main way to explore Denali, but you can't just drive your own car past **Mile 15**, so the park's **shuttle buses** are what you'll use to go further. These buses take you deep into the park, where the scenery gets even more amazing, and it's the only way to get to spots like **Toklat River**, **Eielson Visitor Center**, and the end of the road at **Kantishna**. You'll start at the **Denali Bus Depot**, which is near the park entrance, and you'll need a ticket to ride, so book your seats early, especially in summer when everyone wants to visit. Tickets cost about **$30 to $60**, depending on how far you want to go, and it's best to reserve them online or at the park's website.

The buses leave early, starting around **6:00 AM**, and run throughout the day. The **Transit Shuttles** let you hop on and off as much as you want, so you can explore spots along the road and then catch another bus to continue your trip. The **Tour Buses**, on the other hand, are guided and give you a lot of background about the park, but you stay on the same bus for the entire trip. If you want flexibility, stick with the Transit Shuttles. If you're into stories and learning more about the park, go for the tours—they're pricier, but the guides are really good.

The road itself is unpaved after Mile 15, so it's a bit bumpy, but that's part of the adventure. The further you go, the more wild and untouched the surroundings get. Stops along the way include places like **Teklanika River (Mile 30)** for a quick rest or **Toklat River (Mile 53)**, which has some cool displays about the park's geology and wildlife. If you go as far as **Eielson Visitor Center (Mile 66)**, you'll get incredible views of Denali itself if the weather is clear. This stop also has exhibits and restrooms, so it's a great place to stretch your legs. For those who want to go all the way, **Kantishna (Mile 92)** offers a glimpse into the park's history as an old mining town.

You'll need to pack carefully because there are no shops or places to buy food inside the park. Bring enough snacks, water, and maybe even a small meal, especially if you're going on a longer ride. Dress in layers because the weather can change quickly, and don't forget a rain jacket just in case. The buses stop at a few rest areas with basic facilities, so you don't have to worry about being stuck for hours without a bathroom.

Wildlife is a huge part of the experience. You might spot **grizzly bears**, **caribou**, or **moose** from the bus, so keep your eyes peeled and your camera ready. The drivers are great at pointing out animals, but remember, these are wild creatures, so you have to stay on the bus and keep a respectful distance.

ALASKA ACTION PLAN

Getting to the park is pretty easy. If you're driving, the entrance is on the **George Parks Highway**, and there's plenty of parking near the Visitor Center and Bus Depot. If you're coming by train, the **Alaska Railroad** stops nearby, and it's just a short shuttle ride to the Bus Depot. Once you're in the park, the bus system is well-organized and simple to use.

7.3.2 Wildlife Viewing

Denali is one of the most incredible places to see animals living their best wild lives, and the Park Road is where it all happens. This long road takes you deep into the park, and it's the perfect spot to spot **grizzly bears**, **moose**, **caribou**, and sometimes even **wolves**. You don't have to go hiking off into the wilderness to see them either; just riding along in a shuttle or tour bus gives you amazing chances to see these animals in their natural world.

Grizzly bears love the open tundra around the **Teklanika River (Mile 30)** and **Eielson Visitor Center (Mile 66)**. They're huge, powerful animals, but most of the time, they're just grazing on berries or digging for roots. You'll have the best luck spotting them early in the morning or late in the afternoon when they're most active. Caribou are a little easier to find because they travel in groups and graze in wide-open areas like **Polychrome Pass (Mile 46)**. If you see a herd, you'll know right away—it's pretty amazing to watch them move together.

Moose are massive, and you can often find them

hanging out near **Savage River (Mile 15)** or the wetlands around **Horseshoe Lake**, which is just a short walk from the Visitor Center. They like to stay near water, and early mornings are the best time to catch a glimpse of one wading or grazing. Seeing a moose up close—well, not too close—is unforgettable because they're so big, especially the males with their huge antlers.

Wolves are rare to see, but they do live here, and if you're lucky, you might catch one near **Sable Pass (Mile 39)**. They're super shy and usually avoid people, so it's a treat if you manage to spot one. Bring binoculars or a spotting scope because they're often far away.

To get around, the park's **shuttle buses** are your best friend. They go all along the Park Road, stopping at different points, and the drivers are great at spotting wildlife. If you want to be able to stop and explore more freely, sit on a **Transit Shuttle** because they let you hop on and off as much as you want. The **Tour Buses** are more structured and include guided narration, which is awesome if you want to learn a lot while you ride. The park is huge, so plan your day around the shuttle schedule and decide how far you want to go. If you're only going as far as Savage River, it's perfect for a half-day trip, but if you want to reach Eielson or Wonder Lake, make sure you're ready for a full day out.

If you're driving your own car, you can only go up to Mile 15 at Savage River. The road beyond that is restricted to buses, but don't worry—you'll still see plenty of wildlife in the first stretch of the park. Stop at the **Denali Visitor Center** to grab maps, schedules, and any info you need before heading in. Parking is available here, so you can leave your car and hop on a bus to go further.

When it comes to staying safe, you've got to respect the animals. Always keep a **300-foot distance** from them, and never get out of your bus or car to take a closer look. If you're hiking, carry **bear spray** and make noise so you don't accidentally surprise anything. Never, ever feed the animals—this can harm them and mess up their natural behavior.

For photos, bring a **good zoom lens** so you can capture the animals without getting too close. Early mornings and evenings give you the best light for photos, and that's also when the animals are most active. If you're using binoculars, keep them handy because you might need them to spot a bear on a faraway ridge or a wolf blending into the landscape.

If you need a snack before heading into the park, the **Morino Grill** near the Visitor Center has quick options like sandwiches and soups, with meals costing around **$10–$15**. Once you're inside the park, there's nowhere to buy food, so pack plenty of snacks and water to keep you going through the day. There are picnic tables at some of the shuttle stops where you can relax and eat while enjoying the views.

Late summer is an awesome time to visit because the animals are really active, getting ready for winter. Bears are fattening up, caribou are gathering in big herds, and moose are often out in the open. Fall colors make everything even more beautiful, with the tundra turning shades of red and gold. Just make sure to dress in layers because the mornings and evenings can get cold.

7.3.3 Visitor Centers

The visitor centers in Denali National Park are the best places to get ready for exploring and understanding what's ahead. You start at the **Denali Visitor Center**, which is really close to the entrance, about a mile in. If you're driving, there's parking, but it can fill up fast, so try to come early in the morning. If you don't have a car, the free park shuttle stops here too. The center is open during the summer from **8 AM to 6 PM**, and this is where you'll get all your maps, schedules for the park buses, and advice from rangers who really know their stuff.

When you walk in, there's a short film called *Heartbeats of Denali* that runs throughout the day. It's only about 20 minutes, and it gives you a feel for the park's wild nature and why so many people think it's special. There are displays inside that show you the animals you might see, like bears or moose, and how the giant mountains here were formed. If you have kids, they can grab a Junior Ranger booklet and earn a badge by doing fun activities. Right next door is the **Morino Grill**, where you can grab things like sandwiches or hot soup, which cost around **$10 to $15**, making it a good stop before heading into the park.

If you're visiting in the winter, things shift to the **Murie Science and Learning Center**, which is open all year. It's smaller but has cool exhibits about the science and research that happens here. This place is really helpful if you're coming for things like snowshoeing or skiing since it's quieter and you can get tips from rangers about winter safety.

If you're heading deeper into the park on a bus, the **Eielson Visitor Center** is at **Mile 66** on the **Park Road**. You can't drive there yourself, so you'll need to book a shuttle. The bus ride to Eielson takes about four hours, but the views on the way make it worth it. Once you're there, you'll see some of the best views of the mountain, especially on clear days. Inside, the exhibits focus on the tundra and the animals that live there, like caribou and wolves. If you're up for a hike, there's a trail nearby called the **Thorofare Ridge Trail** that gives even better views, but it's steep, so take it slow. This center is open from **9 AM to 5 PM** during the summer, and while there's no food to buy here, you can fill your water bottle and use the clean restrooms.

If you're not going as far as Eielson, the **Toklat River Contact Station** at **Mile 53** is another good stop. It's smaller, but it has restrooms, a bookstore where you can buy things like postcards or trail guides, and picnic tables where you can take a break. This spot is also good for seeing wildlife or taking photos of the braided river channels that spread out across the valley.

7.3.4 Sled Dog Kennels

The **Sled Dog Kennels** are just three miles from the Denali Visitor Center, and they're one of the coolest things you can check out in the park. These sled dogs aren't just for show; they actually work in the park during the winter, helping rangers patrol the snowy wilderness where cars or machines can't go. The dogs are super tough, smart, and full of energy, and they love what they do.

To get there, you can drive down the **Park Road** or take the free park shuttle. If you're driving, follow the signs from the visitor center, but keep in mind that parking is pretty limited, so the shuttle is usually the easiest way. The kennels are open every day from **9 AM to 4:30 PM**, but you really want to plan your visit around the **daily demonstrations at 10 AM, 2 PM, or 4 PM**. These are the best times to watch the dogs in action, see how they're harnessed, and learn how the sleds work. The dogs get super excited when it's their turn to pull, and you'll feel the energy as they take off.

After the demo, you can walk around the kennels and meet the dogs up close. Some of them love attention and might even let you pet them. If you're lucky, you might see puppies during the summer, and the rangers are always happy to tell you about their training and what life is like for a sled dog. You'll learn how sledding has been part of Denali's history for over 100 years and why it's still used today to protect the park's wilderness.

It's free to visit the kennels, and you don't need to book ahead, which is nice. Make sure you wear comfy shoes because you'll do some walking, and dress in layers because the weather can change fast. There's no food or drink available at the kennels, so bring a water bottle, or grab something at the **Morino Grill** by the visitor center before you head over.

The area around the kennels is peaceful, with trees and mountain views, so you might want to hang out for a bit and soak it all in. If you're into hiking, you can check out the **Rock Creek Trailhead**, which is close by and gives you a chance to stretch your legs after the demo.

7.4 Hiking

7.4.1 Easy Trails

They're short, simple, and give you plenty of time to take in the views, see wildlife, and just relax in nature.

The **Horseshoe Lake Trail** is a perfect choice if you like lakes and a bit of wildlife. It's close to the park entrance, about **1.5 miles down Park Road**, and there's a small parking lot right near the trailhead. If you don't have a car, the shuttle bus can drop you off nearby—just let the driver know your stop. The trail is about **2 miles round trip**, and most of it is flat and shaded by trees, except for one steep hill on the way back. Once you get to the lake, you'll see beaver dams and sometimes the beavers themselves swimming around. It's peaceful and great for a short picnic, so bring some snacks. There aren't any food spots nearby, but if you're hungry after your hike, head to the **Morino Grill** by the visitor center for sandwiches or a warm bowl of soup.

Another easy trail is the **McKinley Station Trail**, which starts right behind the **Denali Visitor Center**. You don't need to go far for this one, and it's perfect for families or if you just want a quiet, flat walk. The trail is **1.6 miles long** and loops through beautiful meadows and forested areas. If you visit during the summer, you'll see wildflowers everywhere, which makes it feel like something out of a postcard. Benches are spread along the path where you can take a break or just sit and watch for small animals like squirrels and birds. Since it's so close to the visitor center, you can grab a map or ask a ranger for advice before starting.

The **Savage River Loop Trail** is one of the most scenic, easy hikes in the park. It's located about **15 miles down Park Road** near the **Savage River Campground**. If you're taking the park shuttle, you can get off right at the trailhead. This trail follows the river for **2 miles in a loop** and has stunning mountain views all around. There's a little bridge at the halfway point where you can stop for pictures or just watch the river flow—it's a great spot to relax. Sometimes you'll see ground squirrels running around or Dall sheep up on the cliffs. There aren't any stores or food here, so pack water and maybe a sandwich or two if you plan to hang out for a while.

If you're lucky enough to make it out to the **Eielson Visitor Center**, don't miss the **Tundra Loop Trail**. It's super short, less than a mile, but it feels like stepping into another world. The trailhead is right outside the visitor center, and you can see the endless tundra stretching out in every direction. On clear days, Denali's massive peak will be right there in front of you—seriously, it's incredible. This is a great place for photos, so don't forget your camera. There are bathrooms and a small shop at the visitor center, so you can grab a snack before or after your walk.

For any of these trails, wear comfy shoes that won't slip if the ground is wet, and dress in layers because the weather can change fast. Always carry a water bottle, some sunscreen, and bug spray. If you want to spot more wildlife, bring binoculars—they're super handy for seeing animals like moose or bears from a safe distance.

After hiking, treat yourself to a good meal. The **Karstens Public House**, near the park entrance, serves hearty dishes like burgers and local Alaskan favorites. Prices are usually around $15–$25 per plate, and the atmosphere is super cozy, especially after a day out in the fresh air.

7.4.2 Moderate to Challenging Hikes

Savage Alpine Trail

This trail is all about earning those views. It's about **4 miles one way**, and it connects the **Savage River Area** with the **Mountain Vista Rest Area**, so it's not a loop. You'll want to plan ahead, maybe use the **shuttle buses** to get back to your starting point. To find the trail, head about **15 miles down the Park Road** from the visitor center—there's a **public transport stop** near the trailhead, making it super convenient if you're not driving.

The first part of this trail climbs steadily, but don't let that stop you. As you go higher, the views get wild—you'll see the entire **Savage River Valley**, and on a clear day, you might even spot **Denali** in the distance. If you're lucky, you could even catch some wildlife far below or soaring above. Bring layers because the wind can get strong up there. Also, pack water, snacks, and maybe a sandwich to enjoy when you take a break. Afterward, you could swing by the **Savage River Campground** to chill or grab a bite near the **Denali Visitor Center**—something like a hearty sandwich from **Morino Grill** for around **$10–$15**. It's close, casual, and perfect for recharging.

Mount Healy Overlook Trail

This one starts easy but gets steeper as you go—it's about **2.5 miles one way** from the **Denali Visitor Center** area. You can park nearby, or hop on a **shuttle bus** that drops you right where you need to be. The trail is well-marked, so you won't get lost, but it's uphill most of the way.

The coolest part? The higher you climb, the more incredible the views become. You'll see the **Nenana River** winding below and mountains stretching endlessly. The final stretch is the toughest, but once you're at the overlook, it's like nature's own reward for all your effort. The space at the top is great for sitting, taking photos, and just breathing it all in. You'll want good hiking boots for this one and maybe trekking poles if you're into that. No food or water along the trail, so carry your own. When you get back down, there's nothing better than grabbing a quick drink or snack near the visitor center.

Triple Lakes Trail

This trail is long but worth every step. It's **9.5 miles one way**, so it's more of a half-day adventure unless you want to turn around sooner. The trail starts either at the **Riley Creek Campground** or near the **visitor center**, so it's easy to find. If you're not up for the full hike, just stop at the first or second lake—they're all gorgeous.

What makes this trail cool is how it changes—you'll walk through forests, across little boardwalks, and next to the most peaceful lakes you've ever seen. The water is so clear and calm; it's like a mirror for the sky and trees. This is one of the best spots to catch sight of moose, so keep your camera handy. You'll need to carry everything you'll need, though—there's no food, water, or restrooms along the way. When you're done, reward yourself with a pizza at **Prospectors Pizzeria & Alehouse** on the **Parks Highway**—trust me, their wood-fired pies are worth it.

7.4.3 Backcountry Camping

You need to plan really well to make sure you have the best time and stay safe. First, you'll need a **permit**, and you can only get that at the **Backcountry Information Center**, right by the main **Denali Visitor Center**. You should go early in the morning because they don't take reservations, and spots fill up quickly. They'll also give you a **bear-resistant food container** to keep your snacks safe from curious bears, and you'll watch a safety video to make sure you know what to do out there.

To get into the backcountry, you'll use the **shuttle buses** that run along the **Park Road**. These buses have specific stops where they'll drop you off and pick you up, but you'll want to book your seat ahead of time, especially in the summer. The shuttle schedule is available at the **Denali Bus Depot**, and if you're staying in nearby **Healy**, some local lodges offer their own transportation to the park entrance. The buses run on a set schedule, so plan your hiking or camping start time carefully.

Safety is the most important part. You'll likely see bears, so keep all food and scented items locked in the bear-resistant container and store it far from your tent. Make noise while you walk, like talking loudly or clapping, so you don't surprise any wildlife. Bring **bear spray** with you; you can find it at the Denali Visitor Center or at stores in Healy. A **map and compass** are must-haves because there are no marked trails. GPS might not work well in this area, so don't rely on your phone.

For packing, think **layers** because the weather changes fast. During the day, it could be warm, but at night it gets freezing, so you'll need a **good sleeping bag** and a strong tent that can handle wind. Bring lightweight, high-calorie foods like nuts, energy bars, and dried meals, plus a **water filter** to clean water from streams. Don't forget a **first-aid kit**, bug spray (you'll thank me later), and extra socks because your feet are going to work hard.

The views out there are unreal. You might hike over wide, open tundra with mountain peaks in the distance one day, and then the next day you're crossing rivers or climbing ridges. You'll probably spot animals like caribou or even a wolf if you're lucky. At night, if the skies are clear, the **northern lights** might even make an appearance. It's quiet, beautiful, and feels like you're on another planet.

Before you head into the park, stop by **Healy** for last-minute groceries or outdoor gear. For food, grab a filling breakfast at **49th State Brewing Company**, or stock up on snacks at **Denali Park Market**. It's best to visit between **late June and early September** when the weather is a bit friendlier, but still, be ready for sudden rain or cold.

7.5 Accommodation near Denali

7.5.1 Campgrounds

Camping near Denali gives you the chance to stay right in the middle of nature, surrounded by mountains, rivers, and wildlife, making it feel like a true wilderness experience. **Riley Creek Campground**, just inside the park entrance, is a great choice if you want a balance of comfort and accessibility. It's right off the **George Parks Highway**, so whether you're driving yourself or arriving by bus, it's super easy to get there. You'll find toilets with running water, drinking fountains, and picnic tables, plus a small store nearby for last-minute supplies. The cost is about **$20 a night**, and it's perfect if you're looking for a convenient but still scenic place to set up camp. If you're hungry, the **Karstens Public House** is nearby with good food like burgers and fish dishes, typically priced between **$15-$25**.

If you're up for a quieter spot with stunning views, **Savage River Campground**, located about **15 miles** down **Park Road**, is ideal. You'll feel a bit more removed from the crowds here, and the surrounding landscape of mountains and open tundra is breathtaking. It's not fancy—just pit toilets and basic water access—but that's part of its charm. You can easily explore the nearby **Savage River Loop Trail**, a gentle path where you might see caribou grazing in the distance. Plan ahead, though, because there are no shops nearby. Stock up on snacks and supplies in **Healy** at **Three Bears Grocery** before heading in. Camping here costs about **$15 a night**, and the peace and quiet are absolutely worth it.

For those who want to dive deeper into the park, **Teklanika River Campground** is where you'll really feel like you're in the wild. It's **29 miles** down **Park Road**, so you'll need to commit to staying there since you can't drive farther in after setting up camp. You'll have to rely on the park's shuttle buses to get around, which is part of what makes the experience unique—you're deep into nature with fewer people around. The campground is rustic, with pit toilets and no running water, so you need to bring everything you'll need, from food to drinking water. But it's a stunning location where you might spot wildlife like moose or even bears wandering nearby. Staying here costs about **$16 per night**, and it's perfect for those looking for solitude and adventure.

If you're not ready to rough it, campgrounds like **Denali Grizzly Bear Resort** in **Healy** offer more comforts, like hot showers, a shop for supplies, and even Wi-Fi. Located just **6 miles** north of the park entrance, it's convenient and still close to nature. You can park an RV with full hookups or set up a tent. After a day of exploring, head to the nearby **49th State Brewing Company** for great food and local beers. Meals here are usually around **$15-$30**, and their reindeer sausage is a must-try. A stay at the resort costs between **$35-$50 per night**, depending on your setup.

When camping near Denali, remember that the weather can

change quickly. **Even in summer, nights can get cold**, so bring warm clothing, a solid sleeping bag, and waterproof gear in case of rain. Always keep food stored in bear-proof lockers provided at the campgrounds—**never leave it out**, not even for a minute. If you need bear spray or extra supplies, you can pick them up in **Healy**.

Getting to these campgrounds is straightforward. If you're driving, just follow the **George Parks Highway**. Buses from Anchorage and Fairbanks also drop you near the park entrance, making it accessible even if you don't have your own car.

7.5.2 Lodges and Hotels

For something super close to the park entrance, you can check out **McKinley Chalet Resort**. It's right along **George Parks Highway**, just a few minutes from the park entrance. What makes it great is the convenience—you get a free shuttle to and from the park, so you don't have to stress about driving or parking. The rooms are cozy and well-kept, and there's a central area with a restaurant where you can try dishes like fresh-caught salmon or something as simple and comforting as a juicy burger. Prices start at **$250 per night**, which isn't cheap, but it's worth it for the location and ease of access.

If you're into something with a view, then you'll want to look at the **Denali Bluffs Hotel**, which is located just a short drive from the park. It sits higher up on a hill, so you get these stunning views over the **Nenana River**, especially in the evening when everything just feels calm and peaceful. They also run shuttles to help you get around, and the rooms have this warm, mountain-lodge vibe that makes you feel like you're right in the middle of nature without sacrificing comfort. Rooms here go for about **$230 a night**, and when you're ready to eat, you can head to the on-site restaurant or grab a pizza at **Prospector's Pizzeria**, just a short ride away.

Now, if you really want a place that feels luxurious but still keeps you close to the wilderness, the **Grande Denali Lodge** is where you'll want to stay. It's perched right on the side of a mountain, so every room comes with these unbeatable views of the valley and the surrounding mountains. It's located just a couple of miles from the park entrance, and like the other places, they've got shuttles, so you don't even need to worry about driving. The lodge itself is comfortable, with spacious rooms and cabins if you're looking for extra privacy. Prices range between **$200 and $350 per night**, depending on when you book and the type of room. If you want to enjoy some local flavor, head to **49th State Brewing Company**, where you can have a cold beer paired with hearty Alaskan dishes like bison chili.

For travelers on a budget, there's the **Denali Park Hotel**, located a bit further out in **Healy**, which is about a 10-mile drive from the park entrance. It's not fancy, but the rooms are clean and practical, perfect if you just need a place to rest after a long day of exploring. The hotel is unique because it's built using converted train cars, which adds a quirky charm. Prices start at around **$150 per night**, and you'll need a car to get to the park and nearby spots like **Rose's Cafe**, where you can grab a simple, affordable breakfast to fuel your day.

For those who are all about adventure and immersion, **Camp Denali** takes things to a whole new level. It's located deep inside the park, so you're far from the crowds and surrounded by untouched wilderness. The cabins are basic—don't expect running water—but the experience is one-of-a-kind, with sweeping views of **Mount Denali** right from your porch. Meals are included, and the food is all locally sourced, so it's fresh and hearty. This is a premium experience, starting at **$750 per person per night**, but that includes your lodging, meals, and guided hikes, so you're getting a full package that's all about connecting with nature.

7.6 Dining

If you want a lively place with a lot going on, head to **49th State Brewing Company** in **Healy**. It's about a 15-minute drive from the Denali park entrance, super easy to find along the **George Parks Highway**, and some hotels or shuttles might even take you there if you're not driving. You've got to try their famous **bison burger**, which costs around **$18**, or their creamy **smoked salmon dip**, about **$12**. They brew their own beer, so get something like the **Denali Gold Lager** to really enjoy the vibe. They sometimes have live music too, which makes the whole experience even better.

For pizza, there's **Prospector's Pizzeria & Alehouse** right near the park entrance. It's easy to walk to if you're staying nearby or using the local park shuttles. They do these amazing wood-fired pizzas, and you can even get toppings like reindeer sausage, which is super unique. A pizza here costs about **$12 to $22**, depending on what you order. The place is laid-back and perfect if you want to relax after a long day outside.

If you're grabbing breakfast or just need coffee to start your day, check out **Black Bear Coffee House**, which is also close to the park entrance. You can get their **breakfast burrito**, stuffed with eggs, cheese, and bacon or sausage, for about **$10**, or grab a fresh pastry and coffee if you're in a rush. It's a small, cozy spot, so it's great for a quick bite before heading back to your adventures.

For something fancy, go to **The Overlook** at the **Grande Denali Lodge**. It's up on a hill with stunning views of the mountains, so it's not just about the food—it's the whole experience. The best part is their **Alaskan halibut**, which costs about **$35**, and the restaurant itself feels special if you're celebrating or just want a great dinner. You'll need a car or hotel shuttle to get there since it's a little out of the way, but the view alone is worth it.

Another standout is **229 Parks Restaurant and Tavern**, which is all about fresh, local food. It's about 10 minutes south of the park entrance, and they switch up their menu with the seasons. Their **smoked salmon chowder** is incredible, and you can also try something like their **roast duck**, but expect to spend about **$25 to $50** depending on what you order. It's not just a meal here—it's like a foodie experience.

If you're sticking to a tighter budget or just want something simple, **Rose's Cafe** in Healy is perfect. It's a diner with big portions of comfort food, and they do a great **meatloaf and mashed potatoes** for about **$15**. It's super casual and feels like home, which is really nice if you're just looking for good food without all the extras.

You'll notice a lot of the places near Denali focus on local ingredients like salmon, halibut, or even game meat, so it's a great way to taste what this area has to offer.

CHAPTER EIGHT
SEWARD

8.1 Introduction

Seward is this small, pretty town right by the ocean, with huge mountains around it and super blue water. You'll notice the harbor first because that's where everything happens—fishing boats are coming in with fresh catches, tour boats are getting ready to take people out, and you might even see kayakers heading out on the calm water. It's a fun spot to just hang out and watch. There are also little places to eat nearby where you can try super fresh seafood while looking out at the water. Sometimes you'll even see a sea otter floating by or a bald eagle flying overhead.

The main street, **Fourth Avenue**, is where you'll find small shops, art galleries, and cafes. Everything feels warm and friendly here. You can grab a cup of coffee, a slice of pie, or pick up something cool like handmade jewelry or a local souvenir. The people who own these places are super nice and love to share tips about what to do around town. It's the kind of place where you feel welcome just by walking around.

What's really special about Seward is how close you are to big adventures. It's the gateway to **Kenai Fjords National Park**, where you can get on a boat and see glaciers up close. If you're lucky, you might spot whales, sea lions, or puffins while you're out on the water. These tours usually start right at the harbor, so it's super easy to join one. Even if you stay in town, you can walk along the water and still see amazing views of the bay and mountains.

If you like hiking, there are trails nearby where you can walk and see incredible views. Some are easy, so you don't have to be an expert hiker, and you can even bring the family. Just make sure you have a jacket because it rains a lot, but honestly, the rain makes everything look even cooler with mist over the mountains.

8.2 Getting to Seward

To get to Seward, you have three main options: train, car, or bus, and each one gives you a chance to enjoy incredible views along the way.

If you're taking the **Alaska Railroad**, it leaves from **411 W 1st Avenue in Anchorage**, and the journey to Seward takes about **4 hours**. The train ride is stunning, with huge windows letting you take in the views of mountains, forests, and Turnagain Arm. You might even spot some wildlife like moose or bald eagles. If you want a premium experience, go for the **GoldStar Class**, which gives you access to an outdoor viewing platform and complimentary meals. Tickets range from **$100 to $200**, and when the train arrives in Seward, you're dropped right at the harbor, making it easy to start exploring.

Driving along the **Seward Highway** is probably the most flexible and scenic option. It's a **127-mile trip** that usually takes **2.5 to 3 hours**, but you'll want to stop often because the views are jaw-dropping. Start by filling up your gas tank in Anchorage—stations like **Holiday Stationstore at 2900 C Street** are convenient—and then head south on the highway. Along the route, you'll find spots like **Beluga Point**, where you can stop to look for whales, or **Girdwood**, where a quick detour can get you amazing coffee and baked goods at **The Bake Shop** for around **$15 per meal**. The **Alaska Wildlife Conservation Center**, closer to Seward, is also worth a stop, especially if you want to see rescued animals like bears and moose up close; admission is usually under **$20 per person**.

If you don't want to drive, buses are a good alternative. Companies like **Seward Bus Line** run daily services, particularly in summer, and they pick up from places like the **Downtown Transit Center on 6th Avenue in Anchorage**. The ride takes about **3 hours**, and tickets typically cost **$50 to $70**. The bus drops you off near the **Small Boat Harbor**, which is central to everything in Seward.

When you arrive, you'll find that the town is small enough to navigate easily on foot or by renting a bike. The **Small Boat Harbor** area is the hub, where you can book wildlife tours or kayaking trips. If you're hungry, head to **The Cookery on 3rd Avenue** for fresh seafood; dishes like halibut or crab are usually **$20 to $40**. For a comfortable place to stay, **Hotel Seward on 221 5th Avenue** offers cozy rooms starting at **$150 per night** and is within walking distance of the harbor and restaurants.

8.3 Visiting

8.3.1 Alaska SeaLife Center

The **Alaska SeaLife Center** is right on **301 Railway Avenue**, near the waterfront of Resurrection Bay. You'll see it easily—it's in a beautiful spot and super close to everything in Seward. If you're driving, just follow **3rd Avenue** until you reach **Railway Avenue**. There's parking around the center and on nearby streets like **Adams Street**. If you're staying by the harbor, it's a quick 15-minute walk along the **Waterfront Trail**, which is nice because you get views of the bay. If you're not walking or driving, taxis or shuttles cost about **$10 to $15** to get there from anywhere in town.

What You Can See and Do

The center is open from **10 AM to 5 PM**, but times might change a little depending on the season, so double-check before you go. Tickets are **$30 for adults, $25 for seniors**, and **$15 for kids aged 4 to 12**. Little ones under 3 get in free. If you're visiting as a family, sometimes they offer group deals.

Inside, you'll get up close to marine animals you might never see otherwise. The **Underwater Viewing Dome** is the first thing you should check out—it's where you'll see seals and sea lions swimming right past you, and it's so cool how close they get. Then head to the **touch pools**, where you can actually feel things like starfish and sea anemones. If you have kids with you, they'll love it. Plan to stick around for the feeding sessions because it's fun watching sea otters and other animals get their meals while the staff explains more about them. There's also an **aviary area** where puffins and seabirds dive into the water—it's like watching them in the wild.

The center does more than just show off animals. You'll learn a lot about how they rescue and care for stranded or hurt marine creatures. For an extra fee, you can even do a behind-the-scenes tour, which lets you see the science labs and get closer to the conservation work they do. If you care about ocean life or just want a deeper look into what goes on, it's worth it.

After Your Visit

When you leave the center, take a stroll on the **Waterfront Trail** right outside. It's peaceful, with spots where you can sit and watch the bay. You might even catch sight of a sea otter or two. If you're ready to eat, go to **The Cookery** on **4th Avenue**, just a few blocks away. They serve fresh seafood like halibut and crab, with plates costing about **$25 to $40**. Or grab coffee and something quick at **Resurrect Art Coffee House**, a cozy spot where a snack will run you less than **$10**.

8.3.2 Downtown Seward

Downtown Seward feels like a cozy little town where everything is close and easy to explore on foot. You start on **4th Avenue**, the main street where most of the shops and cafes are. If you're driving, there's street parking, or you can park by the harbor and walk up. If you come by train or bus, the stops are just a short walk away, so you won't need a car to get around downtown.

The first thing you'll notice is how charming and colorful it feels. There are murals everywhere, showing the history and wildlife of the area. Start at the **Seward Community Library and Museum** on **6th Avenue**, where you can learn about the town's connection to the Iditarod Trail and Alaska's early days. The museum costs about **$5** to enter, and it's small enough to explore in an hour.

On **4th Avenue**, you'll find shops like **The Ranting Raven**, which has handmade Alaskan art, pottery, and jewelry. It's perfect for picking up something unique to take home. Nearby, there's **Harbor Street Books**, a little bookstore where you can find guides on the area or just something fun to read while you relax. Keep walking, and you'll come to **Benny Benson Memorial Park**, which is small but has a cool story behind it—it honors the kid who designed Alaska's state flag.

For food, you've got great options. At **The Highliner Restaurant** on **4th Avenue**, the seafood is fresh and delicious. The **halibut tacos** and **clam chowder** are super popular, and meals are around **$15 to $30**.

If you want something faster, head to **Red's Burger Stand** on **Railroad Avenue** for a burger under **$15**. You can't leave without trying the gelato at **Sweet Darlings**, also on **4th Avenue**. They make it with local flavors like wild berries, and it's perfect for a quick treat.

If you like unique places, check out **Resurrect Art Coffee House and Gallery** on **3rd Avenue**. It's an old church turned into a coffee shop, and it also sells crafts and art from local artists. Sit down with a cup of coffee and enjoy the cozy vibe.

Walking around is easy because downtown Seward is small and everything is close. It'll take you about **10 minutes** to walk from one end of downtown to the other. In summer, there's even a free shuttle that stops at big spots like the **harbor** and the **museum**.

It's a relaxing place to wander, shop, and eat while soaking up the town's history and atmosphere.

8.3.3 Seward Boat Harbor

The **Seward Boat Harbor** is where all the action happens. It's at the edge of **Resurrection Bay**, just off **Port Avenue**. You can walk there from downtown Seward, and in summer, the **Seward Free Shuttle** makes it super easy to get around. The shuttle runs between **8 AM and 6 PM**, and it stops at most hotels and campgrounds, so you won't have any trouble finding your way.

When you're at the harbor, you'll see rows of boats tied up, and the view of the water with the mountains behind it is just amazing. This is the main place to start if you want to go fishing, hop on a sightseeing cruise, or just watch the boats coming and going. If you're into fishing, you'll find plenty of charters here. They usually leave early in the morning—around **6 or 7 AM**. You can catch halibut, rockfish, and salmon, depending on the season. Most trips cost **$250 to $350 per person**, and they include everything you need, like rods and bait. Just dress warm because mornings on the water can be pretty cold.

If fishing isn't your thing, you can take a cruise to see glaciers and wildlife. Companies like **Kenai Fjords Tours** and **Major Marine Tours** have different trips, from short ones to all-day adventures. You'll get to see puffins, sea otters, seals, and even whales if you're lucky. A full-day cruise, which includes glaciers, costs about **$175 to $250 per person**, and it's totally worth it. Make sure to book early, especially in summer, because spots fill up fast.

For something more hands-on, you can rent a kayak or join a guided tour. Kayaking is awesome here because you can paddle close to cliffs and hidden spots that boats can't reach. Prices start around **$50** for a rental or about **$100 to $200** for a guided trip, depending on how long you're out there.

There's more to do around the harbor, too. If you're hungry, check out **Ray's Waterfront** on **4th Avenue**, right by the docks. It's a great spot for fresh seafood, like king crab or halibut tacos, and a meal here will cost about **$25 to $50 per person**. For a quicker bite, there's **Harbor Street Creamery**, where you can grab ice cream or a coffee to enjoy while walking around.

Even if you're not going on a boat, the harbor itself is fun to explore. There are signs and plaques that talk about the history of Seward and how the harbor was connected to the **Iditarod Trail**. It's a cool way to learn a little history while you're walking around. Plus, you might see bald eagles hanging out on lampposts or sea lions swimming nearby.

8.4 Outdoor Adventures in Seward

8.4.1 Kenai Fjords National Park

Kenai Fjords National Park is close to Seward, on the southern side of the Kenai Peninsula. Most people start their trip from **Seward Boat Harbor**, which you can find at 1300 4th Avenue in Seward. If you're driving, just take the Seward Highway from Anchorage—it's a beautiful 2.5-hour drive. If you're not driving, the **Alaska Railroad Coastal Classic Train** runs every morning in the summer and reaches Seward by late morning. Buses and shuttles also run daily, so you've got plenty of options to get here.

Once you're in Seward, all the tours into the park leave from the harbor. If you're driving, there's parking nearby, but it fills up quickly during summer, so come early. The harbor is also a nice spot to grab coffee or check out shops before your tour.

ALASKA ACTION PLAN

To see the park, you'll need to book a boat tour. These cost around $150–$250 depending on how long you go. Short tours last about four hours, but longer ones (six to eight hours) take you deeper into the fjords and give you more chances to see whales and glaciers. You'll definitely want to see **Aialik Glacier** and **Holgate Glacier**, both massive glaciers that sometimes drop huge pieces of ice into the water. It's incredible to watch.

On the way, you'll see a lot of wildlife—seals, sea otters, puffins, and sometimes even humpback whales or orcas. The guides on the boats are great at pointing things out and explaining what you're seeing. If you prefer something quieter, you can go kayaking. You'll paddle near glaciers and along the fjords. Guided tours leave from **Miller's Landing**, just outside Seward, and cost about $120–$300, depending on how long you go.

Bring a waterproof jacket and dress in layers because it's cold near the glaciers, even in summer. Don't forget sunglasses since the ice reflects a lot of sunlight. Some tours include food, but it's smart to pack snacks or drinks just in case.

After your tour, head to **The Cookery** at 209 4th Avenue for fresh seafood. Their halibut is fantastic, and meals cost about $20–$35. For something quick, check out **Woody's Thai Kitchen** at 804 Fourth Avenue. It's affordable (around $15–$25) and tasty.

If you're staying overnight, check out **Hotel Seward** on 5th Avenue or **Resurrection Lodge on the Bay** for a waterfront view. Rooms range from $150 to $250 depending on what you pick.

Nearby, you can visit the **Alaska SeaLife Center** or drive 15 minutes to **Exit Glacier**, which is one of the easiest glaciers to reach by road.

8.4.2 Exit Glacier and Harding Icefield Trail

Exit Glacier is about 12 miles from Seward, at the end of Herman Leirer Road. To get there, drive for 15 minutes from Seward along the Seward Highway and turn onto Exit Glacier Road. If you don't have a car, summer shuttles from town cost about $15–$20 per person, or some hotels offer free rides. The trailhead is at the **Exit Glacier Nature Center**, where you'll find free parking, restrooms, and water fountains. It's a good idea to stop here for maps and updates from the rangers before starting your hike.

The **Exit Glacier Overlook Trail** is super easy and less than a mile each way. It takes about 30 minutes to an hour total and leads you straight to a spot where you can see the glacier up close. The path is flat and great for anyone, even kids or people who don't hike much. Along the way, signs tell you cool stuff about the glacier and how it's been shrinking over time.

If you want something harder, the **Harding Icefield Trail** starts at the same spot but is much tougher. It's 8.2 miles round trip, climbs over 3,000 feet, and takes 6 to 8 hours to finish. You'll start in a shady forest, then pass through open meadows with wildflowers, and finally, you'll reach the edge of the massive Harding Icefield. The view is crazy—just miles of ice stretching forever. But this trail isn't for beginners. You'll need sturdy boots, plenty of water, and snacks. The weather changes fast, so bring layers and a waterproof jacket.

If you're hungry after your hike, drive back to Seward and grab something to eat. **The Smoke Shack** at 411 Railway Avenue serves awesome pulled pork sandwiches for about $12–$15. Or check out **Sea Bean Café** on 4th Avenue for a sandwich and coffee—it's around $10–$20.

8.4.3 Boat Tours and Cruises

Boat tours in Resurrection Bay start at **Seward Boat Harbor**, which is at 1300 4th Avenue in Seward. It's easy to get there by car—just follow Seward Highway, and it's about 15 minutes from most places in town. If you don't drive, some hotels have shuttles, or you can walk if you're staying nearby. Parking costs about $10–$15 a day, but it fills up fast, so get there early.

Most tours are run by **Major Marine Tours** or **Kenai Fjords Tours**, and they're super reliable. Tours happen daily during the summer, with morning trips leaving around 8:00 or 9:00 AM and afternoon options for shorter cruises. Longer tours, usually 6 to 8 hours, cost around $150–$250 per person. Booking early online is smart because they sell out, especially during the busy season.

Once you're on the boat, you'll head into Resurrection Bay, surrounded by giant cliffs and green mountains. You'll see glaciers like **Bear Glacier**, the biggest one in the bay, and smaller ones tucked away in fjords. The guides are great at spotting wildlife and telling you what's going on. You'll probably see sea otters floating on their backs, seals sunbathing on rocks, and even whales if you're lucky. Humpbacks sometimes breach, and orcas swim in pods nearby. Puffins and seabirds nest in the cliffs, and they're easy to spot.

Wear layers because it gets cold and windy on the water, even if it's sunny when you leave. A waterproof jacket is a must since there's a lot of spray. Non-slip shoes help you move around the deck safely, and sunscreen is a good idea because the sun reflects off the water.

Some tours include meals, like salmon or prime rib buffets, but others only have snacks to buy, so check ahead. If you want food after, go to **Ray's Waterfront** next to the harbor for fresh seafood like halibut or salmon, costing about $20–$40. If you're in the mood for something quick, **Harbor Street Creamery** has good coffee and snacks, and it's just down the street.

8.4.4 Kayaking and Fishing

If you want to kayak in Seward, start at **Miller's Landing** on Beach Drive. It's about 10 minutes from the harbor by car, or you can grab a local shuttle. They rent single and tandem kayaks starting at $40 for a couple of hours. If you're not experienced, go for a guided tour. They'll take you to places like **Bear Glacier Lagoon**, where you can paddle around icebergs, or calm spots in **Resurrection Bay**, perfect for seeing sea otters, seals, and puffins up close. A half-day tour costs about $120, and they'll give you all the gear you need, including dry bags. Just wear layers and bring a waterproof jacket because it's colder on the water.

If you're into fishing, head to **Fourth of July Beach** along Nash Road. It's a popular shore fishing spot, especially during summer salmon runs. Another easy spot is near the **Seward Lagoon Outlet**, close to the small bridge by the harbor. You'll need a fishing license, which costs $15 to $30, and you can get one at **The Fish House** on 4th Avenue. They also sell bait and rent gear.

For bigger catches, like halibut or king salmon, book a fishing charter. **ProFish-n-Sea Charters** and **Crackerjack Sportfishing** are two solid options. Their boats leave early, around 6:00 AM, and take you out into deeper waters. Full-day trips cost around $300–$400 and include all the equipment and bait. They'll even clean your fish for you.

When you're done, grab a meal at **The Cookery** on 4th Avenue. Their halibut tacos are amazing and cost about $20–$35. For something quicker, go to **Chinooks Bar & Grill**, also on 4th Avenue, for fish and chips at $15–$25. Both are close to the harbor, so it's easy to stop by.

8.5 Dining in Seward

If you're hungry in Seward, you've got plenty of good spots to eat. Start with **Ray's Waterfront**, right by the harbor at **1316 4th Avenue**. It's easy to find and has parking nearby. You can sit by the big windows and watch the boats while eating fresh seafood. Their **king crab legs** and **seared halibut** are super popular, and if you want to try a little of everything, get the **seafood platter**. Meals here cost about $25–$40, so it's a bit fancy but worth it if you love seafood.

If you want something more relaxed, go to **The Cookery** at **209 4th Avenue**. It's a small, cozy place where they make great dishes like **halibut tacos** and **fresh oysters**. The food feels special without being too fancy, and it costs around $20–$35. It's close to downtown shops, so you can stop by after walking around.

For bigger portions and a laid-back vibe, check out **Chinooks Bar & Grill** at **1404 4th Avenue**, right near the water. Their **fish and chips** are crispy and filling, and their **seafood chowder** is perfect if you need something warm. Meals cost $15–$25, and it's a great spot to hang out with friends or family after a long day.

If you need a quick breakfast or lunch, go to **Sea Bean Café** on **225 4th Avenue**. They make great coffee, sandwiches, and bagels. Try the **smoked salmon bagel** if you want something local. Prices are about $10–$15, and it's a nice, chill place to take a break.

For dessert, head to **Harbor Street Creamery** at **1221 4th Avenue**, close to the harbor. They make their own ice cream, and the flavors like wild berries are amazing. It's also super cheap, about $5–$10, so it's a fun stop if you're walking around.

If you're in the mood for pizza, **Apollo Restaurant** at **229 4th Avenue** has a seafood pizza with shrimp and halibut that's really good. They also have pasta and grilled fish if you're not into pizza. Meals here cost $15–$30, and it's a lively place that's good for groups.

Everything is close to the harbor or downtown, so it's easy to find and get to. The food is fresh, especially the seafood, and there's a mix of casual and nicer spots, so you'll definitely find something you'll like.

8.6 Accommodation in Seward

For a peaceful spot with amazing views, go to **Resurrection Lodge on the Bay** at **13970 Beach Drive**. It's about 10 minutes by car from the harbor, and parking is free. Rooms start at $200 a night, and you might even see otters or seals from your window. It's quiet and feels close to nature, but you're still not far from town. You can also explore **Lowell Point State Recreation Area**, which is nearby and perfect for a walk or some beach time.

If you want to stay right downtown, **Hotel Seward** at **221 5th Avenue** is super convenient. It's close to shops, restaurants, and the harbor, so you don't need a car to get around. Rooms start at $150, and the hotel has a mix of old-school charm and modern touches. You can walk to places like **The Cookery** for great seafood—it's only a block or two away.

For something by the water and close to the harbor, check out **Harbor 360 Hotel** at **1412 4th Avenue**. It's perfect if you're doing boat tours or fishing trips because it's right next to the docks. Rooms cost between $180 and $250 a night, and some have awesome views of the harbor. Breakfast is included, which is nice if you've got an early start. Plus, the **Alaska SeaLife Center** is just a short drive if you want to check it out.

If you're on a budget, **Moby Dick Hostel** at **504 3rd Avenue** is a good pick. Dorm beds are $40–$50 a night, and they have private rooms too. It's basic but clean, and you can walk to spots like **Sea Bean Café** for coffee or a quick breakfast. It's close to everything downtown, so you don't need a car if you're staying here.

For something more fun and unique, try the **Nauti Otter Inn and Yurt Village** at **13609 Seward Highway**. They have yurts and cabins starting at $80 a night. It's about 10 minutes by car from downtown, and it feels super quirky and chill. The staff is friendly and can help you find cool stuff to do nearby.

If you're camping or have an RV, head to **Seward Waterfront Park**. It's right on the bay and super close to downtown and the harbor. You can park your RV or set up a tent with views of Resurrection Bay, and it costs $20–$40 a night. The spot is simple, but the views make it totally worth it. Book early in summer because it gets busy.

8.7 The Scenic Seward Highway

8.7.1 Points of Interest Along the Way

When you drive the Seward Highway, every stop feels like its own adventure, so take your time and enjoy. About 20 miles from Anchorage, you'll hit **Beluga Point**, where there's a wide turnout right off the road. You can park and look out at Turnagain Arm, where the water stretches forever, surrounded by sharp mountains. In summer, watch for **beluga whales** near the shore, especially at high tide. It's one of the easiest and prettiest stops early in the drive.

A little further, you'll find **Potter Marsh**, which has a long boardwalk over the wetlands. It's just off the highway and easy to park. You'll see birds like swans and ducks, and sometimes a moose if you're lucky. It's quiet and free, a great place to stretch your legs and take a few photos.

As you keep going, stop at **Bird Point**, one of the best spots for views of Turnagain Arm. There's a big parking lot, and it's perfect for catching the **bore tide** if you time it right. That's when the water rushes in like a wave, and it's super cool to see. The mountains around here make it feel like you're in a postcard.

After Bird Point, you'll pass the town of **Girdwood**, about 40 miles from Anchorage. Turn off the highway here and check out **Alyeska Resort** if you want an epic view. The tram ride costs $35, but it takes you straight up the mountain, where you can see glaciers and valleys that seem to go on forever. If you're hungry, stop by **The Bake Shop** in town. Their cinnamon rolls are huge, and they cost about $5. It's a cozy little place that's perfect for a snack.

As you get deeper into the mountains, stop at **Turnagain Pass**, around Mile 70. There's a big parking area, and the views of the wide-open valleys and peaks are amazing. In summer, the wildflowers make it even prettier. You can take a short walk or just sit and enjoy how peaceful it is up here.

Closer to Seward, you'll see **Kenai Lake** with its bright turquoise water. Pull over at **Primrose Campground** or one of the lakeside pullouts. It's the kind of spot where you'll want to just sit and take in the view for a while. The water is so clear it feels unreal, and the mountains reflected in the lake are perfect for photos.

Just before Seward, stop at **Tern Lake**, where the Sterling and Seward Highways meet. The lake is small but so calm that the mountains around it look like a mirror in the water. If you're into birdwatching, this is a good spot to see Arctic terns flying over the water. There's a small parking area, so it's easy to pull over and take a quick break.

Leave early so you don't feel rushed, and fuel up in Anchorage or Girdwood because there aren't many gas stations after that.

8.7.2 Driving Tips and Recommendations

When you're driving the Seward Highway, start by making sure you've got enough gas. Fill up in Anchorage before you leave because gas stations are limited. The best spot after Anchorage is in **Girdwood**, about 40 miles down the highway. If you skip it, you won't see another good stop until you're much closer to Seward, so don't take any chances—just fill up when you can.

The road itself is good, but it's full of curves, steep parts, and spots where the shoulder is really narrow. It's pretty easy to drive if you stay focused, but you've got to keep an eye on your speed because the limits change a lot depending on how tight the turns are. You'll also be sharing the road with big RVs, buses, and sometimes cyclists, especially in the summer. If you're slower than the cars behind you, use the pullouts to let them pass—it's safer and less stressful.

Wildlife is everywhere along this highway, especially moose. They like to come out near the trees early in the morning or late in the evening, and they're big, so you really don't want to hit one. If you see one near the road, slow down and be ready to stop. Bears are around too, but they're usually further back in the woods.

Weather changes fast here. Even if it's sunny when you start, you could hit rain, fog, or even snow if it's early spring or late fall. In winter, it's icy and snowy, so go slow and keep plenty of space between you and the car in front. Turn your headlights on no matter the weather because it helps everyone see you, especially when it's foggy or the light changes in the mountains.

There's no real public transport on this road, so you've got to have your own car. Cell service disappears in some spots, especially in the mountains, so download your maps before you leave. Let someone know your plans if you're driving alone, just in case something happens.

Stop only in the designated turnouts—they're there for a reason. Don't ever stop on the shoulder or in the middle of the road, even if the view looks amazing, because cars and RVs come around corners fast. Use the pullouts like the ones near **Bird Point** or **Turnagain Pass** to take your photos or enjoy the view safely.

Leave early in the morning if you can. The road gets busy in summer, and mornings are calmer, plus the light is perfect for pictures. Bring snacks or grab something in Girdwood. A quick stop at **The Bake Shop** for a cinnamon roll is a good idea—they're cheap, around $5, and super filling.

8.7.3 Wildlife Viewing Opportunities

When you're driving the Seward Highway, it's one of the best places to see wildlife up close if you know where to stop and what to look for. Start at **Beluga Point**, about 20 miles south of Anchorage, which is right along Turnagain Arm. There's a big turnout where you can park safely and look out over the water. This is the spot to watch for **beluga whales**, especially in late summer when they follow the salmon close to shore. High tide is the best time to see them, and if you bring binoculars, it's even easier to spot their white backs in the water. The view here is amazing even if you don't see whales, with the mountains and the arm stretching out around you.

Keep going and stop at **Bird Point**, around Mile 96. This area has a big parking lot, picnic tables, and a little trail where you can walk to see more of Turnagain Arm. Look up at the cliffs and the tall trees because this is a prime spot for **bald eagles**. They like to perch high up, looking for fish, especially during the salmon runs. Sometimes, you'll see them flying low over the water. It's peaceful here and a great place to take a break and enjoy the scenery.

EVERYTHING YOU NEED, NOTHING YOU DON'T

Between **Girdwood** and **Turnagain Pass**, keep your eyes on the edges of the forest and the open fields near the road. This stretch is perfect for spotting **moose**, especially early in the morning or late in the evening. They're huge, so you'll notice them if they're around, but don't get too close. If you see one near the road, slow down and watch from your car or pull over safely. Moose can be unpredictable, and they'll move wherever they want, so it's best to give them space.

At **Turnagain Pass**, around Mile 70, there's a big parking area where you can stop and look around. In summer, the open meadows are full of wildflowers, and you might spot smaller animals like **marmots** running around. In winter, if you look up at the rocky ridges, you can sometimes see **mountain goats** climbing high above. This spot is quiet and feels like the middle of nowhere, which is part of what makes it special.

When you get closer to **Kenai Lake**, especially near **Primrose Trailhead**, look out over the water for **ducks, geese, and swans**. This lake is calm, turquoise, and surrounded by mountains, making it one of the prettiest stops along the way. There are small pullouts where you can park and just watch the birds or enjoy how peaceful it is. It's also a great spot to take pictures because the colors are so vibrant.

Always use the pullouts to stop safely; never pull over on the shoulder or in the middle of the road because the highway is busy, and cars come up fast. Bring binoculars or a camera with a good zoom so you can see the animals without getting too close. If you're stopping for food, Girdwood is a good halfway point, and you can grab something quick like a cinnamon roll at **The Bake Shop** for about $5 before heading back on the road.

This highway is full of life if you're patient and know where to look.

CHAPTER NINE
HOMER

9.1 Discover Homer

Homer is a small town at the end of the **Sterling Highway**, about four hours' drive south of Anchorage. It's right on the edge of **Kachemak Bay**, with mountains and glaciers that look like they were pulled straight out of a postcard. The first thing you'll notice is the **Homer Spit**, a long, skinny piece of land sticking out into the water where most of the action happens. The harbor is there, filled with boats, shops, and restaurants, so it feels busy but still laid-back.

If you're driving, just follow the Sterling Highway straight into town. Make sure to fill up your gas tank in **Anchor Point** or **Soldotna** because there aren't many options near Homer. If you don't have a car, you can take a shuttle like the **Alaska Bus Company**, but they only run once a day, so plan ahead. There's also a small airport in Homer if you'd rather fly, and it's just a short drive from the town center.

The main part of Homer is along **Pioneer Avenue**, where you'll find little art galleries, coffee shops, and stores selling handmade crafts. The town is known for its creative side, so you'll see lots of paintings, pottery, and wood carvings inspired by the bay and the wildlife around here. Stop by the **Bunnell Street Arts Center** if you want to see some of the best local art—everything here feels like it's connected to the nature around it.

The views are everywhere, and they're incredible. From almost any spot in town, you can see **Grewingk Glacier** across the bay, the mountains rising straight out of the water, and boats going in and out of the harbor. The light changes all the time, so the water and the sky always look a little different. Even if you just walk down to **Bishop's Beach**, which is easy to reach from downtown, you'll feel like you're in the middle of something wild and beautiful. Eagles often fly overhead, and sometimes you'll see seals bobbing in the water. It's free and quiet, and it feels like your own little escape.

Homer is also famous for its fresh seafood. At **Captain Pattie's**

Fish House on the Spit, you can try halibut or salmon that was probably caught that same day. Plates cost around $25–$40, and the food is worth every penny. If you want something more casual, head to **The Chart Room** at Land's End Resort, right at the end of the Spit, and grab their seafood chowder for about $15. You can sit by the window and look out at the bay while you eat.

This town has a strong connection to the ocean. The harbor is the heart of everything, with fishing boats unloading their catches and people gearing up for fishing charters or wildlife tours. Even if you're not into fishing, it's fun to walk along the docks and watch everything happening. It's the kind of place where life revolves around the water, and you can feel that in everything from the food to the way people talk about the bay.

9.2 Getting to Homer

To get to Homer, you'll drive the **Sterling Highway**, which starts in Anchorage and takes you all the way to the southern tip of the **Kenai Peninsula**. It's about a 225-mile trip, and it'll take you four to five hours depending on how many times you stop to enjoy the views along the way. The road is smooth and paved, but it gets curvy and narrow in spots, so just take it easy and keep an eye on the speed limits.

Make sure to **fill your gas tank** in Anchorage before you leave. The next good place to refuel is in **Soldotna**, which is about halfway to Homer. If you don't stop there, your last reliable spot for gas is in **Anchor Point**, around 15 miles before you reach Homer. Gas stations are spread out, so don't wait until you're running low.

The drive is beautiful, and you'll see some amazing spots on the way. One of the best views is at the **Kenai River**, near Soldotna, where the water is bright turquoise and surrounded by forests. If you have time, pull over at one of the scenic areas—it's worth it. Closer to Homer, you'll pass **Anchor Point**, where you can see across Cook Inlet to snow-covered volcanoes like **Mount Iliamna** and **Mount Redoubt**. The views just keep getting better the closer you get to Homer.

If you're not driving, the **Alaska Bus Company** has shuttles that run daily from Anchorage to Homer. The ride takes about six hours with stops in Soldotna and Anchor Point along the way. Tickets are around $100 one-way, and the buses are comfortable, but they only run once a day, so you'll need to plan your schedule carefully.

You can also fly into Homer if you don't have time for the drive. Regional airlines like **Ravn Alaska** offer quick flights from Anchorage that take about 45 minutes. When you land at the **Homer Airport**, it's only a 10-minute drive into town. Taxis and rental cars are easy to find right outside the airport, so you'll have no trouble getting where you need to go.

On the way, if you need a break, stop in Soldotna and grab a meal at **Buckets Sports Grill** on **Sterling Highway**. They've got great burgers, and a full meal will cost you about $15–$20. For something lighter, you can stop at **Two Sisters Bakery** in Homer after you arrive, where you can get fresh pastries and coffee for $5–$10.

9.3 Exploring Homer

9.3.1 Homer Spit

The **Homer Spit** is this super cool, skinny stretch of land that sticks out 4.5 miles into **Kachemak Bay**, and it's packed with stuff to do. You'll see fishing boats everywhere, little shops, seafood places, and a harbor that's always busy. To get there, you just follow **Spit Road**, which branches off the main **Sterling Highway** as you roll into Homer. If you're not driving, a bus or shuttle can drop you off in town, and a taxi from downtown to the Spit is about $10. Once you're there, parking is all along the Spit, but in summer, it fills up fast, so try to park toward the start and walk in if you want to explore more easily.

EVERYTHING YOU NEED, NOTHING YOU DON'T

The harbor is the first big stop, and it's buzzing all the time. Fishing charters leave from here, so if you're into catching **halibut or salmon**, this is the place to book your trip. Charters like **Homer Ocean Charters** charge about $275–$350 for a full day on the water, and they provide all the gear you need. Even if you're not fishing, just walking the docks is fun—you'll see giant halibut being unloaded, people chatting about their catches, and maybe even seals hanging around hoping for scraps.

If you're hungry, there's no shortage of food. Right near the harbor, grab some **halibut tacos** or seafood chowder at **The Fish Dock** for $10–$15, or sit down for a fresh, local meal at **Captain Pattie's Fish House**, where plates like grilled halibut cost $25–$40. You can eat outside and enjoy views of the bay while watching the boats.

Keep walking, and you'll hit the **boardwalks**, lined with quirky little shops and galleries. Each one is different—some sell handmade jewelry or pottery, while others have paintings and photos of the local mountains and glaciers. **Captain's Curios** is a fun spot to check out for small, affordable souvenirs like wood carvings or marine-themed gifts. Prices are all over the place, from $20 for smaller items to a few hundred for original art, so there's something for everyone.

Toward the end of the Spit, you'll find **Land's End Resort**, which is a great place to stop and just take in the views. From here, you can see across the bay to glaciers and snow-covered mountains—it's like something out of a movie. The water is so clear, and if you're lucky, you might even see otters floating nearby. It's a quiet, perfect spot to relax after exploring.

The Spit has been around for a long time. It started as a coal shipping hub in the 1800s and grew into this fishing and tourist hub it is today. You'll notice plaques here and there sharing fun facts about its history as you walk around. There's also a **Farmers Market** near the start of the Spit on certain days in summer, where you can grab fresh bread for about $5 or handmade crafts for $10–$15.

It's easy to spend hours here without running out of things to see or do.

9.3.2 Pratt Museum

The **Pratt Museum** is right at **3779 Bartlett Street**, just a quick drive or an easy walk from downtown Homer. If you're coming from **Pioneer Avenue**, the main road in town, turn onto **Bartlett Street** near Safeway, and you'll see the museum clearly marked with plenty of free parking right next to it. If you're not driving, a taxi from anywhere in Homer will cost you around $10–$15.

The museum is open **Tuesday through Saturday from 10 AM to 5 PM in summer**, but the hours get shorter in winter, so check ahead if you're visiting outside the peak season. Tickets are **$15 for adults, $10 for seniors**, and **$5 for kids aged 6–17**, while kids under 5 get in for free.

Inside, you'll find fascinating exhibits all about the history, wildlife, and culture of the area. The **wildlife displays** are incredible—they've got life-sized models of whales and bears, plus interactive stuff like a **tide pool tank** where you can touch live sea stars and anemones. It's one of the most fun parts of the museum, especially for kids, but honestly, it's pretty cool for anyone who likes hands-on learning.

There's also the **Harrington Cabin**, a small log house just outside the main museum. It's a real homestead cabin from the early 1900s that shows how people used to live out here. Inside, you'll see old furniture, tools, and things settlers used every day, giving you a real sense of how tough but resourceful they had to be.

The **art gallery** inside features work from local artists, with paintings, sculptures, and even photos that all showcase the beauty of the bay, the mountains, and the wildlife around Homer. The exhibits change regularly, so there's always something new to see. If you like what you see, some pieces are for sale—prints usually cost around $50, but originals can go for a few hundred.

The museum also dives deep into **Native Alaskan culture**, with exhibits about the **Sugpiaq and Dena'ina peoples**, who've lived around **Kachemak Bay** for thousands of years. You'll see traditional tools, clothing, and artifacts that tell their stories and show how they've thrived in this unique environment.

They hold **special events** too, like storytelling sessions, art workshops, and guided walks around the museum's garden area, which is full of native plants. These extras are often included in the admission price, so if something's happening when you're there, don't miss it.

The outdoor areas are just as great. There's a small garden where you can walk around and relax, plus an observation deck with a peaceful view of **Kachemak Bay**. It's a nice spot to take a breather and soak in the scenery.

When you're done at the museum, you should definitely check out **Two Sisters Bakery** on **Bunnell Avenue**. It's only a 5-minute drive away and perfect for grabbing something fresh and tasty. Their sandwiches and pastries are local favorites, and most cost between $10 and $15. The cinnamon rolls are amazing if you're in the mood for something sweet.

9.3.3 Art Galleries and Local Crafts

Homer has some of the coolest art galleries and shops you'll ever visit, all packed with local creativity. Most of them are along **Pioneer Avenue** and **Bunnell Street**, super easy to find. If you're staying in town, you can walk or drive; there's parking right outside most spots, and if you need a taxi, it's about $10–$15 anywhere around Homer.

Start at the **Bunnell Street Arts Center** on **106 W. Bunnell Avenue**. It's a really chill place, with all kinds of art—paintings, sculptures, even mixed media stuff—that shows off how people see the mountains, the sea, and life around here. A lot of the art is for sale. Prints go for about $50, and the bigger original pieces can be over $1,000, but they're worth a look even if you're not buying. Sometimes they do workshops or artist talks, so it's fun to check their schedule if you're in town.

Next, head over to **Fireweed Gallery** at **475 E. Pioneer Avenue**. This place has a little bit of everything: pottery, photography, and paintings. The pottery is my favorite—it's colorful and all handmade, with mugs and bowls starting around $25. If you like photos of cool landscapes and wildlife, you'll love their prints, which usually cost about $100 and up, depending on the size.

A few steps down the road is **Ptarmigan Arts**, a cozy co-op gallery at **471 E. Pioneer Avenue**. You'll find glass art, hand-knit scarves, and some gorgeous wood carvings. The best part? You'll probably meet one of the artists working there, and they'll tell you all about how they made the stuff. Small things like jewelry or ornaments cost $15–$30, and bigger pieces like paintings or sculptures can go for a few hundred bucks.

If you want to see something really different, visit the **Kachemak Bay Wooden Boat Society**. It's a bit out of the way but worth the trip if you like cool handmade wooden crafts and maritime vibes. They've got small items like carved decorations and bigger pieces related to boat building that show off the skills of local artisans.

If you're in town on the **First Friday of the month**, you're in luck. That's when the **First Friday Art Walk** happens, and all the galleries stay open late, put out snacks, and sometimes have live music or special exhibits. It's such a fun, chill way to see the art scene all in one go.

For a snack while you're wandering, stop at **Wild Honey Bistro** on **Pioneer Avenue**. They make killer crepes for about $12 and serve coffee that's just what you need to keep going. If you're over by Bunnell Street, go to **Two Sisters Bakery**—their pastries are amazing, and most cost around $10–$15.

9.3.4 Alaska Islands and Ocean Visitor Center

The **Alaska Islands and Ocean Visitor Center** is at **95 Sterling Highway**, just as you're coming into Homer. It's really easy to find because it's right off the main road, and the parking lot is big and free, so no stress about where to leave your car. If you're staying in downtown Homer, you could walk here in about 15 minutes, or grab a taxi for around $10 if you don't feel like walking.

Inside, this place is like stepping into a marine world without getting wet. The exhibits are all about the birds, sea creatures, and ecosystems around **Kachemak Bay** and the nearby islands. One of the coolest parts is the **seabird exhibit**, where you can hear the sounds of puffins and kittiwakes, and even see maps of their nesting spots. There's a touchscreen display that lets you zoom in on the rocky cliffs where these birds live. It's not just reading signs—it's interactive and makes you feel like you're out there.

Another favorite is the **underwater exhibit**, where you get to explore kelp forests and see what's living under the waves. There are touchscreens to learn about everything from crabs to fish, and even a tide pool tank where you can touch sea stars and anemones. It's hands-on and great for kids, but honestly, it's fun for anyone who's curious.

Right outside the building, there's the **Beluga Slough Trail**, a flat and easy walking path through wetlands. It's perfect for spotting birds like bald eagles or cranes, and sometimes you might even see a moose wandering in the marsh. The trail takes about 30 minutes to walk, and it's super relaxing with benches along the way if you want to just sit and enjoy the view. If you're into wildlife, bring binoculars—they're handy for spotting birds or getting a closer look at the bay.

The center also offers **free guided tours** of the trail, usually led by someone who knows a ton about the local plants and animals. These walks are great if you want to learn more without having to figure it all out yourself. If you prefer to go solo, there are signs along the trail that explain what you're seeing, so you won't miss out on any of the cool stuff.

The center is open **Tuesday through Saturday from 10 AM to 5 PM in summer**, but in winter, the hours are shorter, so check before you go. Admission is completely free, which is awesome, especially if you're traveling on a budget. Inside, there's a gift shop with really cool things like wildlife-themed mugs, books, and handmade crafts. Most items are affordable—postcards and magnets start at $5, and more unique stuff like prints or small carvings might cost $20–$50.

If you're hungry after your visit, head to **Fresh Sourdough Express**, just a quick drive down **Sterling Highway**. They have amazing sandwiches, soups, and fresh bread, and most meals are priced between $10 and $15. Their sourdough bread is super popular, so try that if you're stopping by.

9.4 Outdoor Activities in Homer

9.4.1 Fishing Charters

Fishing charters in Homer are the real deal if you want to catch big halibut and have a great time on the water. Almost all the charters leave from the **Homer Spit**, which is super easy to find. Just drive straight down **Homer Spit Road**, and you'll see the docks and charter offices everywhere. There's plenty of parking nearby, and if you're staying in town, it's just a quick taxi ride for about **$10 to $15**. Some coffee stands like **Coal Town Coffee** open early on the Spit, so you can grab a hot drink while you wait.

The boats usually leave early, around **6 or 7 AM**, so get there a bit earlier to check in and meet your captain and crew. Most charters offer **half-day trips** that last 4–6 hours, costing around **$175 to $225**, or **full-day trips** that go 8–10 hours for about **$250 to $350** per person. Everything you need—rods, reels, bait, and tackle—is included in the price, so you just need to dress warm, pack a lunch, and be ready for some action.

Once you're on the boat, the captain takes you out into **Cook Inlet** or further into **Kachemak Bay**, depending on where the fish are biting that day. The ride out is amazing, with views of mountains and maybe even whales or sea otters along the way. The crew will help you set up your gear and show you how to fish if it's your first time. Halibut fishing isn't super hard, but these fish are big and strong, so reeling them in can feel like a workout. Most halibut you'll catch weigh between **20 and 50 pounds**, but some people reel in monsters over **100 pounds**, which is insane and makes for a great story.

When you catch a fish, the crew helps make sure it's all by the rules. You're allowed to keep **two halibut per person**, and the crew will clean and fillet your fish back at the dock. If you can't cook it yourself, places on the Spit can vacuum-pack and freeze your fish for about **$1–$2 per pound**, or even ship it home for you. If you want to eat it fresh, some restaurants like **Captain Pattie's Fish House** will cook your catch if you ask ahead.

Make sure you dress smart for the trip. Even in summer, it's cold and windy out on the water, so wear layers, bring a waterproof jacket, and make sure you've got non-slip shoes. Pack snacks, water, and maybe a sandwich since most boats don't provide food, though they usually have coffee or tea. If you're worried about getting seasick, take motion sickness pills before you go—it's way better than spending the day feeling sick.

If you've got extra time after fishing, there are cool shops along the Spit where you can buy gear, snacks, or souvenirs. For a good meal, check out **The Chart Room Restaurant** at **Land's End Resort**, right at the end of the Spit. They've got awesome seafood, and the views from their windows are just as good as what you'll see on the boat.

9.4.2 Kachemak Bay State Park

Kachemak Bay State Park is just across the water from Homer, and getting there feels like the start of an adventure. There's no road to the park, so you'll need to take a water taxi from the **Homer Spit**. The taxis leave from the docks right at the Spit, which is super easy to find—it's just at the end of **Homer Spit Road**, where all the boats and tour companies are lined up. Companies like **Mako's Water Taxi** or **Bay Excursions** can take you across in about 20–30 minutes. It costs around **$75–$100 per person for a round trip**, depending on where you're going in the park. Make sure to book in advance, especially in the summer, because the taxis fill up fast. They'll also set a pickup time for you to get back, so double-check that so you're not stuck there.

The park is huge,

ALASKA ACTION PLAN

with mountains, glaciers, forests, and beaches all packed into one place. Hiking is one of the best things to do here, with trails that range from super easy to really challenging. The **Grewingk Glacier Trail** is a favorite and pretty straightforward. You'll start at the **Glacier Spit Trailhead**, which the water taxi will drop you at, and hike about three miles through forest and open meadows to a glacier lake. The lake has floating icebergs, and the views of **Grewingk Glacier** are insane. The trail isn't too steep, so it's good for most people, but wear sturdy shoes because the ground can get uneven in spots.

If you're up for a harder hike, the **Grace Ridge Trail** is amazing. It's about 9.5 miles long and takes you up to a ridge with views of the bay, the mountains, and even Homer in the distance. It's steep in some parts and takes about 6–8 hours, so you'll want to pack plenty of water, snacks, and layers for the weather. Most people arrange for the taxi to drop them off at **Kayak Beach** and pick them up at the other end near the **South Grace Ridge Trailhead**.

If hiking isn't your thing, kayaking in the bay is just as incredible. You can paddle along the coast, explore little coves, and maybe even see wildlife like sea otters, seals, or puffins. You can rent a kayak in Homer for around **$40–$60 for a half day**, or go with a guided tour, which costs about **$100–$150 per person**. A guide is a good idea if you're not used to kayaking because the tides and currents can be tricky here. They'll also take you to the best spots without you having to figure it out on your own.

Wildlife is everywhere in the park. You'll probably see sea otters floating on their backs or seals popping up in the water. Bald eagles are almost always flying overhead, and if you're lucky, you might spot a black bear near the forest edges. Bring binoculars if you can—it's worth it to get a closer look at everything.

When you go, you'll need to bring everything with you because there's nothing for sale in the park—no shops, no restaurants, nothing. Wear layers because the weather can change fast, and bring a rain jacket even if it looks sunny. Hiking boots or good walking shoes are a must. Pack water, snacks, sunscreen, and bug spray because the mosquitoes can get annoying in the summer. If you're kayaking, dry bags for your stuff are a lifesaver, and if you're hiking, bring a small backpack to carry everything.

Before you head out, grab some food in Homer to take with you. **Two Sisters Bakery** on **Bunnell Avenue** makes amazing sandwiches and pastries that are perfect for a trail lunch. Sandwiches cost about **$10–$15**, and their cookies and cinnamon rolls are around **$5** each. If you're in a rush, stop by **Coal Town Coffee** near the Spit for a quick breakfast sandwich and coffee to-go.

After a long day of hiking or paddling, head back to Homer and treat yourself to a meal at **The Chart Room Restaurant** at **Land's End Resort**, right at the end of the Spit. They serve fresh seafood, like halibut and salmon, with entrees costing between **$20 and $35**. Plus, the views from the dining room are incredible, especially if you catch the sunset.

9.4.3 Bear Viewing Tours

Bear viewing tours from Homer are an amazing way to see wild bears in their natural home. Everything starts at **Homer Airport**, which is just a short drive off **Sterling Highway**. If you're staying in town, it's about 5–10 minutes by taxi, costing around **$10–$15**, or you can park your car at the airport. There's no public transport here, so plan ahead. The tours take you to places like **Katmai National Park** or **Lake Clark National Park**, where bears live undisturbed, and you'll get there in a small plane. The flight itself is incredible—you'll see mountains, rivers, and beaches from above, and it takes about **30–60 minutes** depending on the spot.

Tour companies like **Alaska Bear Adventures**, **Homer Air**, and **Emerald Air Service** are some of the best-known operators. They usually fly small groups, just 4–6 people, so you get a front-row seat and plenty of time to watch the bears. Once you land on a remote beach or gravel bar, your guide—a real bear expert—will take you on a short walk to the best viewing areas. You might stand near a river where bears are catching salmon, watch them dig for clams on the beach, or even see a mother playing with her cubs. You'll stay at a safe distance, but it feels close enough to really take it all in.

These tours run from **May to September**, with July and August being the best months because that's when salmon runs bring the bears out in large numbers. Expect to pay around **$600–$800 per person**, which covers the flight and the guide. It's expensive, but this is one of those once-in-a-lifetime things you'll never forget. Book early, though, because spots fill up quickly in the summer.

Dress for anything because the weather changes fast. Wear layers, bring a waterproof jacket, and don't forget sturdy boots since you might walk through muddy areas. Most companies give you rubber boots or waders for walking near water, but ask when you book. Pack snacks and water because food isn't included. A camera with a zoom lens is a must, or use your phone if it has a good zoom. Binoculars are great too if you have them.

Before your tour, grab something to eat in Homer. **Two Sisters Bakery** on **Bunnell Avenue** is perfect for a sandwich or pastry to take with you. Their sandwiches are around **$10–$15**, and pastries like cinnamon rolls or cookies start at **$5**. If you need coffee or a quick breakfast, stop by **Coal Town Coffee** on **Homer Spit Road**, which is close to where many tours meet.

When you're back in Homer, treat yourself to dinner at **Captain Pattie's Fish House** on **Homer Spit Road**. Their fresh seafood, like halibut or crab, is delicious, with prices for main dishes between **$20 and $40**, and the view of the bay makes it even better.

9.5 Dining in Homer

Start at **Captain Pattie's Fish House**, which is right on **Homer Spit Road**. It's easy to find because it's surrounded by shops and tour offices, and there's plenty of parking. Their halibut tacos, king crab legs, and seafood platters are amazing, and you'll spend about **$20–$40** depending on what you order. The best part? You can eat while looking out at Kachemak Bay—it's the perfect place for a relaxing meal after exploring.

For breakfast or lunch, you can't miss **Two Sisters Bakery** on **Bunnell Avenue**. It's not far from downtown Homer and is known for its incredible cinnamon rolls, scones, and fresh bread. Pastries start at **$5**, and their sandwiches, which are big and filling, cost around **$10–$15**. The place has a cozy vibe with local art on the walls, and it's a great spot to grab something to take with you if you're heading out for a hike or a day on the water.

If you're in the mood for pizza, go to **Fat Olives** on **Lake Street**, near downtown Homer. Their wood-fired pizzas are crispy and delicious, with toppings like smoked salmon or roasted garlic that make them special. Pizzas are around **$15–$20**, and they also have clam chowder and fresh salads if you want something lighter. The restaurant has a casual vibe, and it's perfect if you're with friends or family.

If you need coffee or a quick breakfast, stop by **Coal Town Coffee** on **Homer Spit Road**. It's super convenient if you're heading out for a fishing trip or a bear viewing tour. Their breakfast sandwiches are simple and tasty, costing about **$8–$12**, and their coffee is strong enough to wake you up for a busy day. They also have muffins and bagels if you just need a snack.

For something fancier, check out **The Chart Room Restaurant** at **Land's End Resort**. It's all the way at the end of Homer Spit, and the views of the bay from the dining room are amazing, especially at sunset. They serve dishes like grilled halibut and fresh salmon, and prices for entrees are around **$25–$45**. It's a great spot for a nice dinner to end your day.

If you're craving bagels, head to **The Bagel Shop** on **East End Road**, about a 10-minute drive from downtown Homer. Their lox and cream cheese bagel is the most popular, but they have lots of options. Bagels are around **$3–$6**, and everything tastes fresh and handmade. It's a simple, cozy place where you can grab a quick bite or take something with you.

9.6 Accommodation in Homer

For a place with amazing views and everything you need, **Land's End Resort** at the very end of the **Homer Spit** is a great choice. It's right on **4786 Homer Spit Road**, easy to reach by driving straight down the Spit, and there's plenty of parking. Rooms here start around **$150 a night**, and they've got bigger suites if you want more space. The restaurant downstairs, The Chart Room, serves local seafood, and they even have a hot tub and spa if you're in the mood to relax after a long day.

If you like the idea of staying closer to the beach but not on the Spit, **Ocean Shores Hotel** on **3500 Ocean Drive Loop** is perfect. It's a quick drive from downtown and super quiet, plus you can step right out onto the beach. Rooms are around **$120 a night**, and they have little kitchenettes, so you can cook if you want. It's also close to places like **Two Sisters Bakery** if you want fresh pastries in the morning.

For something smaller and cozier, **Halcyon Heights B&B** on **1200 Mission Road** gives you a more personal vibe. It's up on a hill, so the views of the bay and glaciers are amazing. Rooms go for about **$130 to $180 a night**, and they serve breakfast that's homemade and really good. It's about a 10-minute drive from the Spit, so you'll need a car, but it's worth it for the peace and quiet.

If you're on a budget or traveling solo, **Homer Hostel** on **4690 Sterling Highway** is a solid option. It's simple but clean, with dorm beds starting at **$40** or private rooms for **$70 to $90 a night**. It's close to downtown, so you can easily grab food or get to the main shops and tour spots.

Another nice spot is the **Driftwood Inn** on **135 West Bunnell Avenue** in Old Town. It's close to the beach and things like the **Pratt Museum**, plus you can walk to restaurants and shops. They've got regular rooms, cute little cottages, and even RV spots. Prices start at about **$100** and go up depending on what you choose. It's great if you want something local and laid-back.

For something different, check out **Kenai Peninsula Suites** on **3685 Sterling Highway**. They've got underground cabins that feel really unique and even have hot tubs. It's a bit outside town, but still close enough to get to everything quickly. Rooms start at around **$200 a night**, and the views and privacy are totally worth it.

If you're looking for something fancy and quiet, **Baycrest Lodge** on **3651 Sterling Highway** is a bit further out but super peaceful. The cabins come with hot tubs, fireplaces, and kitchens, so it's great if you're staying a few days or just want to spoil yourself. Expect to pay **$250 to $350 a night**, but it's one of those places you'll remember for a long time.

ALASKA ACTION PLAN

CHAPTER TEN
KETCHIKAN

10.1 Discover Homer

Ketchikan sits on **Revillagigedo Island**, right between the Tongass Narrows and the huge Tongass National Forest. You can only get here by plane or boat, which makes it feel special right away. If you're flying, you'll land at **Ketchikan International Airport**, which is on its own little island. From there, it's just a **5-minute ferry ride** to the main town. If you're arriving on a cruise ship, you'll dock right downtown, so you're already in the middle of everything when you step off.

This town is all about fishing, culture, and nature. People call it the **Salmon Capital of the World**, and when you're here, you'll see why. Fishing boats are everywhere, and you'll probably hear someone talking about the salmon runs, whether you're walking by the docks or grabbing a bite to eat. If you're hungry, head to **Annabelle's Famous Keg and Chowder House** on **Front Street**, where the smoked salmon chowder is amazing and costs about **$12**. Their grilled halibut is a little more expensive, starting at **$25**, but totally worth it.

Ketchikan also has a rich history tied to its Native roots. It's famous for **totem poles**, and you'll find them everywhere—in parks, museums, and even along the streets. These tall carvings tell stories about the Tlingit, Haida, and Tsimshian peoples who've lived here for thousands of years. If you want to learn more, check out the **Totem Heritage Center** on **Deermount Street**, a short walk from downtown. It costs about **$6** to get in, and you'll get to see some of the oldest, most detailed totems in the world.

Walking around town is super easy because everything is close together. Streets like **Creek Street** are especially cool, with colorful wooden buildings sitting on stilts over the water. It used to be the town's red-light district, but now it's full of shops and little galleries. If you get hungry or need a coffee break, stop by **Sweet Mermaids Café** on **Dock Street**. You can grab a coffee for **$5** or try their smoked salmon wrap for about **$14**. They also have a shop with local crafts, so it's a great place to pick up something unique.

If you want to go further out, you can hop on a public bus for just **$2**. The buses run along the main roads and can take you to places like **Saxman Native Village**, which is only a few miles south of downtown. The village has even more totem poles and gives you a deeper look into the culture of the area. If you want to stay downtown, though, everything is within walking distance, so you really don't need a car unless you're heading to the outskirts.

10.2 Getting to Ketchikan

Getting to Ketchikan is all about flying or taking a boat since there are no roads connecting it to other towns. If you're flying, you'll land at **Ketchikan International Airport**, which is on a small island called **Gravina Island**, right across the water from the main town. Once you land, you'll hop on a **ferry** that takes just **5 minutes** to cross the Tongass Narrows to the main side of Ketchikan. The ferry runs every **15–30 minutes**, costs around **$6 per person** or **$7 if you're bringing a car**, and is super easy to use. Once you're on the other side, you can grab a taxi, hotel shuttle, or rental car to get downtown, which is just a short drive away. Most flights to Ketchikan connect through **Seattle**, so booking early can help you save money, especially in the busy summer season.

If you'd rather arrive by water, the **Alaska Marine Highway System** ferries are a great option. These ferries connect Ketchikan to other nearby towns like **Juneau** and **Sitka**, or even to **Bellingham, Washington**, if you're coming from the lower 48. The ferry terminal is located on **Tongass Avenue**, about **4 miles north** of downtown, and you can easily get there by taxi or public bus if needed. Tickets for passengers start at around **$250**, and bringing a car will cost between **$500 and $800**, depending on its size. Ferries are slower than flying, but you'll get to enjoy incredible views of the Inside Passage, and there's even a small cafeteria onboard where you can grab a sandwich or coffee during the ride.

Many visitors also arrive by cruise ship, which is one of the most popular ways to visit Ketchikan in the summer. Cruise lines like **Princess**, **Norwegian**, and **Holland America** all stop here as part of their Inside Passage itineraries. Most cruises leave from **Seattle** or **Vancouver**, and prices usually start around **$1,000 per person** for a week-long trip. When your ship docks, it's right in downtown Ketchikan, so you'll be just steps away from shops, restaurants, and the waterfront.

If you need to get around once you're in town, the local **public buses** run along **Tongass Avenue**, and tickets are just **$2 per ride**. Taxis are also easy to find, and most rides within town cost between **$10 and $20**.

10.3 Exploring

Creek Street is right near downtown, super easy to find, and it's one of the coolest places to walk around. It's a wooden boardwalk built over the water along **Ketchikan Creek**, and the whole area feels like stepping back in time. Back in the early 1900s, this was the town's red-light district, full of brothels and bootleggers during Prohibition. The most famous spot is **Dolly's House** at **24 Creek Street**, where Dolly Arthur, a well-known madam, used to live and work. Now, it's a museum where you can walk through her old house and see everything just how it

was back then. It costs **$10** to get in, and it's worth it because the stories are wild and the history is super interesting.

These days, Creek Street is packed with little shops, art galleries, and cafes, but it still has all that old-school charm. The buildings are colorful and sit right on stilts over the water. You can start at the entrance off **Stedman Street** and just wander along the boardwalk. It's all really walkable, so you don't need a car or anything. One place you have to check out is **Soho Coho**, an art gallery with fun and quirky fish-themed prints by Ray Troll. You can grab a cool poster or piece of art for around **$15**, or just look around—it's really unique.

If you're here in the summer, keep an eye on the water below the boardwalk. During the salmon run, usually from **late July to September**, you'll see salmon swimming upstream, and it's amazing to watch, especially if they're jumping out of the water. There are benches along the way where you can sit, relax, and just take it all in. If you're into photography, this is the perfect spot—the creek, the wooden buildings, and the reflection on the water make for awesome shots.

At the end of Creek Street, you'll find the **Married Man's Trail**, which is a short, easy path that takes you into the woods above the boardwalk. It used to be a sneaky route for men coming and going from the brothels back in the day. Now, it's just a quiet little trail where you can stretch your legs and enjoy the trees and creek views. You don't need hiking boots or anything fancy, just wear comfy shoes.

If you get hungry, there are some great places nearby. A few steps away on **Dock Street**, you can stop at **Sweet Mermaids Café** for a coffee or a light lunch. Their smoked salmon wrap is super tasty and costs about **$14**, and their coffee is around **$5** if you just want a quick pick-me-up. There's also an ice cream shop nearby if you're in the mood for something sweet, with cones starting at about **$4**.

10.3.2 Totem Heritage Center

The **Totem Heritage Center** is at **601 Deermount Street**, and it's the place where you'll see real, original totem poles that are more than a hundred years old. These poles were brought here from old Native villages like **Old Kasaan** and **Village Island**, where they were left behind as communities moved. These aren't copies or decorations—they're the real deal, carved by Tlingit, Haida, and Tsimshian people to tell stories about their families, history, and culture.

It's super easy to get here. If you're downtown, just walk up **Deermount Street** for about **15 minutes**, and you'll find it. If you don't want to walk, you can grab the **local bus** for around **$2**, or a taxi will get you here for about **$10**. There's also parking if you're driving. The center is open every day in summer from **9 AM to 5 PM**, and it costs just **$6** to get in, which is a good deal because kids under 12 are free.

When you walk in, you'll feel how calm and respectful the space is—it's all about learning and really seeing the details on the totem poles. These poles are huge, with carvings of animals like ravens and bears, which are super important in Native stories and clans. Each one has signs that explain what the carvings mean, so you'll actually understand the stories they're telling. If you're curious, just ask the staff—they know everything about the poles, like how they were made and why they're so special.

There's more than just the poles here. You'll see tools the carvers used, old pictures of the villages, and other artifacts that give you a better idea of what life was like for the people who made these. You can take photos too, but no flash, so the carvings stay safe. If you want to take a little piece of the experience home, check out the gift shop. They sell books about the totems, cool prints, and crafts inspired by the designs, with prices starting at around **$10**.

You'll probably spend about an hour here, but it's worth taking your time. Afterward, if you're hungry, head down to **Dock Street**, which is just a short walk back toward downtown. Stop by **Sweet Mermaids Café** for a coffee, which costs about **$5**, or try their smoked salmon wrap for around **$14** if you want something local and tasty.

10.3.3 Southeast Alaska Discovery Center

The **Southeast Alaska Discovery Center** is right at **50 Main Street**, super easy to find if you're downtown. It's just a **5-minute walk** from the cruise docks, and if you're coming from farther away, taxis cost about **$10–$15**, or you can hop on the **local bus** for **$2**. If you're driving, there's parking close by. This place is all about showing you what makes the area special—its forests, animals, and the people who've lived here for thousands of years.

When you walk in, the first thing you'll see is all the cool exhibits about the **Tongass National Forest**, which is the biggest in the whole country. They've got displays showing how everything in the forest is connected, from the huge Sitka spruce trees to the salmon that swim in the streams. You can touch samples of tree bark, feel animal furs, and even hear sounds from the forest like birds and rushing water. It's like being in the middle of the woods, but without leaving town.

There's also a section about **salmon**, which is a big deal here. You'll see how they're born in streams, swim out to the ocean, and then come back to lay eggs. It's all explained with videos and displays, so it's easy to understand why salmon are so important—not just to the animals but also to the people here.

The part about **Native cultures** is amazing, too. You'll see tools, masks, and carvings made by the Tlingit, Haida, and Tsimshian peoples. Each piece has a story, and the signs explain everything really well, like what the carvings mean or how certain tools were used. If you have questions, the staff here knows their stuff and will happily explain more.

One of the best spots inside is the **theater**, where you can sit down and watch short films about the wildlife, history, and people of the area. It's included in the ticket price, which is just **$5 for adults**, and kids under 16 get in free. The center is open from **8 AM to 4 PM** in the summer, though hours might be shorter in the off-season, so check ahead if it's not peak tourist time.

If you're hungry after your visit, there are some great places nearby. Just a block away on **Front Street**, check out **Annabelle's Famous Keg and Chowder House** for a bowl of clam chowder, which costs about **$15**, or their fresh halibut tacos for around **$20**. For coffee, head over to **Raven's Brew Coffee** on **Stedman Street**—a cup of their strong, locally roasted coffee is about **$5**.

You'll probably want to spend at least an hour at the Discovery Center, maybe longer if you watch the films or really take your time with the exhibits. There's also a **gift shop** where you can grab field guides, maps, or small souvenirs. Field guides are around **$10**, and there are handmade ornaments and wildlife prints for about **$15–$30**.

10.3.4 Saxman Native Village

Saxman Native Village is at **2841 South Tongass Highway**, just a short **2.5-mile drive south from downtown**. You can get there easily by car, with plenty of parking available right near the entrance. If you don't have a car, taxis from downtown cost around **$10 to $15**, and the **Route 1 bus** will take you there for only **$2**, dropping you off close to the village. It's super convenient, and many guided tours from cruise docks or hotels include transportation.

When you arrive, the first thing you'll notice is the **totem pole park**, which is filled with massive, beautifully carved poles. Each one tells a story—about a family, a legend, or an event. These aren't just decorations; they're full of meaning, and if you take a guided tour, you'll get to hear what they're all about. The guides are great at explaining what the carvings represent, like why the raven means creation or how the bear stands for strength. If you love stories, this is the best way to understand the totem poles because they're like history books carved into wood. Tours cost about **$40 to $60** and usually last **1.5 to 2 hours**, so they're worth it if you want all the details.

The **Clan House**, a giant cedar building in the village, is where you can watch traditional Tlingit performances. Inside, dancers in bright, traditional regalia share songs and stories through movements passed down for generations. The sound of the drums and the way the performers move makes it feel like you're watching history come alive. Performances are usually included in guided tours, and they happen in the late morning and early afternoon when the village is busiest, so plan your visit accordingly.

If you're lucky, the **carving shed** might be open. This is where local artists work on creating new totem poles using old techniques. You can see them carving intricate details into massive logs and even ask questions if they're available. It's amazing to watch, and it gives you a sense of how these traditions are still alive today.

The village is free to visit if you're just walking around the totem poles, but access to the Clan House and performances may require a small fee, depending on how you plan your visit. It's open every day during the summer, from **9 AM to 4 PM**, but hours can change during the off-season, so it's a good idea to check ahead.

After your visit, head back downtown for something to eat. Just a few minutes away, on **Front Street**, you'll find **Annabelle's Famous Keg and Chowder House**, where you can try their famous clam chowder for about **$15** or halibut tacos for **$20**. If you're in the mood for coffee, grab a cup at **Raven's Brew Coffee** for around **$5**.

10.4 Outdoor Activities in Ketchikan

10.4.1 Fishing

Fishing here is so fun and easy to jump into, whether you've done it before or this is your first time. Most charters are right by the docks downtown, near **Front Street** and **Dock Street**, so if you're staying in the area or getting off a cruise ship, it's just a short walk. If you're coming from farther out, taxis are cheap, about **$10 to $15**, or you can catch the **Route 1 bus** for just **$2**, which stops close to the main spots. Some charters even pick you up from your hotel, so ask when you book.

You can expect to catch salmon—like king, coho, or pink—or even big halibut. Half-day trips cost between **$150 and $300**, and full-day trips go for around **$250 to $500**. The price covers everything you need: rods, reels, bait, and a guide who knows exactly where to go to find the fish. You'll need a **fishing license**, which costs **$15 for one day**, and if you're going for king salmon, you'll need a special stamp for another **$15**. Licenses are easy to grab online or at shops like **Tongass Trading Company** or **The Alaska Fish House**, both super close to the docks.

Most charters leave early, around **6 or 7 AM**, so you'll want to be ready to go. The guides are awesome and will teach you how to cast, reel, and handle the fish, so even if you've never fished before, you'll have a blast. The water is calm, the views are incredible, and there's always a chance to reel in something big. If you catch a fish, companies like **Cedars Lodge Fish Processing**, just steps from the docks, can fillet and vacuum-seal it for you, starting at **$2 per pound**. They can even ship it home for you, so you don't have to worry about carrying it.

If you're traveling with kids or don't want to spend a full day fishing, you can book shorter trips, usually **2-3 hours**, which are super fun and less intense. These cost around **$100 to $150 per person** and focus more on enjoying the experience than catching a ton of fish.

Some of the best charters include **Baranof Fishing Excursions** and **Ketchikan Charter Boats**. They're reliable, friendly, and easy to find near the waterfront. Book ahead, especially in summer when everyone wants to fish, because spots fill up fast.

It's really important to dress for the weather, which can change quickly. Wear layers, bring a rain jacket, and make sure your shoes are waterproof. Most boats let you bring snacks and drinks, so pack something to keep you energized, or check if your charter offers food.

After you finish, you'll probably be hungry. Right near the docks, there's **The Alaska Fish House** on **Dock Street**, where you can grab freshly cooked salmon or halibut fish and chips for about **$20-$30**. If you're in the mood for something quick, their smoked salmon chowder is awesome and costs just **$10**. For coffee or dessert, try **Sweet Mermaids Café** on **Front Street**, where a coffee or treat will run you about **$5**.

10.4.2 Hiking Trails

Hiking is one of the best things you can do. The trails are close, easy to find, and show off some of the most amazing views you'll ever see. The **Deer Mountain Trail**, starting at the end of **Deer Mountain Road**, is one of the top hikes. It's about **7 miles round trip** and climbs really high—over **3,000 feet**—so it's not an easy walk, but if you're up for it, the view at the top will blow your mind. You'll see the water, the islands, and even the mountains far away. If you're feeling adventurous, you can keep going to **Blue Lake**, but make sure you have plenty of water, snacks, and good shoes because this trail will take most of your day. Parking is free, and a taxi from downtown will cost about **$10 to $15** if you don't have a car.

For a much easier hike, try the **Rainbird Trail**, which is super close to town. It starts near the **University of Alaska Southeast campus** on **Seventh Avenue** and is just **1.3 miles**. The trail is flat, surrounded by trees, and even has spots where you can look out at the water. It's great if you just want a short walk or don't have much time. You can take the **Route 1 bus** for **$2** to get there or park nearby if you're driving.

Another great spot is **Carlanna Lake Trail**, which is at the end of **Carlanna Lake Road**. This one is also easy, about **2 miles round trip**, and takes you to a peaceful lake surrounded by big trees. It's quiet, super pretty, and great if you're looking for a calm hike. If you want more of a challenge, you can follow a rough trail that goes up the hills, but it's less maintained, so be careful. Taxis from downtown cost about **$10 to $20**, and parking at the trailhead is free.

If you're up for a little trip outside of town, head to **Settlers Cove Loop Trail** in the **Settlers Cove State Recreation Site**, about **18 miles north** along **North Tongass Highway**. The loop is only **1.2 miles**, so it's perfect for a short but beautiful walk. You'll pass through a mossy forest, see a little waterfall, and end up at a rocky beach where you can just sit and enjoy the waves. It's a peaceful, easy hike that's great for families. If you don't have a car, a taxi ride here will cost about **$40 to $50**, so maybe split the ride with others if you can.

Make sure to dress for rain because it happens a lot here. Wear waterproof shoes and bring a jacket so you stay comfortable. The trails can get slippery when it's wet, so watch your step, especially on Deer Mountain.

When you're done, grab something to eat. Go to **Sweet Mermaids Café** on **Front Street** for soup and sandwiches, which cost about **$15**, or head to **The Alaska Fish House** on **Dock Street**. Their smoked salmon chowder is just **$10** and is the perfect way to warm up after a hike.

10.4.3 Misty Fjords National Monument

he cliffs are so tall they seem endless, with waterfalls spilling down into the still, glassy water. You can only get there by **boat** or **floatplane**, which makes the trip feel even more special. It's about **22 miles east of town**, and tours leave from the docks downtown, close to **Front Street** and **Berth 2**. If you're walking from anywhere near the waterfront or getting off a cruise ship, it's super easy to reach.

If you go by **boat**, you'll spend about **5 to 6 hours** cruising

ALASKA ACTION PLAN

through the fjords. The ride is slow, so you get plenty of time to take in the huge granite cliffs, endless green trees, and all the wildlife. Expect to see **seals**, **sea lions**, and maybe even **orcas or humpback whales** swimming by. Bald eagles are everywhere—flying overhead or sitting high in the trees. Boats have big windows and outdoor decks, so you can stay warm inside or head outside for even better views. Tickets for boat tours cost around **$150 to $250 per person**, and it's a good idea to book a day or two ahead, especially in summer when it gets busy.

For something faster and even more incredible, a **floatplane tour** is an amazing option. Planes take off from the **Ketchikan Harbor Seaplane Base**, which is just at the end of **Water Street**. The flight gives you a view of the fjords you just can't get from the water—you'll see cliffs, narrow inlets, and hidden waterfalls from above. Most tours are **1 to 2 hours** long, and many include a stop where the plane lands on the water so you can step out and feel like you're in the middle of nowhere. The price for a floatplane ride is higher, usually **$250 to $400 per person**, but the experience is worth every penny. Make sure you book early since these tours often fill up fast, especially in the summer months.

To get to the docks or the seaplane base, taxis cost about **$10 to $15** from most hotels, or you can take the **Route 1 bus** for just $2, which stops near **Front Street**.

EVERYTHING YOU NEED, NOTHING YOU DON'T

Dress for the weather because it's often cooler on the water or in the air. Bring a rainproof jacket, wear layers to stay warm, and don't forget comfy shoes. If you're going on a boat tour, pack some snacks and water just in case you get hungry during the trip. For floatplane tours, pack light since there isn't much space—just your jacket, camera, or phone.

After you finish the tour, grab something warm to eat. Stop by **Annabelle's Famous Keg and Chowder House** on **Front Street** for their creamy clam chowder or fresh seafood pasta, which costs about **$20 to $30**. If you're in the mood for something quick, head to **Sweet Mermaids Café** on **Dock Street** for a coffee and pastry, priced around **$5 to $10**.

10.5 Dining in Ketchikan

If you want to eat here, the seafood is the main thing you can't miss. Start at **Annabelle's Famous Keg and Chowder House** on **326 Front Street**, which is right downtown and easy to walk to if you're staying nearby or coming from the cruise docks. Their clam chowder is super creamy and costs about **$10**—it's perfect if you want something warm and filling. Their halibut fish and chips are really popular too, with crispy batter and soft fish, and that's about **$25**. If you're extra hungry, the seafood pasta loaded with shrimp and scallops is around **$28**, and it's a big portion that'll fill you up.

For something quicker, head to **The Alaska Fish House** on **Dock Street**. It's close to the water, so you can eat and look out at the harbor. Their smoked salmon chowder, which costs **$12**, has this amazing smoky flavor, and their halibut tacos, at **$15**, are fresh and light but still satisfying. The vibe is casual, and it's a good spot if you're on a tight schedule.

If you want a burger or something simple, try **Burger Queen** on **518 Water Street**. This place is small but really popular for their halibut sandwiches, which cost about **$14**, and they're crispy and delicious. Their cheeseburgers are about **$12**, and everything is made fresh. It's more of a grab-and-go place because there's not a lot of seating, but you can take your food and eat by the waterfront.

For a nicer meal with a view, go to **Cape Fox Lodge**. You can get there by the **funicular** near **Married Man's Trail**, or just drive up **Ketchikan Lakes Road**. Their cedar-plank salmon is probably the best thing on the menu—it's about **$35**, and it's cooked perfectly with a smoky flavor. If you want to share something, the crab-stuffed mushrooms are **$16**, and they're a great way to start your meal. The lodge has huge windows, so you'll get an awesome view of the water while you eat.

If you just want coffee or a light snack, check out **Sweet Mermaids Café** on **5 Creek Street**. They make really good lattes, and their pastries are always fresh. A coffee and a muffin will cost around **$8 to $12**, and it's a cool place to sit and relax because the whole café has quirky art and fun decorations everywhere.

For dessert, stop at **Sweet and Dry** on **Mission Street**. They have ice cream flavors you won't find anywhere else, like spruce tip or smoked salmon, which sound weird but are actually really good. A scoop costs **$4 to $6**, and it's fun to try something totally different.

All these places are pretty close to each other if you're staying downtown, and you can get to them by walking or taking the **Route 1 bus** for just **$2**. Parking is available if you're driving, but you probably won't need a car for most spots.

10.6 Accommodation in Ketchikan

If you need a place to stay, there are lots of good choices here depending on what you like and how much you want to spend. **The Landing Hotel** on **3434 Tongass Avenue** is a solid option if you want something easy and close to everything. It's right by the ferry terminal and about five minutes from the airport. They even have a free shuttle to help you get around. Rooms start at around **$150 per night**, and they're cozy and simple. If you're hungry, their on-site restaurant is great for breakfast or seafood dinners, so you won't have to go far.

For something with more charm, **The Inn at Creek Street** is on **Creek Street**, which means you'll be surrounded by cool boardwalks and shops. It's super close to downtown, so you can walk everywhere. Rooms here are a mix of old-school charm and modern comforts, and they start at about **$130 per night**. Some rooms have views of the water, and during the salmon run, you might even spot fish swimming in the creek. They offer a free shuttle too, which is super handy.

If you're looking for peace and quiet, try **Black Bear Inn** on **5528 North Tongass Highway**. It's about a 10-minute drive from town, so it feels more private. Rooms here start at **$180 per night**, and it's a super relaxing spot surrounded by trees and water. The owners are really helpful and can give you tips on where to go or what to do, like finding good trails or fishing spots.

For a budget-friendly option, **My Place Hotel** on **10885 Tongass Avenue** is great. It's near the airport and ferry terminal, so it's super convenient if you're just passing through. Rooms are simple, with kitchenettes so you can save money by cooking your own meals. Prices start at about **$120 per night**, and it's a practical, no-frills option if you're not looking for anything fancy.

If you want something fancy with amazing views, check out **Cape Fox Lodge**, which sits high above downtown. You can get there by driving up **Ketchikan Lakes Road** or taking the funicular near **Married Man's Trail**. The lodge has stunning views of the water, and the rooms are really nice, starting at about **$220 per night**. They also have a great restaurant where you can try cedar-plank salmon while looking out at the harbor.

CHAPTER ELEVEN
SITKA

11.1 Unique Heritage

It's on Baranof Island, in a spot surrounded by water, mountains, and thick forests. You can get here pretty easily. Flights land at Rocky Gutierrez Airport, with connections from places like Juneau or Seattle. If you're coming by ferry, the Alaska Marine Highway brings you in, and from the terminal, you're just a quick taxi or a short ride on the public bus for about **$2**. Once you're in the town center, most places are close enough to walk.

The streets tell stories. Lincoln Street is where you'll find a lot of the action—restaurants, shops, and landmarks are all lined up, making it a good starting point. This was a key hub when Russia controlled Alaska, and its role in the fur trade left a big mark. At the same time, this is Tlingit land, with thousands of years of traditions tied to the forests and sea. When you walk around, you'll see Russian churches with onion domes sitting close to Tlingit totem poles, a mix that shows how the past and present come together here.

If you want to understand the history, visit Castle Hill, the spot where the United States officially purchased Alaska from Russia in 1867. It's an easy walk from downtown and gives you a great view of the harbor. Not far away is Totem Square, where tall carvings tell Tlingit stories and showcase their culture. Everything here feels connected to the land and its people.

When you're hungry, check out Ludvig's Bistro on Katlian Street for dishes like salmon risotto, which costs around **$28** and blends local ingredients with Mediterranean flavors. For something laid-back, Beak on Lincoln Street serves fresh halibut tacos for about **$16** and has a great view of the water. If you just want coffee and a pastry, Wildflower Café on the same street has treats starting at **$4**.

11.2 Getting to Sitka

EVERYTHING YOU NEED. NOTHING YOU DON'T

Getting here is simple, and you've got a few good options depending on how you like to travel. The easiest way is flying. Planes land at **Rocky Gutierrez Airport**, which is only about **5 miles from downtown**. Alaska Airlines runs daily flights from **Juneau, Seattle**, and other big spots. A flight from Juneau takes just **45 minutes**, and if you're coming from Seattle, it's about **2.5 hours**. Once you're here, you'll find taxis waiting outside the airport. A ride to the center of town will cost you around **$10-$15**. If you're staying at a hotel, check ahead because many of them have free shuttles to pick you up. Renting a car is also an option if you want to explore beyond the main streets, and there are car rental desks right at the airport.

If you're not in a rush and want to enjoy the journey, taking the **Alaska Marine Highway ferry** is a really cool option. The ferry terminal is on **Halibut Point Road**, just a couple of miles from the main downtown area. Ferries come from **Juneau, Ketchikan**, and even as far south as **Bellingham, Washington**, so you can hop on wherever it's convenient. The ride is slow but worth it because you get to see amazing views of the water, mountains, and maybe even some whales. If you're coming from Juneau, the ferry ride is about **10 hours**, so bring snacks and something to keep you busy. Once you dock, you can grab a taxi to town for about **$10** or hop on the **Route 2 public bus**, which costs just **$2** and runs every hour or so.

Cruise ships also stop here all the time. They dock super close to downtown, either at the **Old Sitka Dock** or **Halibut Point Marine Terminal**. If your ship stops here, you can easily walk or take a short shuttle into town. Cruise season is usually **May to September**, so if you're visiting during this time, the area is buzzing with activity.

If you're planning your trip, make sure to book flights or ferry tickets early, especially in summer, because everything fills up fast. For ferries, book online or call ahead, especially if you're bringing a car—there's limited space, and summer can get crazy busy. Flights are pretty reliable, but prices can jump if you wait too long to book.

Once you're in town, getting around is easy. If you're staying downtown near **Lincoln Street**, you can walk almost everywhere. Taxis are around if you need them, but it's a small place, so you won't really need one unless you're heading out of town. For anything further, like a day trip, renting a car is a smart choice, but most of what you'll want to see is close by.

11.3.2 National Historical Park

The **National Historical Park** is at **103 Monastery Street**, just a short walk from downtown, so you won't need much effort to get there. It's all about history and culture, with trails that take you through the story of the Tlingit people and the time when Russian settlers came here. What makes it special are the **totem poles**. These tall, carved poles are like storytellers—they show you pieces of the Tlingit's life, myths, and struggles. They're not just decorations; they mean something, and you'll see them everywhere along the trails.

Start at the **visitor center**, which is open daily from **8 a.m. to 4:30 p.m.**, though hours might change in winter. It's free to enter, so no worries about tickets. Inside, you'll find exhibits with old Tlingit tools, clothing, and carvings, and there's even a section where you can watch real artists carving new totem poles or weaving. It's cool to see how these traditions are still alive. The **Totem Hall** is also inside, where you'll get an up-close look at some of the poles with detailed explanations about what they mean.

After you check out the visitor center, head outside to the **Totem Trail**. It's an easy **1-mile loop** that winds through the forest and along the water. The trail is flat and well-maintained, so you can take your time. Along the way, you'll see more totem poles standing in clearings. Each one has a small sign explaining its story, so you'll know what you're looking at. The trees around you are massive and old, and the ocean is just a few steps away in some places, making the whole walk peaceful and calming. Toward the end of the trail, you'll reach the **Battle of 1804 site**, where the Tlingit fought to keep their land from the Russians. It's quiet now, but thinking about what happened there gives the place a deeper meaning.

If you don't have a car, getting here is simple. You can take the **local bus** for about **$2**; it stops close to the park entrance. There's also parking if you drive, but the lot is small, so getting here early is a good idea. Walking from downtown is easy and takes about **10 minutes**.

Once you've finished visiting, grab a coffee or snack nearby. Head to **Backdoor Café** on **Lincoln Street**, where they have strong coffee and fresh pastries for **$4-$5**. If you're hungry for more, try **Larkspur Café**, also on Lincoln, where you can get seafood chowder or sandwiches for **$12-$15** while enjoying views of the harbor.

11.3.2.1 St. Michael's Cathedral

St. Michael's Cathedral is right in the middle of downtown at **240 Lincoln Street**, super easy to find, and just a short walk from anywhere in the area. This church is a big deal because it was the very first Russian Orthodox cathedral built in North America, way back in the **1840s**. Even though the original building burned down in **1966**, what you see today is a perfect rebuild, made with a lot of the pieces that people saved during the fire. Walking inside feels like stepping into the past.

The first thing you'll notice inside is the **iconostasis**, which is this big wall covered in colorful icons with gold accents. These icons aren't just pretty pictures—they're all about stories of saints, biblical events, and spiritual symbols. A lot of them are originals that were saved from the fire, so they're not just old, they're important. The whole place feels peaceful, with hanging chandeliers adding a warm glow to everything. You can see crosses, chalices, and other church treasures up close, and it's amazing how much detail is in each piece.

You can visit most days between **9 a.m. and 4 p.m.**, though it's smart to double-check the hours if you're going in winter. They suggest a **$5 donation** at the door, which helps keep the place looking great. If you're walking, it's just a few minutes from the harbor, and if you're using the **local bus**, it stops right near the church for about **$2**. Driving is an option too, but parking downtown can get tight, especially when it's busy, so walking might be your best bet.

When you're done exploring, there are some great spots nearby to grab a bite. Just a block or so down Lincoln Street, **Highliner Coffee** is perfect for a quick snack, with coffee and pastries for **$8-$10**. If you're hungrier, check out **Ludvig's Bistro** over on **256 Katlian Street**. They're famous for their seafood, like smoked salmon fettuccine or their cioppino stew, with meals costing about **$18-$30**. The vibe there is cozy, and it's the kind of place where you can sit back and relax after taking in the cathedral.

What's cool about this spot? It's a symbol of how Russian and local cultures blended here.

11.3.3 Russian Bishop's House

The **Russian Bishop's House** is right on **Lincoln Street**, easy to walk to from downtown, and it's one of the oldest buildings still standing from when the Russians controlled this area. It was built in **1842** to be the home and office of the Russian Orthodox bishop, and when you step inside, it feels like you're walking into a piece of history. The whole place is made from hand-carved wood, and the walls have this cool old-school vibe that really shows you what life was like back then.

When you go inside, the first floor is all about the bishop's work life. You'll see his office, which is full of old books, documents, and religious items like fancy crosses and chalices. The upstairs is where he lived, and it's super simple—just basic wooden furniture, a small dining area, and little details like handmade tools and decorations. There are exhibits everywhere that explain how the church helped shape the area, from teaching locals to translating religious texts into Native languages.

The **National Park Service** takes care of the house, and it costs just **$5** to get in, which is a steal considering how much history you'll

EVERYTHING YOU NEED. NOTHING YOU DON'T

see. If you're under 15, you get in free. They're open every day from **9 a.m. to 4 p.m.**, but during winter, the hours might be shorter, so it's smart to double-check before you go. The best part? They have rangers who guide you through and tell stories that make everything way more interesting.

Getting there is super easy. If you're downtown, it's just a **5-10 minute walk**. If you're not up for walking, the **local bus** stops nearby, and it's only about **$2**. If you're driving, there's street parking close by, but during the busy season, it can be tricky to find a spot, so maybe stick with walking or the bus.

After you're done exploring, you'll probably be hungry. There's a great spot called **Mean Queen** nearby where you can grab pizza or burgers for around **$12-$20**. If you want something fancier, head to **Ludvig's Bistro** on **256 Katlian Street**, where they serve fresh seafood like smoked salmon pasta for about **$20-$35**. For coffee and dessert, check out **Backdoor Café**, where you can grab a slice of pie and a latte for about **$6-$10**.

11.3.4 Sheldon Jackson Museum

ALASKA ACTION PLAN

The **Sheldon Jackson Museum** is right on **104 College Drive**, and it's super easy to get to. If you're walking from downtown, it'll take you about **10 to 15 minutes**. If you're using the **local bus**, it stops close by, and a ride costs about **$2**. If you're driving, there's a **free parking lot** right outside, so you won't have to stress about finding a spot.

Inside, it's like stepping into a whole other world. The museum is packed with **over 5,000 artifacts** that show how Native Alaskan groups like the Tlingit, Yup'ik, Haida, and Iñupiat lived and thrived. You'll see all kinds of incredible stuff—like **ceremonial masks** that were used in dances and rituals, and they're covered in beautiful carvings and designs. There are **tools made from bone, wood, and stone**, things like harpoons for hunting or fish traps that are so smartly designed you'll wonder how they made them without modern tools.

You've got to check out the **kayaks** on display. These are made from stretched seal skin over wooden frames, and they're perfectly crafted for traveling the icy waters. The clothing on display is just as impressive, with parkas made from animal hides, all stitched together with such care. Everything tells a story, and it's really cool how you can see the connection between people and the land they lived on.

The museum is open **Tuesday to Saturday, from 10 a.m. to 4 p.m.**, and tickets are just **$7 for adults**. If you're under 18 or a local, you get in for free. Sometimes they even have events where you can watch Native artists demonstrate traditional crafts or hear talks about the artifacts, so it's worth checking their schedule online or asking when you get there.

After you've soaked up all that history, you'll probably want to grab something to eat. Just down the road, there's **Bayview Pub**, where you can dig into fish tacos, burgers, or seafood chowder for around **$15 to $25**. If you're in the mood for coffee and something sweet, head to **Raven's Brew Coffee**, where their strong blends and pastries cost about **$8 to $12**.

11.4 Outdoor Activities in Sitka

11.4.1 Whale Watching Tours

EVERYTHING YOU NEED, NOTHING YOU DON'T

If you want to see whales up close, this is one of the best places to do it, and it's really easy to make it happen. Most whale-watching tours leave from **Sitka Sound Harbor**, which is right off **Katlian Street**. If you're staying near downtown, it's a quick **10- to 15-minute walk** to the harbor. If you're coming from farther away, you can use the **local bus system**, which costs about **$2** and stops close to the docks. Driving? No problem. There's a **free parking lot** right near the harbor, so you won't have to worry about where to leave your car.

The tours are run by experienced guides who know exactly where to find whales and other marine life. **Sitka Whale Watching Company** is great if you like smaller boats with just a few other people onboard. It feels more personal, and you'll have plenty of space to see everything. Their trips are usually **2 to 3 hours long** and cost around **$125 to $150 per person**. If you want something bigger or are traveling with kids, **Allen Marine Tours** offers larger boats with more room and a smoother ride, and tickets cost about **$100 to $120 per person**.

The best time to go is during **May to September**, which is when the humpback whales are migrating through these waters. It's an incredible sight to watch them breach, slap their tails, or blow water from their spouts. Orcas are often seen too, swimming in groups and moving gracefully through the water. The guides will also point out sea lions, porpoises, and even sea otters floating on their backs. Bald eagles are everywhere, soaring above the water or diving for fish—it's like a wildlife show all around you.

Dress warm because it can get pretty cold out on the water, even in summer. Wear **layers**, bring a jacket that blocks the wind, and maybe pack gloves and a hat just in case. A lot of tours provide rain jackets and even binoculars, but it's always a good idea to bring your own if you have them. Don't forget your camera or phone because when a whale breaches or an orca comes close to the boat, you'll definitely want to capture that moment.

After the tour, you'll probably be hungry. Just a short walk from the harbor, **The Mean Queen** on **Lincoln Street** is a great spot for something hearty, like their smoked salmon pizza or clam chowder. Meals here cost about **$15 to $30**. If you're in the mood for something

ALASKA ACTION PLAN

lighter, head to **Raven's Brew Coffee** on **Lake Street**, where you can grab a strong coffee and a fresh pastry for about **$8 to $12**. For something fancier, check out **Beak Restaurant** on **Seward Street**, where the menu is full of fresh, locally sourced seafood like halibut or salmon, with dishes costing around **$20 to $40**.

11.4.2 Hiking on Baranof Island

Harbor Mountain Trail starts at the end of Harbor Mountain Road, about 20 minutes from downtown. The road is steep and narrow, so drive carefully. There's a parking area at the trailhead. The hike is 6 miles round trip and has steep sections with rocky terrain. At the top, you get clear views of the ocean, islands, and mountains, especially on sunny days. Wear good hiking boots and bring water and snacks. If you don't have a car, call a taxi or rent a bike to get close.

Indian River Trail is off Indian River Road, about 10 minutes from town. It's a 4.5-mile trail that follows the river through the forest. The trail ends at a viewpoint near the river's upper section. You'll see small waterfalls and wooden bridges along the way. The terrain is less steep but can be muddy after rain. Use sturdy shoes. A bus stops half a mile from the trailhead and costs $2 if you're not driving.

Thimbleberry Lake Trail is an easy, 1-mile trail off Sawmill Creek Road. There's a parking lot at the start. The trail leads to a quiet lake surrounded by trees and mountains. It's great for a quick hike or picnic. The path is clear and good for families. Bring a light jacket since it can get chilly.

Baranof Island's weather changes quickly. Always bring a rain jacket and wear layers. Carry water, snacks, and bear spray. Make noise to avoid surprising bears, especially on Indian River Trail.

After hiking, grab food at **Ludvig's Bistro** on Lincoln Street for seafood like halibut tacos, costing $20 to $40. For something quick, try **Highliner Coffee** on Lake Street for coffee and pastries around $10. Near Harbor Mountain, **Bayview Pub** on Halibut Point Road has burgers and fish for $15 to $25.

11.4.3 Kayaking and Wildlife Viewing

Kayaking here gets you close to nature and marine life. Start at **Sitka Sound Ocean Adventures** on **Smith Street**, a short walk from downtown. Rentals cost about **$40 per hour** for single or tandem kayaks. Guided tours cost around **$100 per person** and take you to quiet inlets where you can see otters floating, seals resting on rocks, and sometimes humpback whales surfacing. Eagles are easy to spot perched in trees or flying above. Bring waterproof gear because water sprays are common.

From **Harrigan Centennial Hall**, near the harbor, you can rent kayaks for **$30 to $50 per hour**. This spot has calmer waters, great for beginners or families. Kayak to bays where starfish and fish are visible under clear water. Guides often include information about the local wildlife.

For a quieter trip, head to **Halibut Point Recreation Area**, about 15 minutes by car from downtown. Buses stop nearby, costing **$2** one way. Rentals here are about **$35 per hour**. This area is known for shoreline paddling where you might see deer or even bears close to the water.

Dress in layers and bring a rain jacket. Rentals include life jackets, but you'll want a dry bag for your phone and camera. If you're joining a tour, many guides provide binoculars for better views of whales or distant wildlife.

After kayaking, stop at **Beak Restaurant** on **Seward Street** for fish tacos or salmon burgers costing **$15 to $25**. For coffee and a pastry under **$10**, head to **Highliner Coffee** on **Lake Street**. Near Halibut Point, try **The Nugget**, where fish and chips cost **$15 to $20**.

11.5 Dining in Sitka

If you want a nice dinner, go to **Ludvig's Bistro** on **256 Lincoln Street**. This small restaurant is famous for fresh seafood like salmon risotto and scallops, and it has a Mediterranean twist. Dinner costs about **$25 to $40**, so it's great for a special night out. Make sure you book ahead because it's small and fills up fast. It's easy to find, just a short walk from the harbor, and after your meal, you can wander nearby to check out some small shops or enjoy the quiet streets.

For something casual, try **The Mean Queen** on **315 Harbor Drive**. They have wood-fired pizza and big bowls of pasta with seafood. It's close to the harbor, so you can enjoy views of the water while you eat. Meals are about **$15 to $25**, and they're great if you want a relaxed vibe. It's also near public transport stops, or you can find parking close by if you drive. After you eat, take a walk by the docks to soak in the views.

Beak Restaurant on **205 Seward Street** is the spot for creative food. They make things like smoked salmon mac and cheese and fresh halibut burgers. Prices are around **$15 to $25**, and the location is right by Crescent Harbor, so you get a nice view while you eat. It's easy to walk here from downtown, and the atmosphere is super friendly. After your meal, you can explore the harbor area or just enjoy the relaxing view.

If you're looking for coffee and something quick, head to **Highliner Coffee** on **327 Lake Street**. They do great coffee, fresh pastries, and sandwiches. It's cheap, around **$5 to $10**, and perfect for a light meal. It's also near some local shops, so you can grab breakfast here and then explore. There's parking out front, and buses stop nearby if you don't have a car.

For a chill spot, check out **Bayview Pub** on **407 Halibut Point Road**. They serve big portions of burgers, fish and chips, and hearty chowder. Meals cost about **$15 to $25**, and they have a lot of local beers on tap. It's a little outside the main downtown area, but there's parking and a bus stop nearby. It's perfect if you want something filling after a long day.

If you have a sweet tooth, stop at **The Backdoor Cafe** behind Old Harbor Books at **201 Lincoln Street**. They bake fresh cookies, brownies, and pies, and serve coffee and tea. It's cheap, about **$3 to $7**, and super cozy. You can grab a snack here after shopping or sightseeing since it's right in the middle of everything.

11.6 Accommodation

Start with **Westmark Sitka Hotel** on **330 Seward Street**. It's super close to everything downtown, so you can just walk to shops, restaurants, and even places like St. Michael's Cathedral. Rooms here cost around **$150 to $200 per night**, and you get free Wi-Fi and parking. There's even a restaurant inside, which is handy if you don't feel like going out after a long day.

For something a bit smaller but still central, you could try the **Sitka Hotel and Restaurant** at **118 Lincoln Street**. It's right by the harbor and just steps away from the main downtown spots. Rooms are usually between **$130 and $180 per night**, and a lot of them have views of either the ocean or the mountains. Plus, their restaurant serves fresh seafood, so you don't have to go far for a good meal.

If you want something fancy, the **Totem Square Hotel & Marina** at **201 Katlian Street** is a great option. It's right on the water, so you can wake up to views of the marina. It's close enough to walk to most places downtown, and rooms here cost between **$180 and $250 per night**, depending on what kind of view you want. They also have parking, which is great if you're driving around.

If you're trying to save money, check out **Aspen Suites Hotel** at **210 Lake Street**. It's a bit farther from downtown, but it's easy to get there by car or public bus. Rooms cost around **$120 per night**, and they all have kitchenettes so you can cook your own meals and save some cash. It's super practical if you're staying for more than a few days.

For something totally different, there's the **Sitka Lighthouse B&B** on its own little island. You'll need to take a water taxi to get there, but it's a once-in-a-lifetime kind of stay. It costs about **$300 per night**, but you'll have the whole place to yourself, with ocean views and all the peace and quiet you could want. It's great for a romantic trip or if you just want something memorable.

If you prefer something cozy and local, go for the **Alaska Ocean View Bed and Breakfast** on **1101 Edgecumbe Drive**. It's a little outside the town center, about a 10-minute drive, but the hosts are super friendly, and the homemade breakfast is amazing. Rooms are priced between **$120 and $160 per night**, and you'll even get some tips from the hosts on the best things to do around town. Some rooms have views of Mount Edgecumbe, which is a nice bonus.

Most of these places are easy to get to, whether you're driving or

ALASKA ACTION PLAN

taking a bus, and they're close to everything you need.

CHAPTER TWELVE
VALDEZ

12.1 Introduction

Valdez is this small, beautiful town at the edge of Prince William Sound, surrounded by huge mountains and glaciers that feel like they're straight out of a movie. You'll find it about 300 miles east of Anchorage, at the end of the Richardson Highway. Getting here is an adventure itself. If you're driving, the Richardson Highway gives you stunning views, especially as you pass through Thompson Pass. It's steep, snowy in winter, and absolutely breathtaking. If driving isn't your thing, you can hop on the Alaska Marine Highway ferry from places like Whittier or Cordova, which drops you right at the Valdez Ferry Terminal on North Harbor Drive. Flights are another option, with small planes landing at Valdez Pioneer Field, just five minutes from the town center.

Once you're in town, everything is close and easy to get to. The main streets, Egan Drive and Meals Avenue, have most of the shops, restaurants, and places you'll need. Around the harbor, the town feels alive with boats coming and going. You'll see fishing boats unloading fresh catch, people heading out on tours, and locals grabbing coffee or chatting near the docks. It's small but has this friendly, hardworking vibe.

The town's history is everywhere. During the gold rush, people came here thinking they'd found the easiest way to the Klondike, but the Valdez Glacier Trail turned out to be deadly. Later, the 1964 earthquake destroyed the old town, and they had to rebuild it in a safer spot. That toughness is part of what makes Valdez special—you feel it in the stories people tell and how connected they are to the land.

The outdoor stuff here is incredible. You can take a boat tour to Columbia Glacier, where you'll see massive chunks of ice breaking off into the water. It's wild and feels like something you'd only see on TV. If you want to get closer to a glacier, drive along the Richardson Highway to Worthington Glacier. There's a parking lot, and you can walk right up to the ice. For waterfalls, check out Bridal Veil Falls and Horsetail Falls, both just a short drive from town. They're right off the road, so you don't even have to hike to see them.

When you get hungry, seafood is the big thing here. The Halibut House on Egan Drive has fresh halibut and fish and chips for about $15–$20, and the portions are generous. Another great spot is Fat Mermaid on North Harbor Drive, where you can try fish tacos or seafood chowder for around $15–$25. If you're craving something sweet or need a good coffee, Sacred Grounds near the ferry terminal is perfect, with drinks and pastries costing $4–$6.

For places to stay, you've got choices. If you want something simple and close to everything, Totem Inn on Richardson Highway is a solid pick, with rooms starting at $130. Glacier Sound Inn on Pioneer Drive offers great views of the water and starts at $150 per night. If you're into camping, Valdez Glacier Campground is awesome, with spots starting at $25 and easy access to nearby trails.

12.2 Getting to Valdez

Getting to Valdez is simple, and you've got three main choices: driving, taking a ferry, or flying. If you want a road trip, drive the **Richardson Highway**. It's a long, scenic route that starts in **Glennallen** and takes about two hours to Valdez, but if you're coming from **Anchorage**, it's a 300-mile trip, which takes six or seven hours. You'll pass amazing views like **Thompson Pass**, where the mountains are massive and covered in snow most of the year, and the **Worthington Glacier**, where you can pull over and see the ice up close. The road can be curvy and steep, especially near Thompson Pass, so take it slow. Make sure to fill up your gas tank in **Glennallen** or **Copper Center**, because there aren't many fuel stations after that. Snacks and restrooms are also easy to find in those towns before the last stretch.

If you like the idea of traveling by water, take the ferry. Ferries leave from places like **Whittier** and take you straight to Valdez. The ferry terminal is at **139 Harbor Drive**, close to downtown Valdez. The ferry ride itself is beautiful, with views of glaciers and wildlife like seals and maybe even whales. Tickets cost around $50–$100 per person, and if you're bringing your car, you'll pay extra. During summer, ferries fill up fast, so book your tickets early. If you're driving to Whittier to catch the ferry, remember the **Anton Anderson Tunnel** only allows cars to go through at certain times, so check the schedule in advance.

Flying is the fastest way. Small planes run by airlines like **Ravn Alaska** will take you from **Anchorage to Valdez Pioneer Field Airport** in under an hour. The airport is only a five-minute drive from downtown Valdez. Flights cost between $150 and $300 for a round trip, depending on the season, and they often sell out quickly, so book early if you can. Once you land, you'll find taxis or rental cars right at the airport.

12.3 What to visit

12.3.1 Valdez Museum and Historical Archive

The **Valdez Museum and Historical Archive** sits right on **217 Egan Drive**, easy to spot if you're heading through the main part of town. You can park nearby, or if you're walking from the harbor, it's just a quick five-minute stroll. If you're using local buses, they drop you close, so it's simple to get there without a car.

Inside, the museum feels packed with stories. The first thing that will grab your attention is the display about the **1964 Good Friday Earthquake**. This wasn't just any earthquake—it wiped out the old town completely, and the tsunami that came after was devastating. You'll see photos of the destruction, videos showing how intense it was, and even some objects people pulled from the ruins. What's cool is that the museum also explains how they rebuilt the whole town further inland, which is where you're standing now.

Then there's the section about the **gold rush**. Imagine people hauling heavy gear over icy passes, chasing dreams of striking it rich. The tools and maps they used are right there in front of you, showing just how tough they had it. There's also a section on the **Trans-Alaska Pipeline**, which brought big changes to Valdez, making it a key port for shipping oil. You can learn how the pipeline works and see some of the equipment they used to build it.

One of the most fascinating parts is the focus on **Native Alaskan culture**. The museum has traditional tools, clothing, and even ceremonial pieces. You'll get a sense of how people thrived in this tough environment long before modern tools existed.

You'll probably want to spend at least an hour here—two if you're the kind of person who reads everything. The museum is open daily in the summer from **9 AM to 5 PM**, and during winter, it shifts to **10 AM to 4 PM**. Tickets are around **$8 for adults** and **$5 for kids**, and they offer discounts for families or seniors. It's not a huge price for what you'll walk away learning.

After the museum, you might feel like grabbing some food. Just down the street, at **226 Pioneer Drive**, is **Rogue's Garden**, where you can grab a quick sandwich or a smoothie if you want something light. If you're more into seafood, head to **The Fat Mermaid** at **143 N. Harbor Drive**. Their fish tacos and clam chowder are super popular, and the prices are decent—think **$10 to $20** depending on what you order.

12.3.2 Old Town Valdez

Old Town Valdez is about 4 miles east of the current town along Dayville Road. This was the original spot where the town stood before the huge earthquake and tsunami in 1964. You can get there in 10 minutes by car, and it's super easy to find because there are signs guiding you. If you don't have a car, a taxi works too, but there's no bus or public transport going that way. Parking is free, so no stress about finding a spot.

When you get there, it's quiet and kind of eerie. There aren't buildings anymore, just some foundations left behind, but there are signs all over the place telling you the story of the town. This was where people first set up shop during the gold rush in the late 1800s. Back then, it was a busy place with miners coming through, hoping to strike it rich. The signs also explain how everything changed in 1964 when a massive tsunami hit after a big earthquake. The water just destroyed everything, and the town had to move to where it is now.

You can walk around and follow the path that takes you through the old streets. It's a short walk, maybe 30 to 45 minutes if you take your time. Wear shoes that are good for walking because the ground can be a bit uneven. Morning is the best time to visit because it's quiet, the light is better for taking pictures, and it feels peaceful with the mountains in the background.

If you're into history, you'll love the little details on the signs. They show where the post office used to be and some of the homes, so you can imagine what life was like back then. It's not a big, fancy place, but it's meaningful. You get a real sense of what people went through and how they rebuilt their lives afterward.

After you're done walking around, you might want to grab something to eat. Head back into town and stop by The Fat Mermaid on North Harbor Drive. They have great seafood, like halibut dishes, for around $20. It's a cozy spot, perfect for relaxing after exploring.

12.3.3 Maxine & Jesse Whitney Museum

The Maxine & Jesse Whitney Museum is right on the **Prince William Sound College campus** at **303 Lowe Street**, super close to downtown Valdez. If you're driving, there's free parking right at the entrance, and if you're walking, it'll only take you about 10 minutes to get there from downtown. The museum is open **Monday to Friday, from 9 AM to 5 PM**, and during the summer, they're also open on Saturdays. You don't have to pay to get in, but they do accept donations if you want to help out.

Inside, you'll see one of the **largest collections of Native Alaskan artifacts** anywhere. It's full of stuff like **beautifully carved masks**, **woven baskets**, and even **hunting tools and clothing** made by Alaska's first people. The masks are really amazing, with intricate designs that tell stories about the people and their traditions. You'll also find a big collection of **taxidermy animals**—everything from a **grizzly bear** to an **arctic fox**. It's cool because you get to see these creatures up close, which is way different than spotting them from far away in the wild.

The museum also has some pieces from the **gold rush days**, like tools and photos, which show how hard life was for the people who came here looking for gold. You can really feel the history while you're walking around.

After you're done inside, you might want to grab a bite to eat. **Magpie's on the Fly**, which is just down the road at **310 Pioneer Drive**, serves an awesome salmon sandwich for around $15, and they've got homemade pie that locals love. It's simple, tasty, and close by.

The museum is also a good spot to take some pictures of the mountains around Valdez. The views are crazy beautiful, and it's a good idea to bring your camera or phone for some shots. If you're lucky, you'll catch the perfect lighting on the mountains when the clouds clear up.

12.4 Outdoor Adventures

12.4.1 Prince William Sound

Prince William Sound is like stepping into a giant postcard, with glaciers, mountains, and tons of wildlife. Everything starts at the **Valdez Small Boat Harbor** on **North Harbor Drive**, right in the middle of the town. You just head there to catch your boat tour or rent a kayak. If you're driving, there's parking nearby, but during summer it can get busy, so go early. If you don't have a car, the **Valdez Bus Service** can drop you off right by the harbor.

For boat tours, you can't go wrong with **Stan Stephens Glacier & Wildlife Cruises**. They take you out to see **Columbia Glacier** or other stunning spots in the Sound. You'll see massive chunks of ice breaking off and crashing into the water, which is super cool (literally). These tours usually last between 6 and 9 hours, cost about **$150 to $200 per person**, and you need to book ahead because they fill up fast. They start around **9 AM**, so plan your morning.

If you want to paddle instead of sit on a boat, go for kayaking. **Anadyr Adventures**, near the harbor, rents kayaks and offers guided trips. Rentals start at **$60**, and guided tours are about **$100 to $150**. Guided is better if you're new because they help you with gear and show you cool spots like **Shoup Bay** or hidden coves. The water is calm, so it's great even if you're not super experienced. You might see otters playing, seals popping their heads up, and even whales if you're lucky.

Wildlife is everywhere. Look up, and you'll spot bald eagles flying or sitting on trees. On the water, it's common to see orcas, humpbacks, and little porpoises. Near the shore, you might catch sea lions sunbathing or puffins nesting. Bring binoculars if you can—it makes spotting things way easier—and definitely take your camera.

Summer, especially **June to August**, is the best time to go because the weather is nicer and all the tours are running. Wear layers since it's cold on the water, even in summer, and pack a waterproof jacket because it can get splashy near the glaciers. For shoes, sturdy ones are great if you plan to step out on trails or rocky areas.

Before or after your trip, grab food at **The Fat Mermaid**, right by the harbor. Their fish tacos and burgers are around **$15 to $20**, and they're super tasty. If you want snacks for the tour, stop at **Rogue's Garden** on **Egan Drive** for fresh sandwiches or trail mix.

The harbor area itself is nice to hang out in. You can watch fishing boats come and go or check out little shops for souvenirs. It's chill and has that peaceful vibe you want before or after an adventure.

12.4.2 Worthington Glacier

Worthington Glacier is super close to the **Richardson Highway at Milepost 28.7**, just a 30-minute drive from Valdez. You'll see a big parking lot with signs, and parking is totally free. There's no public transport here, so you'll need to drive yourself or take a tour shuttle that stops along the highway. It's easy to spot and super simple to get to.

Once you park, the glacier is just a short walk away. There's a smooth, paved trail that takes you to an observation deck where you can see the glacier up close. If you're feeling adventurous, there's a tougher trail called the **Ridge Trail**. It's rocky and climbs up higher, but it gets you super close to the ice. You'll need good hiking shoes because it can get slippery, especially if it's rained recently.

If you're into taking photos, this is the perfect spot. Early morning or late afternoon is best because the light makes the glacier look super blue, and the mountains in the background are just gorgeous. If you want to get really cool shots of the glacier streams, bring a tripod for steadier photos.

It can get chilly, even in summer, so wear a warm jacket, maybe something waterproof if it looks like rain. Don't forget gloves if you plan to spend some time here. Bring a water bottle and snacks, too—there's nowhere nearby to buy food or drinks.

The area also has cool signs along the path that tell you about the glacier and how it's changed over the years. It's a great way to learn while you're taking in the views. You'll notice how the glacier has gotten smaller over time, which makes the experience feel even more special.

After visiting, if you're heading back to Valdez, stop for food at **The Fat Mermaid** for some tasty burgers or go to **Fu Kung Restaurant** for a mix of Chinese and Thai food. Meals are around **$15–$25**, so it's not too pricey, and both spots are close to the harbor area.

12.4.3 Keystone Canyon

Keystone Canyon is about **15 miles east of Valdez on the Richardson Highway (AK-4)**, and you'll know you're there when you see the towering cliffs and waterfalls that make it unforgettable. Driving is the easiest way to get here, and it takes about **20 minutes from Valdez**. You won't find buses or public transport heading this way, so renting a car is your best option if you don't have one. Along the way,

you'll notice scenic pullouts where you can stop, stretch your legs, and take photos.

When you get to the canyon, park near the **Bridal Veil Falls** or **Horsetail Falls**, which are the main highlights. Bridal Veil Falls is closer to the road and perfect for getting up close to the cool mist, while Horsetail Falls is just a short drive down the highway and equally stunning. Both are best in spring and summer when the snowmelt makes the water roar down the cliffs.

The canyon isn't just pretty; it's full of history. Back during the gold rush, this area was a major route for miners heading to Valdez. If you like easy walks, the **Wagon Trail** is a short path, about **2 miles round-trip**, that follows part of that historic route and gives you awesome views of the waterfalls. If you're more into hiking and ready for a challenge, the **Valdez Goat Trail** climbs higher into the canyon and offers crazy good views. It's steeper and about **5 miles**, so bring good hiking boots and some snacks.

If you visit in winter, the waterfalls freeze into huge ice walls that are crazy beautiful and attract climbers from all over. Even if you're not climbing, it's worth seeing because the icy blue formations look unreal. Just make sure you're dressed for the cold with sturdy shoes because it can get slippery.

There aren't food places right at the canyon, so pack some snacks and water if you're planning to stay for a while. After your visit, head back to Valdez for a meal. If you want something nice, check out **Raven's Perch Restaurant** near the airport. They serve amazing local fish dishes like salmon or halibut, and you'll pay around **$25–$30 per meal**. For something quick and casual, **Old Town Burgers** on Pioneer Drive has great burgers starting at **$15**. If you just want a coffee or snack, **Sacred Grounds Coffee** on Egan Drive is cozy and affordable, with drinks and pastries starting at **$5**.

12.5 Dining

If you're hungry, you've got plenty of good places to eat, and most of them are really close to the harbor or along Egan Drive, so it's super easy to find something. You'll love the seafood here—it's fresh and everywhere.

Start with **The Fat Mermaid** on **Harbor Drive**, right by the Small Boat Harbor. It's a fun and colorful place where you can grab some amazing fish tacos, halibut chowder, or even a big burger if you're in the mood for something heavier. Prices are around **$15 to $25** per plate. If it's busy, try to get there early because it fills up fast, especially at dinner.

If tacos are more your thing, you've got to try **Nat Shack**, also on **North Harbor Drive**. It's casual, the portions are generous, and they've got killer fish tacos that are fresh and full of flavor. They also have chicken and veggie options if you don't want seafood. You'll spend about **$12 to $18**, and it's perfect if you don't want to sit for a long meal.

Want something fancy with a view? **Raven's Perch Restaurant** over at **325 Airport Road**, inside the Valdez Harbor Inn, is a great pick. They do dishes like grilled salmon and halibut, and everything comes out looking really nice. Plus, you get these amazing views of the mountains. It's a bit pricier, around **$20 to $35**, but perfect if you want a relaxed dinner after a busy day.

For something cozy, check out **Mike's Palace** on **North Harbor Drive**. It's where you go if you're craving pizza or pasta. The food's solid, the atmosphere is super laid-back, and it's good for families too. Expect to pay around **$15 to $20**, and their pizza slices are huge.

If you're looking for coffee or breakfast, go to **Sacred Grounds Coffee** on **Egan Drive**. They've got all the usual coffee drinks plus some quick breakfast sandwiches and pastries. It's not expensive, around **$5 to $10**, and it's the best spot to grab something before heading out to explore.

For a quick stop, hit **Captain Joe's Gas & Deli** on **Richardson Highway**. Their deli sandwiches and pizza slices are actually pretty decent for gas station food, and it's perfect if you need something fast. Prices are cheap, around **$7 to $12**.

Everything is close by, so you won't have to go far. Parking is free and easy near most places, and if you're walking around town, the main spots are all within a short distance from the harbor.

12.6 Accommodation

ALASKA ACTION PLAN

You'll have lots of places to choose from depending on what you like and how much you want to spend. Most places to stay are close to the harbor and the town, so you'll be near restaurants, shops, and all the fun stuff to do.

If you want something comfy and easy, go to the **Best Western Valdez Harbor Inn** on **100 North Harbor Drive**. It's right next to the harbor, so you can just walk to boat tours and fishing trips. The rooms are nice and clean, and you get free breakfast and Wi-Fi. It usually costs **$180 to $250 per night**, but it's more expensive in summer when everyone visits.

For a cozy and personal vibe, check out the **House on the Rock B&B** on **613 S. Moraine Drive**. The owners are super friendly, and they make amazing homemade breakfasts. The rooms are cute, with local decorations, and it's a quiet place. Prices are between **$150 and $200 per night**, and it's great if you want something calm and peaceful.

If you're looking for something simple and cheap, the **Keystone Hotel** on **Egan Drive** is a good pick. It's super close to shops, food places, and the harbor, so you don't need a car. Rooms start at about **$120 per night**, but in summer, they go up to around **$180**. It's basic but clean, and it's perfect if you're just looking for a place to sleep after exploring.

If you like camping or have an RV, go to the **Bear Paw Camper Park & Campground** on **North Harbor Drive**. It's close to the harbor, and they have spots for tents and RVs with hookups. Prices start at **$35 to $50 per night**, and they have showers, laundry, and picnic areas, so it's really convenient.

For another camping option, try **Eagle's Rest RV Park & Cabins** on the **Richardson Highway**. They have tent spots, RV spaces, and small cabins if you want something more comfortable. Cabins cost about **$90 to $120 per night**, and campsites are around **$40 to $50**. It's a good spot if you're with family or friends, and the mountain views are amazing.

If you like a small, boutique-style place, look at the **Glacier Sound Inn**. It's not right on the harbor, but it's close enough to walk there. Rooms are clean and modern, and prices are about **$150 to

$200 per night. It's a good choice if you want something simple but nice.

CHAPTER THIRTEEN
SKAGWAY

13.1 Historical Overview

This little town, surrounded by huge mountains, feels like it's frozen in the days of the gold rush. Back in 1898, people came here hoping to get rich, and you can still feel their stories in the streets. The main street, Broadway, is where everything happens. The buildings are old and full of character, especially the **Arctic Brotherhood Hall**, covered in driftwood. It's right on Broadway, near 2nd Avenue, and when you walk by, you'll feel like you're part of history.

The streets are easy to explore because everything is close. You can just park your car near the ferry terminal or the main area and start walking. If you're not driving, the ferry drops you off at the edge of town, and from there, you can explore without needing anything else. In summer, there's a small shuttle bus that loops around, but honestly, you won't need it unless you're tired.

Skagway's history is wild. During the gold rush, it wasn't just about digging for gold—it was also about outlaws, chaos, and big personalities like **Soapy Smith**, a famous conman. You can learn about all this at the **Klondike Gold Rush National Historical Park Visitor Center**, right on Broadway and 2nd Avenue. It's free, and they even offer guided walking tours. These tours are great because they take you through the most historic spots while telling you stories that make everything come alive.

When you get hungry, you'll find some really cool places to eat. If you want something with a lot of personality, head to the **Red Onion Saloon**. It used to be a brothel and now it's a bar and restaurant where meals cost about $20 to $30. The vibe there is as much a reason to go as the food. If seafood is more your thing, check out **Skagway Fish Company** by the small boat harbor. They do fresh halibut and salmon for around $20-$25. For something quick and sweet, grab a fried dough treat from **Klondike Doughboy**. It's only about $5 and perfect to munch on as you walk around.

13.2 Getting to Skagway

Getting to Skagway is simple, and you've got a few solid options. If you want to take the ferry, it's part of the **Alaska Marine Highway**, which drops you off right at the waterfront in Skagway. The terminal is on Ferry Way, and from there, everything downtown is close enough to walk to. The ferry connects with towns like Juneau and Haines, and you'll enjoy stunning views of the mountains and water during the ride. Tickets cost around $50 to $150, depending on whether you're walking on or bringing a vehicle. Summer is busy, so book early if you're planning to travel then.

If you're driving, the **Klondike Highway** is an awesome road trip. It links Skagway to Whitehorse in Yukon, Canada, and takes about two hours of driving time. The views are incredible, with lakes, mountains, and deep canyons all along the way. You'll need your passport at the border crossing, so don't forget it. Fill up on gas before you hit the road because there aren't many stops, and Skagway's gas stations don't stay open all night. Plan for extra time to stop at places like **Emerald Lake** or just to take in the scenery.

Flying is the fastest way to get here, especially from Juneau. Small planes operated by **Alaska Seaplanes** fly in less than an hour and land at the local airport, just outside of town. Tickets are usually $150 to $200 one way. Once you land, it's an easy walk into town or a quick taxi ride. Just be ready for weather delays since flights in this area depend on clear skies.

If you're thinking about visiting Haines, you can take a quick ferry ride that's just about an hour. The tickets are affordable—around $40 if you're on foot—and the views on the way are unbeatable. Check the schedule ahead of time, though, since ferries don't always run late in the day.

Once you're in Skagway, it's a small town, so getting around is no hassle at all. Most of what you'll want to see is within walking distance. There's free parking near the harbor if you've driven in, and maps at the visitor center can help you find your way.

ALASKA ACTION PLAN

13.3 Exploring

13.3.1 White Pass & Yukon Route Railway

The **White Pass & Yukon Route Railway** is a really cool train ride that starts in the center of town at **Broadway and Second Avenue**, super close to the port if you're coming off a cruise ship. It's an old railway built back in 1898 during the Gold Rush, and the train climbs high into the mountains all the way to the **White Pass Summit** on the U.S.-Canada border. The views along the way are insane, with waterfalls like **Bridal Veil Falls**, cliffs, deep valleys, and even tunnels.

You'll board vintage-style train cars with huge windows for great views, but the best part is the open-air platforms where you can step out and feel the wind and take photos without any glass in the way. The ride lasts about **2.5 to 3 hours**, and the train climbs over **2,800 feet in just 20 miles**, so it's packed with sights the whole way.

How to Get There

If you're in town, you can just walk to the station. It's super easy to find in the middle of Skagway. Coming from the ferry terminal? There's a shuttle, or you can walk if you feel like stretching your legs. Driving? Park nearby—Skagway is small, so nothing's far.

Tickets and Costs

The main ride, called the **Summit Excursion**, costs around **$130 for adults and $65 for kids**. The train runs from **May to September**, and there are a few departures each day. Book online ahead of time if you can because seats fill up fast in the summer. But if you're here on a quiet day, you might be able to snag tickets at the station.

What to Bring

It gets chilly as you climb higher, so wear or bring a jacket, even if it's sunny when you board. No snacks are sold on the train, so grab something before you go—maybe from **Bites on Broadway**, a café near the depot. You'll want your camera or phone ready because the views are non-stop.

What to Do Nearby

When you're back in town, grab a meal or a drink at places like the **Skagway Brewing Company** on Fifth Avenue if you're hungry for a hearty lunch, or stop by **Glacial Coffeehouse on Third Avenue** for a quick coffee or treat. Everything in downtown is super close, so you can walk and explore after your ride.

13.3.2 Klondike Gold Rush National Historical Park

The **Klondike Gold Rush National Historical Park** sits right in the middle of town, along **Broadway Street** and nearby areas. It's easy to reach if you're walking from the cruise ship docks or any hotel in Skagway because it's all close by. Start at the **Visitor Center**, which is in the old Train Depot on **Second Avenue**. You'll see displays showing tools miners used, photos of Skagway back when everyone was rushing for gold, and stories about the people who risked everything for their chance. Best part? It's **free to enter** and open from **9 AM to 5 PM** during the summer.

You can take a free **walking tour** led by park rangers. These tours are short, usually **45 minutes**, and take you past key spots like restored buildings and streets full of history. You'll hear stories about what it was like back in the 1890s, during the gold rush boom.

There's also the **Jeff. Smiths Parlor Museum**, a short walk from the Visitor Center. This place tells you about a guy named **Soapy Smith**, a scam artist who ran all kinds of schemes in town. It's quirky and gives you a feel for how wild things were back then. Another cool spot is the **Mascot Saloon**, which is now a museum showing how saloons worked back in the day. Imagine smoky bars, loud music, and people spending their last dime on a drink after a tough day.

You don't need a car to get around, but if you're driving, you can park near **Spring Street** or side streets close to downtown. Everything's so close that it's easy to walk. And if you're hungry while you're exploring, head to **Glacial Coffeehouse** on Broadway for a coffee and fresh pastry for about **$10-$15**. For lunch, try the **Red Onion Saloon**, where they serve salmon chowder and other local favorites for **$15-$25**. It's also a fun place because it used to be a brothel, and they've kept a lot of its old charm.

When you're visiting, wear comfy shoes since you'll be walking a lot. Bring a light jacket too because the weather can switch up quickly, even in the summer. If you're into souvenirs, the gift shop at the Visitor Center has books and cool items tied to the gold rush history.

13.3.3 Historic Downtown

Downtown Skagway feels like stepping back in time. You're walking on wooden boardwalks surrounded by buildings that look like they belong in a gold rush movie. It's all centered on **Broadway Street**, and everything is so close you can just park your car or step off the cruise ship and start exploring right away. If you're driving, parking on **Spring Street** is your best bet, but it can get crowded, so come early.

The vibe here is all about history and charm. You'll see old saloons, banks, and shops—like the **Arctic Brotherhood Hall**, covered in driftwood. It's at **Broadway and 2nd Avenue**, and it's hard to miss because it looks so unique. You'll want to stop and grab a photo, trust me. The whole area feels like a living museum, but instead of boring exhibits, there are stores where you can actually buy cool souvenirs, like t-shirts for around **$20** at **The Alaska Shirt Company**, or jewelry at **Corrington's**

Alaskan Ivory and Museum on **Broadway and 5th**. If you're into handcrafted stuff, you'll love it there, though prices can go up depending on how fancy you want to get.

It's super easy to get around because downtown is laid out in a grid, and most of the action happens between **2nd and 7th Avenues**. You won't need a car or a bus—just wear comfy shoes, and you're good to go. When you get hungry, grab a bite at the **Red Onion Saloon**, which used to be a brothel. It's at **Broadway and 2nd Avenue**, and you can try local seafood or a burger for **$15-$25**. If you just want a snack, head to the **Klondike Doughboy** on **3rd Avenue**, where their fry bread costs about **$6** and tastes amazing.

If you're curious about the stories behind this place, there are walking tours that start near **4th Avenue and Broadway**. These guides know all the juicy details about the gold rush and even the shady characters, like Soapy Smith, who ran scams here. It's around **$10-$15** for a tour, and you'll definitely learn something cool while stretching your legs.

For a little side trip, walk about 20 minutes north to the **Gold Rush Cemetery**, where you'll hear even more wild stories from the past. While you're there, check out **Lower Reid Falls**, which is just a short path from the cemetery. It's small but really pretty, and it's free, so why not?

Shops and restaurants usually open around **9 AM and close by 6 PM**, and the busiest time is when the cruise crowds are in town, usually mid-afternoon.

13.3.4 Red Onion Saloon Brothel Museum

The **Red Onion Saloon Brothel Museum** is right on **2nd Avenue and Broadway**, super easy to find when you're in downtown Skagway. Back in the gold rush days, it was a place where miners came to drink and meet "ladies of the night." Now, it's a cool mix of a bar downstairs and a museum upstairs, giving you a real feel of Skagway's past.

If you're walking from the cruise ship area, it's about a 10-minute stroll down **Broadway Street**, so you won't miss it. If you're driving, parking might be tight near the saloon, but streets like **Spring Street**

ALASKA ACTION PLAN

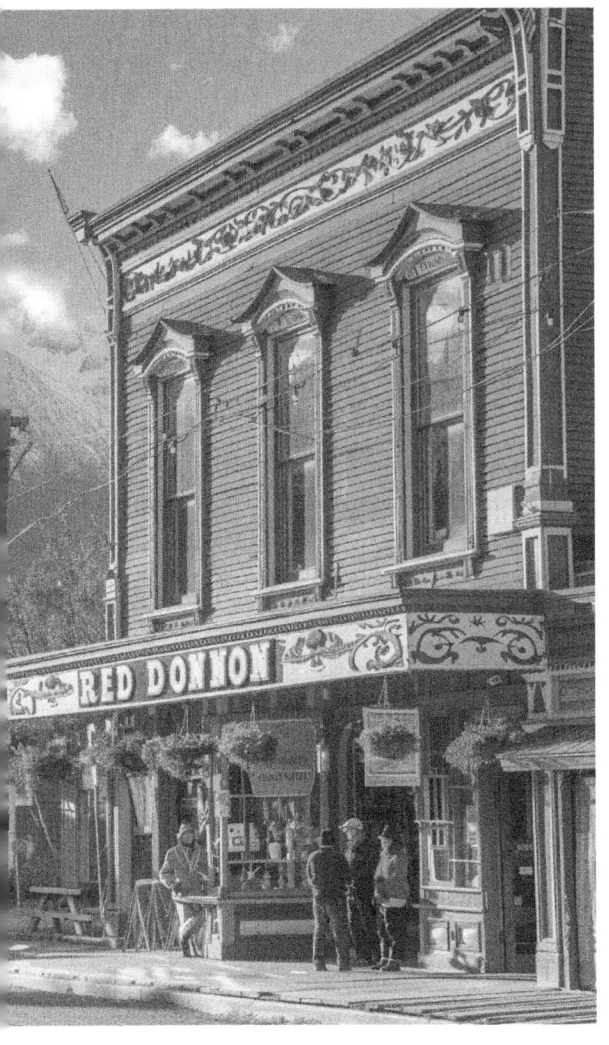

usually have a few open spots. If you're taking a local shuttle or bus, they drop you pretty close to downtown, and it's just a short walk from there.

When you step inside, the downstairs is all about old-school vibes—there's an original wooden bar, old photos on the walls, and staff that dress the part. You can grab a beer or a cocktail here; prices are chill, usually around **$7-$12**, and it's the perfect spot to sit and soak up the atmosphere. Upstairs is where the museum is, and this is the real highlight. For **$10 per person**, you get a guided tour with someone dressed like they're straight out of the 1890s. They'll show you the rooms where the women worked and tell you stories about what life was like back then, mixing the funny, scandalous, and historical stuff in a way that keeps you hooked.

The museum is open during the day, usually from **11 AM to 5 PM**, so plan your visit accordingly. The saloon stays open longer, often until **10 PM**, so you can come back later for drinks if you want. If you're into live music or just want to hang out, this place often has a lively crowd in the evening.

Right around the saloon, you'll find plenty to do. There are cute shops and local restaurants within a block or two, offering fresh seafood like salmon and halibut for **$15-$25 a plate**. If you're still in a history mood, the **Klondike Gold Rush National Historical Park Visitor Center** is just a few minutes away, making it easy to fill your day with more gold rush stories.

For the best experience, visit earlier in the day to catch the museum tours.

13.4 Outdoor Activities

13.4.1 Hiking Trails

You'll find some amazing trails around Skagway, each offering something different. The **Chilkoot Trail** is super famous because it's not just a hike; it's part of gold rush history. You start at the **Dyea Chilkoot Trailhead**, which is about 10 miles from downtown Skagway along **Dyea Road**. You can get there by car or take a local shuttle from the **Skagway Depot** on **Spring Street**. The first part of the trail, up to **Finnegan's Point**, is about 3.9 miles one way. It's mostly flat and runs through a beautiful forest with some cool old gold rush spots along the way. If you're doing just this part, it's an easy day trip.

If you don't want something too far from downtown, try the **Lower Dewey Lake Trail**. You'll find the trailhead right behind the **White Pass Depot** at **2nd Avenue and Spring Street**, so it's super easy to reach. It's a short but steep climb to a peaceful lake where you can hang out, have a snack, or just enjoy the view. The loop is about 3 miles total. If you're driving, park near the depot, but spaces can go fast, especially in summer, so it's better to walk if you're staying nearby.

For something harder, the **Upper Dewey Lake Trail** is a serious workout but totally worth it for the views. Start at the same trailhead as Lower Dewey, and just keep climbing. It's around 6.5 miles round trip, and the views of the lake and mountains at the top are stunning. If you're feeling adventurous, there's even a cabin you can rent for the night—ask at the **Skagway Visitors Bureau** on **Broadway Street** for details. Bring layers and plenty of water because it gets colder the higher you go, and you'll definitely work up a sweat on the way up.

If you're in the mood for something easier and more relaxing, check out the **Yakutania Point and Smuggler's Cove Trail**. It's at the end of **Main Street**, next to the airport. This one is pretty flat, about 2 miles total, and it takes you along the coast with amazing views of the water and mountains. There are benches and spots to chill, so it's a great option if you want to take it slow. Sunset here is awesome because the light on the water is magical. You can walk to this trailhead from downtown, so no need to worry about transport.

Before you head out, grab some snacks from **Bites on Broadway** on **Broadway Street**—their sandwiches and pastries are great and cost around $5 to $10. After your hike, reward yourself with something hearty at **Skagway Brewing Company** on **5th Avenue and Broadway**. Their halibut fish and chips are amazing, and you can pair it with a local beer for about $18 to $25.

13.4.2 Dog Sledding Tours

Dog sledding here is awesome. You take a helicopter ride up to the snowy glaciers, and then you hop on a sled pulled by dogs who live to run. The main place to start is the **Temsco Helicopters base** on **Dyea Road**, which is super close to downtown. Just grab a taxi or shuttle since public buses don't run there. Most flights happen mid-day, but it depends on the weather, so double-check with the company before you go.

The helicopter part is insane. You're flying over sharp mountains, huge glaciers, and ice that's super blue. It takes you to a glacier, like **Denver Glacier**, where the dog camp is set up. Companies like **Temsco Helicopters** and **Alaska Icefield Expeditions** run these tours, and they're easy to book online or through the **Visitors Center** on **Broadway Street**. These tours sell out, especially in summer, so book early.

Once you land on the glacier, you meet the mushers and their dogs. These dogs are so friendly and full of energy. The mushers teach you how they train the dogs and what their life is like. Then, you get on the sled for about 30 minutes, gliding over the snow. If you're up for it, you might even get to drive the sled with help from the musher. It's quiet, except for the dogs running, and it's something you'll never forget.

It costs about **$500 to $600 per person** for everything, including the helicopter and sledding. Plan for two to three hours total. It's cold up there, so wear layers, gloves, boots, and sunglasses because the snow reflects a ton of sunlight. They might give you boots if you don't have the right ones.

When you're done, head back into town and grab a bite. For quick food, **Glacial Smoothies & Espresso** on **Broadway Street** has great sandwiches and smoothies for **$8 to $12**. If you're starving, check out **Skagway Fish Company** near the harbor, where seafood dishes like fish and chips or crab legs cost **$15 to $30**.

13.4.3 Glacier Tours

Most tours start with **Temsco Helicopters**, just off **Dyea Road**, and it's really easy to get there with a quick shuttle or taxi ride. You need to book these tours early because everyone wants to do them, especially in summer when it's busiest. You can either book online or check at the **Visitors Center** on **Broadway Street** if you're already in town.

The helicopter rides are incredible. You'll fly over sharp mountain peaks, glaciers that look like frozen rivers, and icy blue cracks you can't even imagine until you see them. The ride itself lasts about 15-20 minutes, and then you land on the glacier, like **Denver Glacier** or **Laughton Glacier**, where the real fun starts. When you step out onto the ice, it feels like you're in another world. Guides will explain how glaciers form and how they slowly move, which is really cool when you see it right under your feet.

If you want to take it further, you can do a glacier trek. After the helicopter drops you off, you strap on special gear like crampons, and a guide takes you walking across the glacier. You'll see melt pools, icy ridges, and even deep crevasses. It's not super hard, and the guides make sure you're safe the whole time, but it's still a serious adventure. These treks usually last about three hours, so wear layers and a good jacket to stay warm. Also, bring sunglasses—the glare from the ice is intense.

Tours can cost between **$300 and $600 per person**, depending on what you choose. It's expensive, but you're literally flying to and walking on a glacier, so it's worth every penny. They'll give you all the gear

ALASKA Action PLAN

you need, but make sure you've got gloves, warm socks, and waterproof layers so you stay comfortable the whole time.

After you're done, you're probably going to be starving. Walk back into town and grab some food at **Sweet Tooth Cafe** on **Broadway Street**, where you can get a good burger or some warm soup for about **$15 to $20**. If you just need a snack, head to **Bites on Broadway** for coffee and a quick pastry—it's cozy and super affordable.

13.5 Dining

Start on **Broadway Street**, where you'll find a mix of small cafes, casual restaurants, and friendly pubs. Everything is close, and you can walk from one place to the next without breaking a sweat.

You can't go wrong with the **Skagway Brewing Company**, which sits on **5th Avenue and Spring Street**. They're famous for their **halibut burgers** and a beer called **Spruce Tip Ale** that's made with real spruce tips—you've got to try it. A meal here will cost you between **$15 and $25**, and the vibe is laid-back, with wooden interiors that make it cozy. It's also near some shops, so it's easy to grab a bite after walking around.

If you just need coffee or something light, head to **Glacial Coffeehouse** on **Broadway Street**, near **7th Avenue**. They do great **coffee**, sandwiches, and pastries that won't cost more than **$10 to $15**. It's perfect if you're on your way to catch a tour or exploring downtown. If you're staying further out, the SMART bus stops near here too, which makes it super convenient.

For a classic diner feel, check out **Sweet Tooth Cafe**, also on **Broadway Street**, close to **5th Avenue**. It's a cozy spot with big portions of **pancakes, eggs, bacon, or even chicken pot pie** if you're there later in the day. Expect to pay around **$10 to $20**. This place is a favorite for people heading to the train depot for the White Pass & Yukon Route Railway, so it's great for grabbing breakfast before a ride.

If you're in a rush or just want something quick, go to **Bites on Broadway**, a food cart parked near **2nd Avenue**. They do amazing **fish tacos and fries** that are cheap, around **$10 or less**, and it's all made fresh. This is one of those spots where you can eat, walk, and explore all at once.

Seafood lovers will love **Bonanza Bar & Grill** on **2nd Avenue**. They have a simple menu with good options like **fish and chips, chowder, and grilled seafood plates**. It's a good choice for dinner, and prices are around **$15 to $25**. You can also hang out there for drinks if you're winding down for the night.

Don't forget to grab some sweets while you're here. **Alaska Fudge Company**, on **Broadway Street**, has some of the creamiest fudge you'll ever try. Whether you like **chocolate, caramel, or rocky road**, you can grab a box for about **$10 to $15**. It's also a great snack for walking around downtown or to take back home as a gift.

Everything is super close, so you won't need to drive anywhere, but if you're staying further out, you can hop on the SMART bus. It stops near places like **7th Avenue and Spring Street**, so it's easy to get to the center.

13.6 Accommodation

Most spots are downtown, so you don't need to go far to get comfortable. You can find cozy inns, hotels, and even spots for camping, depending on what you like. Everything is close, and you can easily walk from the ferry terminal, the cruise docks, or the train station to most places.

The **Westmark Inn** is on **3rd Avenue near Spring Street**, and it's great if you want something simple but comfortable. The rooms are clean, you get free Wi-Fi, and there's a restaurant on-site. It's close to shops and restaurants, so you don't need a car. Expect to pay around **$150 to $200 per night** in the summer.

If you like something historic and charming, the **Skagway Inn Bed & Breakfast** on **7th Avenue** is a really nice pick. It's in an old building that feels like stepping into the gold rush days, with rooms that have a cozy, vintage vibe. They even make a big breakfast for you, which is included. It costs about **$130 to $180 per night**, and it's quiet but still close to everything.

For something cheaper, the **Pullen Creek RV Park and Campground** on **1st Avenue** has cabins, tent spots, and RV spaces. The cabins are basic, but they're clean and cost around **$80 to $100 a night**. It's close to the downtown area and good if you're into outdoor stuff like camping.

Another great option is the **White House Inn**, located on **5th Avenue and Main Street**. This place is small and peaceful, with nicely decorated rooms and free coffee or tea. It's close to the Skagway Museum and costs about **$120 to $160 a night**.

If you want something that feels really special, try the **Historic Moore Homestead** on **2nd Avenue**. It's got rooms that make you feel like you're part of Skagway's history. It's near cool spots like the Red Onion Saloon and costs around **$100 to $150 per night**.

No matter where you stay, you're super close to everything in town. You can walk to restaurants like the **Skagway Fish Company**, which is near the ferry terminal, or grab a casual meal at **Bonanza Bar & Grill** on **4th Avenue**. Food is fresh and not too pricey, around **$15 to $25 per meal**. Book early if you're coming in summer because Skagway gets busy with visitors. It's easy, simple, and everything is close, so you'll feel right at home.

CHAPTER FOURTEEN
HAINES

14.1 Introduction

Haines is a small town right by the water, where the **Chilkat River** meets the **Lynn Canal**. You can get there by driving along the Haines Highway, which is a super scenic road that connects to Canada's Yukon. If you're coming by ferry, the **Alaska Marine Highway terminal** is just outside the main part of town, and it's a quick drive or taxi ride in. Small planes also fly into **Haines Airport** from Juneau, and the airport is just a few minutes from the town center. There isn't a lot of public transport here, so you'll probably want a car or bike to explore.

The main street in Haines is where most things happen. It's small, so you can walk around easily, checking out little shops, cafés, and galleries. Everything feels really close to nature, and the mountains and water are always in sight. The **Sheldon Museum**, located right on Main Street, is great for learning about the town's gold rush history and Native Tlingit culture. Tickets are about $10, and it's worth visiting to see old photographs, tools, and stories about how life used to be here.

If you're here during **fall**,

the **Chilkat Bald Eagle Preserve** is a huge deal. It's about 15 minutes outside town, and in October and November, hundreds of eagles come to feed on salmon. Even if you're here another time, the preserve is peaceful and a great spot for wildlife spotting. Bring a good jacket because it can get cold by the river.

For food, you've got to try local seafood. The **Pilotlight Restaurant** on 1st Avenue serves fresh fish dishes, and you can eat while looking out over the water. Meals here usually cost between $20 and $30. If you're just looking for something quick, the **Mountain Market** on 3rd Avenue has sandwiches, soups, and really good coffee for under $15. They also sell snacks and stuff if you're packing for a hike.

Speaking of hiking, the **Battery Point Trail** is easy and only about 2 miles round trip. It starts near the **Port Chilkoot** area and takes you through a forest to a quiet beach with amazing views of the water. If you want more of a challenge, the **Mount Ripinsky Trail** goes all the way up for some epic views, but it's steep and long, so only try it if you're ready for a tough hike.

14.2 Getting to Haines

You've got three main ways. If you like water, take the **ferry with the Alaska Marine Highway System**. It's a smooth ride from places like Juneau or Skagway, and the ferry lands at the terminal on **Lutak Road**, just five minutes from the center of town. The ferry costs around **$50 to $100 per person**, and if you're bringing a car, that's about **$100 to $300 more**, depending on the size. Ferries come more often in summer, so it's easier to plan, but in winter, you'll need to double-check the schedule.

If you prefer flying, book a quick flight from **Juneau with Alaska Seaplanes**. The ride is only **30 minutes**, and the views of mountains and water are incredible. You'll land at the **Haines Airport**, just three miles from downtown. Flights usually cost between **$150 and $250 one way**, and from the airport, you can catch a taxi or rent a car to get to your lodging or the center of town.

Driving is another option if you're up for a road trip. The **Haines Highway** connects through the Yukon, starting at **Haines Junction**.

ALASKA ACTION PLAN

The drive takes around **four to five hours** from Whitehorse, with gas stops available in Haines Junction. The highway is beautiful, passing mountains, rivers, and glaciers. In winter, the road can be icy, so be ready with snow tires or chains, and always check the weather before you leave.

Once you arrive, having your own car helps a lot since public transportation is limited. The ferry terminal and the town are connected by good roads, and parking is usually easy. If you're near the terminal, check out **Fort Seward**, where you can explore local galleries or grab a bite at **Fireweed Restaurant**, with fresh seafood dishes for around **$20–$40**, or sip on cocktails at **Port Chilkoot Distillery** for about **$12–$15**.

14.3 Exploring Haines

14.3.1 American Bald Eagle Foundation Museum

The **American Bald Eagle Foundation Museum** is at **113 Haines Highway**, super close to downtown. You can just walk or drive there in a few minutes. The place is all about teaching people about wildlife, especially eagles and other birds of prey. Inside, you'll see **cool exhibits with taxidermy animals, dioramas, and fun interactive stuff** that let you learn how these animals live, what they eat, and how they survive in the wild.

The best part is the **live raptor center**, where you'll see eagles, owls, and hawks up close. These birds are rescued and taken care of here, and the staff does little shows where they tell you everything about them—like what they eat and how they were rescued. These demos happen a few times a day, so it's good to check the timing when you get there.

The museum is open **daily from 9 AM to 5 PM** in the summer (May to September) and shorter hours in the off-season. Tickets are around **$15 for adults** and about **$10 for kids and seniors**, and kids under five usually get in for free. You can call ahead or check their website to make sure they're open when you want to visit.

If you're staying downtown, it's super easy to get there. It's a short drive or walk, and there's free parking right outside. There aren't public buses, but taxis and shuttles can help if you're coming from the ferry dock or airport.

After visiting, grab a bite at **Mountain Market and Cafe** on Second Avenue, just a few minutes away. They've got sandwiches, soups, and really good coffee, and you'll spend around **$10 to $15** per person. If you just want a snack, check out **Big Al's Coffee**, also nearby, where you can grab a muffin or coffee for about **$5**.

You only need **1–2 hours** to see everything here, so it's easy to add more to your day. Maybe walk around **Fort Seward** nearby, or head to the waterfront for killer views of the Lynn Canal.

14.3.2 Sheldon Museum and Cultural Center

The **Sheldon Museum and Cultural Center** is right in **downtown Haines** on **11 Main Street**. You can get here super easily. If you're coming by ferry or cruise ship, it's just a **10-minute walk** straight up the main street from the dock. If you're driving, park right out front or along the nearby streets. If you don't feel like walking, just grab a **taxi** or ask the local shuttle to drop you off at **Main Street**.

Once you step inside, the museum feels cozy but packed with interesting stuff about the **history and culture of Haines**. You'll see a lot about the **Tlingit people**, who were here long before anyone else. One of the coolest things they have is the **Chilkat blankets**. These aren't just regular blankets – they're handwoven from **mountain goat wool**, dyed with natural colors, and made with so much detail that the patterns tell stories. They even show you how these blankets are made, so you can see why they're such a big deal.

The museum also tells you about the **Gold Rush days** when Haines was a stop for miners heading to the Klondike. There are **old tools, maps, and photos** from that time. You'll see how the town looked over 100 years ago and what life was like for the miners who passed through. It's simple but super interesting if you like history.

There's also stuff about the **wildlife in the area**, like **bears**, **bald eagles**, and **salmon**. They have displays that explain how important these animals are for the valley and for the people who live here. If you're lucky, you might even visit when there's a **workshop or live demonstration**, like storytelling sessions or cultural events. The people who work there are locals, and they're really nice – they'll tell you even more if you ask questions.

The museum is **open from 10 AM to 4 PM**, but in winter, it's better to check ahead since the hours might change. Tickets are super cheap – around **$5 to $8 for adults**, and kids either get in for free or pay just a couple of dollars. It's totally worth the price for what you get to see and learn.

When you're done, **downtown Haines** is right there, so you can easily grab a bite to eat or walk around. If you're hungry, stop by **Mountain Market & Cafe** just a block away. They have really good sandwiches, hot soups, and fresh coffee for about **$10 to $15**. It's super cozy, and the food is made fresh.

You can also take a short walk down to the **Port Chilkoot Dock** to see the water and the mountains. Sometimes you'll spot bald eagles flying around or sitting on the piers. It's a great spot to just relax and enjoy the view.

14.3.3 Hammer Museum

The **Hammer Museum** in **Haines** is exactly what it sounds like, and somehow so much more. You'll find it right in the middle of town, at **108 Main Street**, with a **giant 20-foot hammer** standing outside that you literally cannot miss. It's one of those places that makes you stop and think, "Wait, really? A hammer museum?" But trust me, once you walk through the doors, you'll be surprised how interesting and fun it

EVERYTHING YOU NEED. NOTHING YOU DON'T

actually is.

This small, cozy museum has **over 2,000 hammers** on display, and it's the only museum in the world that's all about hammers. And no, it's not boring. You get to see hammers from every time period and for every job you can think of. There are **prehistoric hammers** made of stone and bone that were used by early humans. Then there are **medieval hammers** used for blacksmithing and building. You'll even find tiny, detailed **goldsmithing hammers** that look like little works of art and massive tools used in shipbuilding. Some are so unique, like the **hammer-pistol hybrid**, which is part hammer and part firearm – yeah, that actually exists.

The museum is small, so you can see everything in about **45 minutes to an hour**. It's super easy to explore, and the people who work there are **really friendly**. If you ask them questions, they'll happily share cool stories about the weirdest and rarest hammers in the collection. Some tools date back over **2,000 years**, and there's a lot of history packed into this one room. You'll probably leave thinking, "I didn't know there were so many kinds of hammers," because they've been used for everything from **crafting jewelry** to **building entire cities**.

Visiting Details:
- The museum is open during summer, **May to September**, from **10 AM to 5 PM**. If you're visiting in the winter, you'll need to call ahead because hours are limited.
- Tickets are cheap: it's about **$5 for adults** and **$3 for kids**.
- Location: **108 Main Street**, Haines, Alaska. If you're coming from the ferry dock, it's about a **15-minute walk** or a quick taxi ride. From downtown, it's right there, so you can't miss it.

When you finish, just take a stroll around **downtown Haines** because everything is super close. You can grab a hot coffee and a snack at **The Rusty Compass Coffeehouse**, which is nearby, for around **$5 to $10**. Their cinnamon rolls and pastries are a must-try. If you're hungrier, walk over to **Mountain Market & Café** for a fresh sandwich or soup for about **$10 to $15**.

The Hammer Museum is quick, fun, and a little bit quirky. It's not like anything else you'll see on your trip, and that's what makes it special.

14.4 Outdoor Activities in Haines

14.4.1 Chilkoot Lake State Recreation Site

Chilkoot Lake State Recreation Site is about **20 minutes from downtown Haines** along **Lutak Road**, a beautiful drive with amazing views of **Lutak Inlet**. The road is smooth, and you'll follow it straight until you see signs for the lake. There's a small parking area right near the **boat launch**, so it's easy to stop and get out. You'll need a **car** to get here since there's no public transport to this area.

Once you arrive, it feels like stepping into a postcard. The **lake** is calm and surrounded by tall, green mountains, with the sky reflecting on the water. It's so quiet you can hear the water lapping at the shore. This is a great place to do **fishing**, **boating**, or just relax with a picnic and enjoy the view. If you like **fishing**, the **Chilkoot River** is famous for its **sockeye salmon** runs in the summer, especially from **July to September**. You'll see salmon swimming upstream, and if you're lucky, you might spot **bears** catching fish right along the shore.

Wildlife here is everywhere, so keep your eyes open. You'll often see **brown bears** near the river, **eagles** flying overhead, and sometimes **harbor seals** swimming close to the lake's edge. If you're visiting for bears, it's best to come **early in the morning or late afternoon** when they're most active. Bring a **bear spray** and stay a safe distance – don't ever approach them.

If you want to get on the water, you can **rent a kayak or canoe** in Haines for about **$40 to $75** for a half day. It's an easy way to explore the lake and feel surrounded by nature. The water is calm, so even if you're not experienced, you'll be fine. It's also perfect for taking photos of the mountains reflected on the water.

You won't find any food or shops here, so grab something to eat before heading out. In Haines, stop at **Mountain Market & Café** near **Third Avenue** and **Haines Highway** for sandwiches, coffee, and snacks. A sandwich will cost you about **$10 to $15**, and they're perfect for a picnic by the lake.

There are **basic restrooms** at the parking lot, but that's about it for facilities, so plan ahead. Bring **bug spray** in the summer since the mosquitoes can get annoying, and wear **layers** because the weather can change fast. A good pair of **binoculars** will help you spot bears, eagles, or other wildlife in the distance.

14.4.2 Hiking and Biking Trails

If you're looking to hike or bike in **Haines**, you've got some really cool trails to check out. I'm talking about easy, fun ones and a few that are more challenging but totally worth it if you're up for it. **Battery Point Trail** is the one you start with if you just want something easy and beautiful. It begins at the end of **Beach Road**, super close to downtown – you can drive there in about 5 minutes or walk in 20. There's free parking right by the trailhead, and you'll find yourself on a nice, **flat dirt path** surrounded by tall spruce trees. It's quiet and peaceful, and you'll love the way it opens up to a view of the **Lynn Canal** once you hit Battery Point. Sit on the rocks, bring a snack, and just take in the blue water and snowy mountains. It's about **3 miles round trip**, so you won't need much gear – just good shoes and maybe a water bottle.

If you want to step it up a little, head over to the **Seduction Point Trail** near **Chilkoot Lake State Recreation Site**. To get there, drive along **Lutak Road** for about 15 to 20 minutes – you'll see signs for the recreation area. If you don't have a car, arrange for a ride because public buses don't go this far. This trail is **8 miles one way**, and it's a mix of forests, open meadows, and some coastline views that are pretty unreal. You'll see streams, small rocky beaches, and lots of places where you can stop and just look out at the water. If you're here during **salmon season**, you might even spot some bears nearby, so you **need bear spray** and some awareness. If you're biking, be ready for rugged terrain – it's not smooth, but it's perfect if you want a bit of a challenge.

Then there's **Mount Ripinsky Trail**, and this one is for you if you're looking for something that'll test your legs. You start at **Young Road**, about a mile from downtown. You can drive there and park at the trailhead or just walk over if you're nearby. This trail is **7 miles round trip**, but it's steep – you're climbing most of the time. You'll start under trees, but as you get higher, the views just keep getting better. Once you hit the top, you'll see the **Lynn Canal**, the **Chilkat River**, and mountains all around you. It's like standing on top of the world. Bring layers because it gets cold and windy at the top, plus snacks and plenty of water. If you're biking, the ride down is technical and fast – definitely for experienced riders only.

Before you head out, go to the **Haines Visitor Center** on **Main Street** to grab a trail map and check the weather. If you don't have a bike, you can rent one at **Sockeye Cycle Co.** on **Union Street** for about **$40 to $75 a day**, depending on what you need. And if you want food for the trail, stop by **Mountain Market & Café** on **3rd Avenue**. Their sandwiches and drinks are perfect to pack, and they'll cost you around **$10 to $15**.

14.4.3 River Rafting and Kayaking

If you want to see **Haines from the water**, river rafting and kayaking are the **best ways** to really experience the wilderness. You'll float through quiet rivers surrounded by **mountains and wildlife**, or paddle on a clear lake where the only sounds are the splash of your paddle and the wind through the trees. It's something you'll never forget.

For **river rafting**, head to the **Chilkat River**, about **25 minutes** north of Haines by car on the **Haines Highway**. If you don't have a car, most companies like **Chilkat River Adventures** or **Haines Rafting Company** will pick you up downtown. The river is calm, not fast, so it's perfect for relaxing and looking around. You'll see **bald eagles perched in trees**, sometimes **bears fishing for salmon**, and maybe a **moose** wandering along the shore. It's quiet and peaceful, with views of snow-topped mountains all around. Tours last about **3 to 4 hours** and cost between **$110–$150** per person, including waterproof gear and life jackets. Pack a snack or grab a sandwich from **The Bamboo Room** on Main Street before you go – it's easy, affordable, and perfect for the trip.

For **kayaking**, the best spot is **Chilkoot Lake** at the **Chilkoot Lake State Recreation Site**, about **25 minutes** north of town along **Lutak Road**. If you don't have your own kayak, you can rent one from **Sockeye Cycle Co.** on **2nd Avenue** or book a tour with a group like **SEABA**. The lake is calm and surrounded by **mountains with waterfalls** flowing down the sides. In **salmon season (July to September)**, you'll see salmon swimming below your kayak and maybe a **black bear** catching fish near the shore. Early mornings are the best because the water is smooth, and the light makes everything look perfect. A guided kayaking trip costs about **$90–$120** for **2–3 hours**, and they'll provide you with all the gear you need. If you're doing it yourself, there's parking right by the lake where you can launch easily.

When you're done, stop by **Haines Packing Company** near the ferry terminal on **Lutak Road** for a fresh **salmon sandwich** or some **smoked fish** for about **$12–$18**. It's a great way to end the day. Or head back to downtown and grab a soup and coffee from **Mountain Market & Café** on **3rd Avenue** – it's cozy and always fresh.

Make sure you **dress in layers** and bring a waterproof jacket because the weather can change fast.

14.5 Dining in Haines

Haines may be small, but the food is all about **fresh, local, and homemade flavors**. You're in a place surrounded by water, mountains, and wilderness, so you get **wild-caught seafood, freshly baked bread, locally raised meats, and strong coffee** at nearly every spot. There are no big fast-food chains here, so everything feels personal, cooked by locals who actually care about the food they serve. The best meals here are simple but made with quality ingredients—**crispy halibut fish and chips, thick clam chowder, juicy burgers, wood-fired pizzas, and fresh berry pancakes**. Everything tastes better because it's **fresh, caught or grown right here, not shipped from far away**. The prices are reasonable for Alaska, but don't expect huge menus—restaurants are small, and they serve what's in season. Just remember, **places close early, usually by 8 or 9 PM, and some spots are only open in the summer**.

Right in downtown, **The Bamboo Room** is the go-to for **legendary halibut fish and chips**, golden and crispy on the outside, flaky inside, served with thick fries and homemade tartar sauce. They also do **rockfish tacos, burgers, and bowls of steaming clam chowder**. It's simple, filling, and exactly what you want after a long day outside. Next door, the **Pioneer Bar** has cold Alaskan beer on tap and a laid-back crowd of locals and travelers swapping adventure stories.

If you need **breakfast or a quick coffee**, **Mountain Market & Café** serves up **strong espresso, smoked salmon bagels, fresh pastries, and hearty breakfast burritos** packed with eggs, cheese, and meat. The café is inside a small grocery store where you can grab **local honey, jam, fresh fruit, and snacks for the road**. It's an easy 5-minute walk from downtown, and if you're heading out early for a tour, this is where you grab something quick to go.

For something more relaxed with an **ocean view**, **The Pilotlight** sits right on the waterfront. The **menu changes daily based on what's fresh**, but expect **seared halibut, crab bisque, smoked salmon flatbread, and grilled local meats**. If you're here for brunch, the **eggs benedict with smoked salmon and fresh berry pancakes** are the best in town. The vibe is casual but **one of the best places for a slow, scenic meal** with a drink in hand.

If you want **pizza done right**, **Fireweed Restaurant** makes **hand-stretched, wood-fired pizzas** with crispy crusts and fresh toppings. It's only open in the summer, but when it is, it's packed every night because the food is good, the portions are big, and they've got **local craft beers to go with your meal**.

If you're in a rush or heading out for a tour, **Sarah J's Espresso Shoppe** is a **tiny, roadside espresso stand** near the ferry terminal, serving **quick breakfast burritos, fresh muffins, and strong coffee**. It's perfect if you just need to grab something and go.

During the **warmer months**, you'll find **seafood stands and food trucks** down by the harbor, selling **fresh crab legs, grilled salmon plates, fish tacos, and hot bowls of chowder**. These places serve some of the freshest seafood in town, and you can eat while watching the boats come in and out of the harbor.

Most places in Haines **close early**, so if you're planning on dinner, **eat before 8 PM or risk missing out**. If you're on a **budget**, Mountain Market is your best bet for **cheap, filling meals**. If you want the best seafood, **stick to halibut or salmon**, since it's **caught right here and never frozen**. For a sit-down dinner, **The Pilotlight has the best atmosphere, and Fireweed makes the best pizza**. If you're here in the summer, **check out the food trucks—they're quick, cheap, and serve some of the freshest seafood in town**.

14.6 Accommodation in Haines

Haines has **a few solid places to stay**, whether you want a **basic but comfortable motel, a cozy lodge, a budget-friendly hostel, a cabin surrounded by nature, or a campground where you can sleep under the stars. Everything is close**, so no matter where you stay, you'll be **minutes from the harbor, restaurants, and main attractions**. In the **summer**, prices go up because of the tourists, but in **winter**, you'll find cheaper rates, though some places shut down for the season. If you **want a modern stay**, pick a **hotel or a lodge with all the amenities**. If you **want something personal**, go for a **cabin or a family-run inn**. If you're **watching your budget**, a **hostel or a campsite** will do the job.

Right in town, **Aspen Suites Hotel** is **the most modern choice**, offering **big rooms, kitchenettes, Wi-Fi, and parking**, making it **great for longer stays. Captain's Choice Motel** on **Front Street** has **harbor views and clean rooms**, a **mid-range price**, and easy access to **restaurants and shops**. If you **want something with character**, **Halsingland Hotel** is inside an **old military building**, giving it a **unique historical vibe**, with **big rooms, free breakfast, and a bar**, just a short walk from downtown.

For a **more personal experience**, you'll find **small inns and lodges** like **Bear Den Inn**, where you get **a quiet stay, Wi-Fi, and a shared kitchen**. If you want **a rental-style stay**, **Port Chilkoot Rentals** offers **apartments and homes with kitchens, laundry, and mountain views**. If you're looking for **something rustic and peaceful**, **Hidden Cove Farm Lodge** has **cabins by the water with full kitchens and amazing views**. If you **love waking up to nature**, the **Cabin by the Beach** is a **simple, private spot right near the harbor**.

For **budget travelers, The Funny Farm Lodge & Hostel** is **the cheapest option**, offering **dorm-style beds or private rooms, Wi-Fi, a shared kitchen, and a relaxed, social vibe**. **Chilkoot Haven** is a **quiet guesthouse near the river**, with **affordable rooms and a peaceful setting**.

ALASKA ACTION PLAN

If you're **camping or traveling in an RV, Oceanside RV Park** sits **right on the waterfront**, offering **tent sites, RV hookups, showers, and picnic tables** where you can **watch the ferries come and go**. **Haines Hitch-Up RV Park** is **closer to town**, with **full hookups, Wi-Fi, laundry, and clean facilities**. If you **want a true wilderness experience**, **Chilkoot Lake Campground** is the best option, surrounded by **mountains, forests, and plenty of wildlife**, where you can **see bears fishing for salmon**. The campsites have **fire pits and outhouses but no running water or electricity**, so **come prepared**.

If you **want the best comfort**, **Aspen Suites Hotel** is the top pick. If you **want a historic stay, Halsingland Hotel** has charm. If you're **on a budget**, **The Funny Farm Lodge** is cheap and social. If you **want an unforgettable view**, book a **cabin at Hidden Cove Farm Lodge** or stay at **Oceanside RV Park**.

EVERYTHING YOU NEED. NOTHING YOU DON'T

CHAPTER FIFTEEN
KODIAK - THE EMERALD ISLE

15.1 Introduction to Kodiak

Kodiak is **Alaska's second-largest island**, surrounded by **rough seas, green mountains, and deep forests**. The **Alutiiq people** have lived here for **over 7,500 years**, depending on **fishing, hunting, and traditions tied to the land and sea**. Russian fur traders arrived in the **1700s**, leaving behind **churches, culture, and history still visible today**. The island later became **a major U.S. fishing hub**, with **boats pulling in salmon, halibut, and massive Kodiak king crab**.

Kodiak is **one of the biggest fishing ports in the country**, and the local economy **runs on the ocean**. You see it everywhere—**boats lined up in the harbor, fishermen loading gear, seafood markets selling fresh catches, and restaurants serving wild salmon, crab, and halibut**. The town itself is **small but lively**, with **shops, historic buildings, and docks always busy with activity**.

The island's **wildlife is legendary**, especially the **Kodiak bear**, the **largest brown bear species in the world**, often spotted **fishing in rivers or roaming the forests**. Eagles crowd the trees, whales pass through the waters, and the landscape is packed with **hiking trails, lakes, and coastline waiting to be explored**.

The weather **changes fast—rain and fog can roll in suddenly**, but clear days offer **incredible ocean and mountain views**. Summer is **cool and green**, perfect for **hiking, fishing, and wildlife tours**. Winter is **stormy and rugged**, drawing visitors who want to experience **Kodiak's remote beauty without the crowds**.

15.2 Flying – The Fastest Option

The **quickest and most convenient way** to reach the island is by **taking a commercial flight from Anchorage**, which runs **multiple times a day** and **takes just about an hour. Alaska Airlines operates these flights year-round**, and if you're traveling in **peak summer months (June through August), book early** because seats fill up fast, and prices climb as demand goes up. **Winter and spring can bring flight cancellations**, thanks to Kodiak's famous fog, storms, and gusty winds, so if you're flying between **October and April**, be prepared for **possible delays** and **have some flexibility** built into your schedule.

If you're not into **commercial airlines** and want **something more adventurous**, you can **charter a small plane or hop on a seaplane** with carriers like **Island Air Service or Andrew Airways**, which serve **remote lodges, villages, and backcountry areas** around the island. Seaplanes don't land at the airport—they **drop right into the water**, giving you a pretty unforgettable **Alaskan arrival**. These flights can be pricey, but if you're headed **to a fishing lodge or exploring the wild parts of the island**, they're often **the only way in or out**.

Kodiak Benny Benson State Airport (ADQ) is **where all commercial flights land**, and it's just **five miles southwest of downtown**, so once you arrive, **it's an easy taxi or shuttle ride into town**. If you're renting a car, **book ahead**, because rental options are **limited compared to bigger cities**.

Taking the Ferry

For a **slower, scenic approach**, you can **take the Alaska Marine Highway ferry** from **Homer**, which is **250 miles south of Anchorage** and reachable by car, bus, or plane. The ferry ride **across the Gulf of Alaska takes between 9 to 12 hours**, depending on conditions, and **operates year-round**, though the **schedule changes by season**, with **fewer sailings in winter**.

Summertime ferries book up early, so **reserve your spot months in advance** if you're traveling from **June to August**. If you're bringing **a vehicle**, book **even earlier**, because car spots **are limited** and fill up quickly. While ferries have **private cabins available**, budget travelers **often sleep on deck or in the lounge areas**—so if you're going this route, **bring a warm sleeping bag, a pillow, and maybe an eye mask** if you're planning to rest while onboard.

There's **a cafeteria on the ferry** with **basic hot meals**, but if you're **picky or don't want to spend extra, pack your own food and drinks**. You can also walk around **outside on the deck**, where you might see **whales, puffins, or sea otters** as you cruise past Alaska's rugged coastline.

When you get to the **Kodiak ferry terminal**, it's about **three miles from downtown**, and taxis **usually wait at the dock** for incoming passengers. If you're heading to **a lodge or rental**, check if they **offer shuttle service**, since many places **pick up guests directly from the ferry**.

15.3 Kodiak National Wildlife Refuge

Kodiak National Wildlife Refuge is one of the wildest places you can step into, covering **over two million acres of rugged mountains, deep forests, winding rivers, and untouched coastlines**. There are **no roads inside the refuge**, so you can't just drive in like a normal park—you **have to fly in on a floatplane, take a boat, or hike in from certain points along the road system**. This is home to **the Kodiak brown bear, the largest bear species in the world**, along with bald eagles, river otters, red foxes, and hundreds of migrating seabirds. If you want **true Alaskan wilderness**, this is it.

ALASKA ACTION PLAN

Getting In and Best Ways to Travel

There's **no easy way in**, so if you want to reach the heart of the refuge, **you need to book a floatplane or boat**. The most common way is **flying from Kodiak's main town** with air taxi services like **Island Air Service, Andrew Airways, or Kingfisher Aviation**. These small planes **land on lakes or coastal waters**, dropping you off **in complete isolation**. If you're staying at a remote lodge, **they usually arrange flights for you**.

If you want a **more budget-friendly way**, some areas of the refuge **can be reached by boat from Kodiak's harbor**. This takes **longer** but gives you a chance to **see marine wildlife along the way**. If you're just looking for a **quick experience**, you can also **hike into the refuge** from spots like **Buskin River or Saltery Cove**, which don't require expensive flights.

Kodiak Brown Bears – What You Need to Know

This is **bear country, no question about it**. Kodiak's brown bears are **massive, sometimes over 1,500 pounds, standing more than 10 feet tall**. They roam the refuge **in high numbers**, especially along rivers where **salmon run thick from July to September**. If you want to **safely see them up close**, guided bear-viewing tours take you to prime spots like **Karluk Lake, Frazer Lake, and Uganik Bay**, where you can watch them **fishing for salmon just feet away**.

If you're hiking or camping alone, you need bear spray, a way to store your food safely, and the knowledge to handle a bear encounter. Never leave food out, never hike silently, and never, ever get too close for a photo. **This is their home—you're just visiting**.

Best Times to Visit

Summer (June to August) is the best time if you want **long daylight hours, better weather, and active wildlife**. This is when bears are **most visible**, and you'll also see **whales, sea otters, and bald eagles**. The downside? **Mosquitoes are relentless, and flights book up fast**, so you need to plan ahead.

Fall (September to October) is quieter, with **fewer visitors and peak bear activity** before hibernation. The weather can be **cold and rainy**, but the landscape turns **beautiful shades of red and orange**, making it **a great time for photography**.

Winter (November to March) is a different world—bears are in hibernation, and everything is **covered in deep snow**. It's **harsh, remote, and unforgiving**, but if you're looking for **solitude and raw wilderness**, this is it.

Spring (April to May) is when the bears wake up, but trails are **still muddy, and the weather is unpredictable**. This is **prime time for birdwatching**, with hundreds of species returning from migration.

Hiking, Camping, and Exploring on Foot

If you're not flying into the deep backcountry, **there are a few places where you can hike into the refuge**.

The **Saltery Cove Trail** is a rough, rugged path where you might see **bears, eagles, and wild salmon runs**, but you need **serious hiking experience**.

The **Buskin River Trail** is easier, taking you **through forested areas and riversides**, giving you a good taste of the wilderness **without going too deep into bear territory**.

Camping is allowed, but you need to know what you're doing—this is not a place for beginners. **There are no marked campsites, no facilities, and no safety nets**, so if you go in, you **must pack out everything, store your food properly, and be prepared for extreme weather changes**.

Weather and What to Prepare For

Kodiak's weather is **unpredictable year-round**, with sudden fog, rain, and wind gusts. **Flights get delayed or canceled often, and ferry crossings can be rough in fall and winter**. Pack for **cold, wet conditions no matter what season it is**, and **always assume the weather will change**. If you're taking the ferry, bring **seasickness meds**, because the Gulf of Alaska can be a rough ride.

15.3.1 Fort Abercrombie State Historical Park

Fort Abercrombie is where **history, nature, and incredible views** all come together in one spot. You walk in, and it feels like **a time capsule from World War II**, with huge concrete bunkers and old coastal defense structures hidden between thick spruce trees and steep cliffs dropping straight into the ocean. This place was built to protect the coastline, and today, it's one of the **best places on Kodiak Island to explore abandoned wartime ruins while being surrounded by pure Alaskan wilderness**.

You can **step inside the bunkers**, where soldiers once stood guard, and imagine what it was like to **watch the sea for enemy submarines**. The old gun emplacements still sit there, aimed toward the Pacific, reminding you how serious things were back then. **Some of these structures are falling apart, covered in moss and rust, giving the whole place an eerie but fascinating atmosphere.** If you're into history or just love places that feel untouched by time, this is where you want to be.

But this park is more than just its past. You have **incredible hiking trails** that wind through the forest, opening up to **steep cliffs with unreal views of the ocean**. One of the best trails loops around **Lake Gertrude**, a peaceful, glassy lake surrounded by towering trees where you can **walk, spot wildlife, or just sit and take in the view**. If you follow the paths toward the coastline, you'll get to **rocky bluffs overlooking the water**, where you can see **sea otters floating, bald eagles soaring overhead, and—if you're lucky—whales passing by in the distance**.

If you love photography, **this place is unbeatable**. The best shots? **The bunkers**, where light creeps through the cracks and moss grows over the walls, making everything look like something out of an old war movie. **The cliffs**, where the ocean stretches endlessly in front of you, making you feel like you're standing at the edge of the world. **Lake Gertrude at sunrise or sunset**, when the trees reflect perfectly in the water, turning everything into a postcard scene.

Getting here is **quick and easy**, just **4 miles north of downtown Kodiak**, about **a 10-minute drive** if you have a rental car. If you don't, **you can take a taxi or even bike** since the park is easy to explore on foot once you're there. **There's no entrance fee**, and it's open **year-round**, but if you come in the winter, expect **snowy trails and icy paths** that make hiking tougher. The best time to visit is **spring through early fall**, when the trails are dry, the wildlife is active, and you can join **ranger-led tours** to learn even more about the area's history.

You can't visit Kodiak without seeing this place. **It's not just about history—it's about standing in a spot where the past and present collide, where nature takes over old bunkers, and where you can hike, explore, and take in some of the best views on the island all in one stop.**

15.3.2 Alutiiq Museum

The **Alutiiq Museum** isn't big, but what's inside carries **thousands of years of history**, telling the story of the **Alutiiq people** who have lived on this island for generations. The moment you walk in, you're surrounded by **ancient artifacts, traditional tools, intricate masks, and beautifully crafted objects** that show how the Alutiiq adapted to the land and sea long before modern times.

What makes this place **stand out** is that it's not just a collection of old items—it's **a living, breathing space where history and culture continue to thrive**. You don't just look at things behind glass; you **hear stories, watch demonstrations, and sometimes even touch materials** that Alutiiq ancestors used for survival. **Hunting tools carved from bone, woven grass baskets that carried food**, and **masks once worn in powerful ceremonies** all give you a **deep connection to Kodiak's past**.

The museum regularly changes its **exhibits and interactive displays**, keeping things fresh for visitors. One day, you might see **a show-**

case of ancient fishing gear, and another time, you might walk into an exhibit about **Alutiiq spiritual beliefs, featuring painted masks and carvings used in storytelling and rituals**. Some displays let you **listen to the Alutiiq language**, which is still being preserved today, and you might even catch a **live storytelling session or cultural workshop**, where local artists demonstrate traditional skills like **skin sewing, beadwork, or wood carving**.

Located **right in downtown Kodiak on Mission Road**, the museum is **easy to reach on foot** if you're staying in town. It's **open year-round**, but hours can vary, so checking ahead is always a good idea. Admission is **affordable, usually under $10**, making it **one of the best and most accessible ways to learn about Kodiak's deep Indigenous roots**.

15.4 Outdoor Activities in Kodiak

15.4.1 Fishing and Hunting

Kodiak is one of the best places in the world for fishing and hunting, where the ocean is full of massive halibut and king salmon, and the forests are home to Sitka black-tailed deer. Whether you're standing on the shore, casting your line into the cold waters, or heading deep into the backcountry on a guided hunt, **this island gives you an adventure that feels raw and wild.**

If you're here for **fishing, summer is the best time.** Charter boats leave **daily from Kodiak Harbor**, taking you into waters teeming with **halibut that can weigh over 200 pounds, feisty king salmon, rockfish, and lingcod.** Many captains have been fishing these waters for decades, so if you're new to deep-sea fishing, they'll help you with everything from **choosing bait to reeling in a catch that will test your strength.** If you **prefer to fish from land, there are plenty of spots along the shore**, including the **Buskin River**, where **silver salmon run strong in late summer.** Permits are required, and you can pick them up at local shops before heading out.

For hunters, fall is the prime season. Kodiak's backcountry is **rugged and remote**, so this isn't a place where you just walk into the woods with a rifle—you **need a guide unless you're an experienced backcountry hunter.** The most sought-after target is the **Sitka black-tailed deer, which thrives in the island's dense forests and alpine meadows.** Some hunters come here for the **mountain goats**, while others take on the ultimate challenge: **hunting the massive Kodiak brown bear. Bear hunting requires special permits, and only a limited number are issued each season.** Because of the sheer size and power of these bears, **most hunters work with licensed guides who know the terrain and the safest way to approach a hunt.**

15.4.2 Kayaking and Boating

Kodiak's waters are full of wildlife, sea cliffs, and hidden coves, and the best way to explore them is by kayak or boat. You can rent a kayak in Kodiak Harbor and paddle along the coast, spotting sea otters floating in the kelp, bald eagles soaring overhead, and seals curiously watching from the rocks. If you want a guided trip, outfitters in town offer tours that take you to more remote areas, like Near Island or Long Island, where you can paddle through calm waters, explore rocky shorelines, and maybe even see a whale surface nearby.

For a more challenging route, experienced kayakers head to Chiniak Bay, Uganik Bay, or Blue Fox Bay, where you paddle past steep cliffs, sea caves, and open ocean swells. The further you go, the wilder it gets, with stretches of coastline where you won't see another person for miles. If you're up for a real adventure, multi-day kayaking trips take you deep into untouched areas, where you camp on remote beaches and paddle in waters teeming with puffins, sea lions, and sometimes even bears fishing along the shore.

If you want to cover more ground or reach remote islands, taking a boat is the way to go. Wildlife tours and fishing charters leave from Seward Boat Harbor, taking you through channels where orcas and humpback whales surface, sea lions lounge on rocky outcrops, and seabirds dive for fish. Some trips take you to uninhabited islands where you can hike, explore tide pools, or fish for halibut and salmon.

The water around Kodiak changes fast, so always check the weather and tides before heading out. Even in summer, the ocean is cold enough to be dangerous, so rental shops offer dry suits for kayakers. If you're new to paddling, stick to sheltered areas or go with a guide to avoid strong currents and rough waters.

15.4.3 Bear Viewing Tours

Kodiak is home to the world's largest brown bears, and seeing them in the wild is something you'll never forget. These giants roam the island's rivers and forests, but if you want a guaranteed sighting, you need to go where the salmon run. The best spots are Frazer Lake, Karluk Lake, and Uganik Island, and the only way to reach them is by boat or floatplane.

Most bear viewing tours start in Kodiak and fly you over the island's rugged landscape, landing in remote locations where bears gather to fish. Some trips take you to platforms overlooking salmon-filled rivers, while others let you watch from a boat, drifting along the shore as bears wade into the water, swiping at fish with their massive paws. The best time to go is July to September when salmon runs are strongest, and bears are out in full force, feeding before winter.

These bears are huge—males can weigh over 1,500 pounds—and watching them in their natural habitat is both thrilling and humbling. You'll see them fighting over prime fishing spots, standing on their hind legs to get a better view, or playfully splashing in the water. Some tours offer longer excursions where you hike with an experienced guide to find bears away from crowded viewing areas.

You'll need to dress warm, even in summer, because the weather can change fast. Wear layers, waterproof gear, and bring a good camera with a zoom lens—getting too close isn't an option. Most guides carry bear spray and follow strict safety rules, keeping a respectful distance while letting you experience the wild up close.

15.5 Dining in Kodiak

You're on an island surrounded by some of the best seafood in the world, so you should eat like it. The salmon here is wild-caught, rich, and fresh off the boats, whether it's grilled, smoked, or turned into a thick, creamy chowder. Halibut is another must-try—fried for fish and chips, seared with butter and herbs, or wrapped in a taco with crunchy slaw and house-made sauce. If it's crab season, don't leave without cracking into some local king crab legs, sweet and tender, dripping with melted butter.

Restaurants line the harbor, serving plates piled high with fresh seafood while fishing boats unload the day's catch nearby. Some places go simple—**just-caught fish, golden fries, and a cold beer—but if you want something fancier, you can find seafood grills with dishes like pan-seared scallops, blackened salmon with honey glaze, or halibut paired with roasted vegetables.

Not everything here swims in the ocean. Kodiak has big, juicy burgers made from local beef, and if you want something wilder, some places mix in elk or venison for extra flavor. Reindeer sausage is another local favorite—grilled and topped with caramelized onions and mustard, served in a toasted bun. Bakeries and small cafes serve fresh bread, hot coffee, and pastries perfect for a quick breakfast before heading out to explore.

Kodiak's breweries make small-batch craft beers that go perfectly with seafood, burgers, or a long day of adventure. Some of them use glacial water or local ingredients to give their brews a true Alaskan taste. Whether you're sitting by the docks with a plate of fresh halibut, grabbing a quick bite from a food truck, or warming up with a hot bowl of chowder, you're eating food that comes straight from the island's land and sea.

15.6 Accommodation

You have two choices when staying in Kodiak—keep it comfortable in town or go full adventure mode in the wilderness. If you want easy access to shops, restaurants, and the harbor, downtown inns and hotels give you a warm bed and all the basics. These places range from budget-friendly motels to mid-range hotels with ocean views, Wi-Fi, and cozy lobbies perfect for unwinding after a long day.

Fishing lodges are a big deal here, especially if you're coming for halibut, salmon, or king crab. Many of them sit right on the water, where you can step outside and cast a line from the dock or book a charter that leaves straight from the lodge. Some places even include meals, gear rentals, and professional guides who know the best fishing spots. These are great for serious anglers but also for travelers who want the full Kodiak experience without worrying about the details.

For the most epic stay, go off-grid in a remote lodge or an oceanfront cabin tucked deep in the island's wild landscape. Some cabins are only accessible by boat or small plane, meaning you'll be surrounded by nothing but forests, mountains, and the sound of the waves. You'll wake up to fresh air, hike straight from your front door, and maybe even spot bears or eagles without leaving the porch. Some lodges offer guided bear-watching tours, sea kayaking, and backcountry hiking, turning your stay into a full outdoor adventure.

If you're camping, there are campgrounds near town with basic facilities, but the real thrill comes from setting up a tent in the backcountry, where you'll have Kodiak's wild beauty all to yourself. Just be prepared for rain, bring the right gear, and follow bear safety rules—this isn't a place where you want to leave food out overnight.

EVERYTHING YOU NEED, NOTHING YOU DON'T

CHAPTER SIXTEEN
WRANGELL-ST. ELIAS NATIONAL PARK AND NEARBY TOWNS

16.1 Overview of Wrangell-St. Elias National Park

This isn't just another national park. It's the biggest one in the United States— more than **13 million acres of glaciers, towering peaks, and valleys so deep they seem endless.** Imagine a place where the mountains rise so high they disappear into the clouds, where glaciers move like frozen rivers, carving the land over thousands of years. **The Wrangell, St. Elias, Chugach, and Alaska Ranges collide here, creating a landscape that looks like it belongs on another planet.**

If you want to see pure, untouched nature, **this is where you come.** There are no crowds, no traffic, and no easy way in or out. This is **one of the last true wilderness areas on Earth.** With nine of North America's **tallest peaks, hundreds of miles of glaciers,** and **valleys so remote few humans have ever set foot in them,** this place is wild in every sense of the word. **The air is crisp, the silence is deep, and the scenery is so massive it makes you feel small.**

The isolation is what makes it special. Unlike other national parks, you won't find paved roads leading to every attraction. **You either fly in on a bush plane, drive along rough gravel roads, or hike deep into the backcountry.** Once you get here, you step into a world where nature controls everything. **Storms roll in fast, rivers rise without warning, and the mountains demand respect.** But that's what makes this place a paradise for true adventurers.

16.2 Getting to the Park

Wrangell-St. Elias is not a place you just stumble into. This is the **biggest national park in the United States**, and getting here is already part of the adventure. You can't just drive up like it's a city park. **There are no highways, no easy paved roads—only two long, rough gravel roads that take you deep into some of the most untouched land**

ALASKA ACTION PLAN

you'll ever see. You need to be prepared for the journey before you even think about what you'll do once you arrive.

If you're **driving**, you've got **two choices: McCarthy Road or Nabesna Road.** Neither is smooth. **Both are full of potholes, loose gravel, washouts, and almost no services.** McCarthy Road is **60 miles** from **Chitina to McCarthy** and takes at least **2-3 hours** to drive. Some parts have **old railroad spikes still buried in the gravel**, so a **flat tire is a real risk.** Nabesna Road is **42 miles long** starting at **Slana**, with fewer visitors but **even rougher terrain**—deep mud, rocky creek crossings, and sections that can completely wash out after heavy rain.

There are no gas stations, no food stops, no phone signal once you get past Chitina or Slana. You have to **bring your own extra fuel, a spare tire, food, water, and emergency gear** because if something goes wrong, you won't find a tow truck or help for miles. **You drive slow, you watch for loose gravel, and you don't rush because getting stuck out here is no joke.**

If you don't want to risk the drive, you can **fly instead. Bush planes** from **Anchorage, Glennallen, or Chitina** can land right in **McCarthy**, dropping you into the middle of the park with no need to deal with the roads. It costs more than driving, but if you **only have a short time and want to get straight to the scenery, flying is the best way.**

Weather is unpredictable all year. Even in **summer**, you can get **cold winds, sudden rainstorms, and even snow in the higher elevations.** The best time to go is from **June to early September** when the roads are clear and the rivers are low, but even then, **you have to check conditions before heading out** because washouts and rockslides can happen anytime.

You **don't just "swing by" Wrangell-St. Elias.** Getting here is a challenge, but if you're prepared and ready for rough roads, no services, and real wilderness, you'll be stepping into a place that **almost no one else in the world has ever seen.**

16.2.1 Kennecott Mines National Historic Landmark

Kennecott isn't just an abandoned town—it's a **snapshot of history**, frozen in place against the backdrop of **towering peaks and massive glaciers.** In the early 1900s, this was one of the richest **copper mining operations in the world**, pulling millions of dollars' worth of ore from the rugged mountains. Today, the old **red mill buildings**, rusted mining equipment, and forgotten homes **still stand**, telling the story of the workers who lived and labored in this **isolated corner of Alaska.**

You don't just drive up to Kennecott. To get here, you first have to **reach McCarthy**, which is at the end of the **rough 60-mile McCarthy Road.** From there, you **cross a footbridge over the Kennicott River** (cars aren't allowed past this point), then either **hike five miles up to the mill site or take a local shuttle**. Most visitors arrive **between June and September**, when the roads are clear and the tours are running. The area is **snow-covered and inaccessible in winter**, except by **snowmobile or bush plane**.

Once you arrive, **you can explore at your own pace or take a guided tour** inside the **14-story wooden mill building, which is one of the most impressive industrial structures left in Alaska.** The tour takes you through **the old conveyor belts, crushers, and ore chutes**, where workers once processed thousands of tons of copper. **The inside of the mill is steep, with narrow staircases and tight walkways,** but the experience is worth it. Seeing the **massive** machinery still in place, coated in rust and history, is like stepping straight into the past.

For those who prefer to explore without a tour, **there are self-guided walking trails around Kennecott.** The trails take you past **old worker housing, storage barns, and the general store**, all of which still **hold echoes of the past.** One of the best short hikes is **the trail to Root Glacier**, where you can **walk right up to the ice**, see deep blue crevasses, and even join a glacier trekking tour if you're feeling adventurous.

Kennecott isn't just another historical site—it's a place that **feels untouched by time.** The red buildings, the quiet air, the towering mountains in the background—it all comes together to create a place that **tells a real story.** Walking through here, you don't just see history—you **feel it.**

16.2.2 Hiking and Backpacking

Wrangell-St. Elias is not a park with easy trails or clear signs pointing you where to go. This is wild land, no maintained paths, no crowds, just massive mountains, glaciers, deep valleys, and unpredictable weather. If you are hiking here, you need to know exactly where you're going, have the right gear, and be fully prepared. Root Glacier Trail is one of the easiest hikes, starting right near Kennecott and leading straight onto the ice, where you can walk over deep blue pools, cracks in the glacier, and frozen formations that shift over time. You don't need a guide, but you do need crampons or good traction cleats because the ice is slick, and falling here can be dangerous. This hike is about four miles round trip, mostly flat, and takes a few hours. If you want a challenge, Bonanza Mine Trail is a steep climb up nearly 4,000 feet, where rusted mining equipment and century-old structures sit abandoned in the mountains, with a view stretching far over the valley and glaciers below. It's a hard hike, the incline is relentless, and the way down is tough on your knees, but standing at the top, surrounded by nothing but peaks and sky, makes it all worth it.

Backpacking here is for serious hikers. There are no marked backcountry trails, no set routes, just open tundra, high ridges, river crossings, and deep, remote valleys where you might not see another person for days. Some trekkers head into Nizina River Valley, surrounded by jagged peaks and ice fields. Others take on the Erie Mine Trail, climbing steep ridges to reach an abandoned copper mine perched high above everything else. The Seven Pass Route is one of the hardest multi-day treks, cutting through alpine passes, ridgelines, and valleys so isolated that you will feel like the last person on earth. If you get lost or injured out here, no one is coming quickly to help you, so you have to know how to navigate, cross rivers, and deal with unpredictable weather that can turn from sunny to freezing rain in an instant.

Bears are everywhere in this park, grizzlies and black bears, and you have to carry bear spray, know how to store your food in a bear-safe container, and be prepared for an encounter at any moment. The weather is just as unpredictable, and even in the summer, nights can be freezing, storms can roll in with little warning, and river crossings can become dangerous after heavy rain. You need waterproof gear, warm layers, a solid tent, and a plan in case something goes wrong.

To camp overnight, you need a backcountry permit, and rangers will check that you have everything needed to survive out there. There are no set campgrounds, so you have to find a safe, dry spot on your own, away from animal paths and places where rivers might rise overnight. This is not a park where you just show up and go—everything requires planning, caution, and the right equipment. But if you are ready for it, if you can handle the challenges, this is one of the most raw, untouched, and truly wild places left on earth.

16.2.3 Glacier Tours

Root Glacier is one of the most accessible glaciers in Wrangell-St. Elias, and walking on it feels like stepping into another world. The ice is alive, constantly shifting, cracking, and melting in slow motion, creating deep blue crevasses, rushing meltwater streams, and jagged ice formations that change every season. A guided glacier tour is the safest way to explore, especially if you have never hiked on ice before. Guides provide **crampons**, metal spikes that strap onto your boots for grip, and an **ice axe** to help with balance on the slick surface. The standard tour

ALASKA ACTION PLAN

is a **half-day hike**, covering about 4-5 miles round trip from Kennecott. You start on a rocky trail before stepping onto the glacier itself, where the temperature drops, and the wind often picks up.

For a more extreme adventure, **ice climbing tours** let you scale vertical ice walls with ropes and harnesses, using sharp ice tools to dig into the frozen surface and pull yourself up. This requires more physical effort but is open to beginners as long as you have decent fitness and follow the guide's instructions. Some multi-day glacier expeditions go beyond Root Glacier, leading deep into the ice fields and remote valleys, where campers sleep on the ice itself.

Weather can be unpredictable, even in summer, so you need **layers, waterproof clothing, gloves, and sunglasses** to protect your eyes from the glare. Rain can make the ice slippery, and the cold air blowing off the glacier can chill you fast. Drinking water is easy to find—just fill a bottle from a meltwater stream flowing across the ice, some of the purest water you'll ever taste.

16.3 Nearby Towns

16.3.1 McCarthy

McCarthy is **a tiny, off-grid town** deep in the wilderness. There are **no paved roads, no gas stations, no chain stores, and no big hotels**—just dirt streets, old wooden buildings, and a small community of **locals, seasonal workers, and travelers**. The town started as a **boomtown for Kennecott miners** in the early 1900s, where workers came to drink, gamble, and escape the hard life of the copper mines. Today, it's **a remote adventure hub** with **simple lodges, campgrounds, small restaurants, and outfitters** for hiking, glacier trekking, and backcountry exploring.

To get here, you take **McCarthy Road**, a **60-mile gravel route from Chitina** that takes **2-3 hours** because of **potholes, washouts, narrow bridges, and rough terrain**. Rental car companies **often don't allow their vehicles on this road**, so check before you drive. **No gas stations after Chitina**, so **fill up before you go**. There are **no mechanics or tow services nearby**, so a **spare tire and repair kit are smart to have**. If you don't want to drive, there are **seasonal shuttle services from Anchorage, Glennallen, or Chitina**, but seats fill up fast, so you need to **book ahead**.

You **can't drive into town**. When you reach the end of McCarthy Road, you **park and walk across a footbridge** over the **Kennicott River**. A local shuttle or a short walk gets you into town, where everything is **small, simple, and easy to explore on foot**. The town has **a few lodges, bed-and-breakfasts, hostels, and campgrounds**, but **no luxury resorts, no modern hotels, and no fast food**. Lodging **fills up in summer**, so **book months in advance** if you want a place with a bed. Campgrounds and basic cabins are **cheaper** and often available last-minute.

Food is **local and homemade**. Small cafés and restaurants serve **fresh bread, hot coffee, wild game, and seafood**. Expect **simple, hearty meals**, not fancy dining. Some places have **live music, campfire hangouts, and outdoor seating with mountain views**. Groceries are **very limited**, so if you need snacks or supplies, **bring them with you**.

There's **no cell service** in McCarthy. Wi-Fi is available **only at** a few lodges and cafes, but it's **slow and unreliable**. This is a place where **you unplug and focus on nature**.

16.3.2 Chitina

Chitina is **a small, historic town** that sits at the **edge of the wilderness**, where the paved road ends and the adventure into **Wrangell-St. Elias National Park** begins. It was once a **railroad stop for copper miners** traveling to and from **Kennecott**, but after the mines shut down, the town became **quiet and remote**, serving mostly as **a stop for travelers, fishermen, and locals**.

You get here by **driving 85 miles southeast from Glennallen on the Edgerton Highway**, a **paved road that's open year-round**. The drive takes **about 1.5 to 2 hours**, with **gas stations and small stops along the way**. Chitina is **the last place to fill up on gas, buy snacks, or check your gear before heading onto McCarthy Road**, the **60-mile rough gravel route** leading toward McCarthy and Kennecott. There are **no services beyond this point**, so **if you need supplies, this is your last chance to stock up**.

The **Copper River runs right next to town**, drawing **fishermen in summer** for **dipnetting and salmon fishing**. If you're here during the **sockeye salmon run (June-July)**, you'll see **locals catching fish by the dozens**, as dipnetting is **a major part of Alaskan subsistence culture**. If you want to try fishing, make sure you have **a valid Alaska fishing license** and, if using a dipnet, **an Alaskan residency permit**.

There are **a few small places to eat**, usually offering **burgers, sandwiches, or fresh fish**. A **general store** sells **basic groceries, fishing supplies, and camping gear**, but it's **not a full supermarket**, so don't expect a huge selection. There are **a couple of motels and cabins**, mostly for fishermen and travelers who need a place to sleep before continuing into the park.

CHAPTER SEVENTEEN
NOME - ON THE EDGE OF THE BERING SEA

17.1 Discovering Nome

Nome is **a small, remote town on the Bering Sea**, about **540 miles northwest of Anchorage**, only reachable by **plane or boat** because **no roads connect it to the rest of Alaska**. It's known for **gold mining, sled dog racing, and Arctic survival**. The weather is **harsh, cold, and unpredictable**, with **long, dark winters** and **cool, windy summers**. The town has about **3,500 residents**, a mix of **Inupiat locals, longtime settlers, and seasonal workers**.

Nome **exploded during the 1899 Gold Rush**, when **thousands of prospectors arrived, hoping to get rich by mining the beaches**. Today, you can still **see people panning for gold** along the shore, using modern dredging equipment or simple gold pans. **Old wooden buildings, rusted dredges, and abandoned mining camps** are scattered across the landscape, reminders of Nome's past.

This town is also famous for **dog mushing**. Nome was the final stop of the **1925 serum run**, when **mushers and sled dogs raced through brutal winter conditions** to deliver diphtheria medicine, saving the town. That journey inspired the **Iditarod**, the world's most famous sled dog race, which **ends in Nome every March** after mushers travel **nearly 1,000 miles from Anchorage**.

Outside of town, the land is **vast, open, and wild**, with **no forests, just tundra, rolling hills, and icy rivers**. You might see **musk oxen, moose, reindeer, or even grizzly bears** roaming the terrain. The **Northern Lights** dance in the sky during winter, while summer brings **long daylight hours, fog, and migrating birds**. Nome is **a place where nature dominates**, and survival depends on **respecting the land and its extreme conditions**.

There are **a few hotels, stores, and restaurants**, but life here is **simple and rugged**. People hunt, fish, and rely on **small planes to**

ALASKA ACTION PLAN

bring in fresh food and supplies. Internet is slow, and winters are isolating, but **the people who live here are tough, resourceful, and proud of their home**. Nome isn't just a town—it's **a test of endurance, a connection to history, and a true edge-of-the-world experience**.

17.2 Getting to Nome

No highways, no road trips—**Nome is only accessible by air.** The only way to get here is by **flying from Anchorage**, with **Alaska Airlines offering daily flights**. The trip takes about **90 minutes**, but **weather delays are common**, especially in winter when **strong winds, ice, and low visibility** can disrupt schedules. **Flights can be expensive**, so book early, especially around **major events like the Iditarod finish** in March.

Nome's **small airport (OME)** is **basic but efficient**, with **one terminal, a single baggage claim, and no jet bridges**—you walk across the tarmac to board and deplane. There's **no TSA security screening**, which feels unusual for air travel, but flights still follow strict rules for safety. The airport has **limited services**—a small waiting area, a few vending machines, and sometimes a food stand, but no major restaurants or stores.

Once you land, **Nome's streets are unpaved, muddy in summer, and icy in winter**. You can **rent a car**, but most locals prefer **ATVs, pickup trucks, or snowmachines** for getting around. There are **no taxis**, but **a few car rental agencies** offer trucks and SUVs built for the rough terrain. Nome is **spread out**, with three small communities—**Nome, Fort Davis, and Dexter**—so having a vehicle helps if you plan to explore beyond downtown.

Weather here is **unpredictable all year**. Even in summer, **fog, wind, and sudden storms** can cancel flights, stranding visitors for days. Winter is even harsher, with **temperatures well below zero, brutal wind chills, and long, dark nights**. You should always **pack warm layers, waterproof boots, and survival essentials**, even in warmer months. Nome isn't a place where you just show up unprepared—it's **remote, wild, and demands respect for the environment**.

Stepping off the plane in Nome feels **like landing on the edge of the world**. The landscape is **vast and empty**, stretching endlessly in every direction, with **no trees, just open tundra and distant hills**. The air is **cold and sharp**, the people are **tough and independent**, and the feeling of **being in a truly isolated frontier town** is immediate. **You're not just visiting Nome—you're experiencing a piece of the last true wilderness.**

17.3 Exploring Nome

17.3.1 Gold Rush History

 Nome exploded onto the map in 1899 when gold was discovered—right on the beach. Unlike most gold rush towns where prospectors had to **dig deep into mountains**, here, **flakes and nuggets lay in the sand**, waiting to be scooped up. **Within months, thousands of people flooded Nome**, transforming it into **Alaska's largest town** almost overnight. What followed was **chaos, fortune, and hardship**—a town of **tent camps, lawlessness, and nonstop digging**, where **some struck it rich while others lost everything**.

 Today, **Nome's gold rush history is everywhere**, from the **rusted dredges and abandoned mining shacks** scattered across the tundra to the **wooden false-front buildings** that still line Front Street. **Walk past old storefronts**, where saloons once buzzed with rough miners celebrating lucky strikes, and imagine the frozen streets filled with **dog sled teams, supply wagons, and hopeful prospectors** searching for their next claim.

 To dive deeper into the past, **visit the Carrie M. McLain Museum**, right in town. **This small but packed museum tells the story of Nome's wild gold rush days**, with **artifacts, faded photographs, and firsthand accounts** from the people who lived it. **See old mining tools, historic maps, and even pieces of gold** recovered from Nome's famous beaches.

 Gold fever never completely disappeared here. You'll still see **modern-day prospectors panning for gold along the shore** or operating small dredges just off the coast. Some do it for fun, while others **still chase the same dreams of fortune** that brought thousands here more than a century ago. Nome's gold rush **may have faded, but its spirit is**

alive in every grain of sand.

17.3.2 Bering Land Bridge National Preserve

This land once connected Asia and North America, a frozen bridge where mammoths, early humans, and migrating herds crossed between worlds. Today, the Bering Land Bridge National Preserve is **a vast, untouched wilderness**, 100 miles north of Nome, only accessible by **chartered flights, snowmachines, or extreme overland travel** across the tundra. **No roads, no towns—just open land shaped by time, wind, and history.**

The landscape is like nowhere else. Volcanic formations **rise from the tundra**, leftovers from an ancient past when this land was shaped by fire and ice. The most famous are the **Tors of Serpentine Hot Springs**, massive rock pillars standing like ancient sentinels. Here, **a natural geothermal spring bubbles in the middle of the Arctic**, offering steaming waters even in the coldest winters. This was once a healing site for the Inupiat people, and today, it remains **one of the most remote hot springs in the world.**

Wildlife thrives in this empty land. **Muskoxen graze in herds, their shaggy coats built for survival in the harshest weather. Caribou migrate across the tundra, following trails used for thousands of years.** Birds from every corner of the world arrive in the short Arctic summer, turning the preserve into **a nesting ground for species rarely seen anywhere else.**

For those who make the journey, local guides **offer deep insight into the land's history, geology, and cultural significance**. They tell the stories of **the first humans who walked this land, hunting giant mammals and surviving in one of the world's toughest environments.** The Inupiat people still hold this place sacred, their traditions and knowledge passed down through generations.

17.3.3 Iditarod Trail Sled Dog Race Finish

Nome is where the greatest dog sled race on Earth ends, and the entire town comes alive when the mushers arrive. Every March, after **1,000 grueling miles of snow, wind, and wilderness**, the Iditarod Trail Sled Dog Race reaches its dramatic finish under the **Burled Arch**, the iconic wooden arch that marks the end of the trail. **Mushers and their teams push through brutal conditions, some arriving in the middle of the night, exhausted but victorious.**

When the first team reaches Nome, the celebration begins. Crowds gather along Front Street, bundled up in parkas, **cheering as the sleds slide in, headlamps glowing through the dark. Bars, cafes, and local shops stay open late**, serving hot drinks and hearty food as people swap race stories. The entire town feels like a festival, with **dog handlers, race officials, and visitors from all over the**

world packed into Nome's streets.** The excitement doesn't stop when the winner crosses the finish—teams continue arriving for days, each musher receiving a hero's welcome no matter their position.

Visiting Nome during the Iditarod is the best way to feel the heart of sled dog racing. Stop by the **Iditarod headquarters**, where exhibits showcase legendary mushers, record-breaking finishes, and the deep bond between humans and their sled dogs. You'll see **historic sleds, race footage, and stories of famous champions like Balto and Lance Mackey.** Locals and past racers share their experiences, giving visitors **a real sense of what it takes to conquer the trail.**

If you ever wanted to witness true grit, survival, and the spirit of Alaska, this is the moment. Nome isn't just the finish line—it's where the legends of the Iditarod are made. **Whether you're watching the winner arrive or greeting the last musher weeks later, standing under the Burled Arch as teams cross is an unforgettable experience.**

17.4 Outdoor Activities in Nome

17.4.1 Bird Watching

Nome is one of the best bird-watching destinations in North America, attracting birders from around the world to spot species rarely seen anywhere else. The town sits at the meeting point of Arctic, subarctic, and Asian migratory routes, making it a prime location for **rare shorebirds, waterfowl, and raptors. Spring and summer bring a massive migration, with millions of birds passing through, filling the tundra, lagoons, and coastal wetlands.**

Top birding spots include Kougarok Road, Teller Road, and Safety Sound Lagoon. Kougarok Road is famous for its chance to spot the **rare Bristle-thighed Curlew,** a bird that nests in the Alaskan tundra before flying nonstop to the South Pacific. **Teller Road** leads to rugged coastline and open tundra, offering opportunities to see **jaegers, Snowy Owls, and Long-tailed Ducks. Safety Sound Lagoon** is one of the richest birding areas, attracting **Arctic Terns, Loons, Eiders, and rare Asian migrants** carried over by strong winds. The Nome River mouth is another must-visit, where seabirds and shorebirds gather in large numbers.

The best time to visit is from late May to early July, when the tundra bursts to life, and nesting birds are most active. Early summer offers the best lighting for photography, with the **Midnight Sun creating endless daylight.** Fall migration in August and September is also rewarding, as flocks gather before their long flights south.

Birding in Nome requires preparation. The **weather is unpredictable**, with **chilly winds, rain, and even snow possible in late spring.** Dress in **layers, bring waterproof gear, and wear sturdy boots** for walking in the tundra. **Binoculars and a spotting scope** will help identify distant birds, and having a local birding guide or checklist can make spotting rare species easier. **Patience is key—Nome's wild landscapes are vast, but the rewards are unmatched.**

For serious birders, Nome is a once-in-a-lifetime experience. Whether scanning the horizon for a Peregrine Falcon, spotting an Arctic Warbler flitting through willows, or witnessing thousands of shorebirds feeding along the coast, **this remote corner of Alaska offers birdwatching unlike anywhere else.**

17.4.2 Dog Sledding

Dog sledding isn't just a sport in Nome—it's a way of life. Long before modern snowmachines, **sled dogs were the only way to travel across the frozen tundra,** and even today, many locals still rely on dog teams for transportation and survival in remote areas. In winter, you can experience the thrill of **mushing across the Arctic landscape**, feeling the power and speed of a trained sled dog team as they race over the snow.

Several local mushers offer sled dog tours, ranging from short, introductory rides to multi-day expeditions deep into the backcountry. For a quick taste of mushing, some operators offer **one-hour loops,** where you bundle up and ride behind a skilled musher as the dogs pull the sled across the tundra. **For a more immersive experience,** you can join a **half-day or full-day tour**, learning how to handle the sled, command the dogs, and navigate the trails like a true musher.

If you're looking for a real Arctic adventure, some outfitters even offer overnight expeditions, where you camp under the northern lights, hearing nothing but the wind and the rhythmic sound of paws on snow.

Many of Nome's mushers train for the Iditarod, the legendary 1,000-mile sled dog race that finishes right in Nome. Some tours give you a behind-the-scenes look at **Iditarod training,** introducing you to champion dogs and showing you how mushers prepare for one of the toughest races in the world. **You'll see the deep bond between mushers and their dogs, built on trust, teamwork, and survival in some of the harshest conditions on Earth.**

Winter in Nome is brutally cold, and dog sledding is an outdoor sport, so dressing properly is essential. Wear **multiple layers, an insulated parka, windproof pants, thick gloves, and a warm hat. Goggles or sunglasses** help protect against the glare of the snow, and hand warmers can be a lifesaver. **Wind chills can be extreme, easily dropping to -30°F (-34°C) or lower,** so make sure you're well-prepared before heading out.

There's nothing like the feeling of gliding across the snow, with only the sound of the wind and the steady breath of the dogs pulling you forward.

17.4.3 Beachcombing for Gold

Nome's beaches still hold gold, and anyone can try their luck. More than a century after the Gold Rush of 1899, the **Bering Sea continues to wash up fine gold dust and small flakes along the shore,** making Nome one of the few places where you can literally scoop up gold from the sand. **Locals and seasoned prospectors use sluice boxes, suction dredges, and high-powered metal detectors, but you can get started with just a pan and some patience.**

The best places to search for gold are east of Nome, along the beaches near the Safety Sound area and along the Nome-Council Road. The ocean constantly shifts the sands, uncovering new deposits and burying others, so some areas may be more productive than others depending on recent storms and tides. **The ideal time to search is**

from late spring through early fall, before the coastline freezes over and harsh winter conditions make beach mining impossible.

If you want to give it a try, you can rent gold pans and small prospecting equipment in town. Some shops even offer quick lessons on how to pan properly, helping you separate the gold from the black sand. **The process is simple but requires patience—you scoop up a pan of wet sand, swirl the water around to wash away the lighter materials, and look for tiny golden specks left behind.**

Metal detecting is another way to find gold, especially for small nuggets hidden just beneath the surface. Some hobbyists walk along the shore with high-frequency detectors designed to pick up small gold particles. **You might also come across old relics, like rusted mining tools, coins, or even abandoned equipment from the early 1900s.**

Nome still has active gold mining operations, so make sure you're on public land or designated recreational areas before you start digging. Private mining claims exist, and venturing onto someone else's claim without permission can get you in trouble. **If you're unsure where to go, check with the local visitor center for guidance on legal areas for recreational prospecting.**

17.5 Dining and Accommodation in Nome

Food in Nome is all about hearty meals, fresh seafood, and a taste of true Arctic life. You won't find big-name restaurant chains, but **local diners, small cafes, and family-owned eateries serve up filling plates made for long, cold days. Reindeer sausage, muskox burgers, and halibut sandwiches** are local favorites, while fresh-caught **king crab and salmon** bring a taste of the Bering Sea straight to your plate. Expect big portions and warm service—this is the kind of place where you'll find yourself chatting with locals over a hot cup of coffee.

Breakfast spots open early to fuel miners, mushers, and travelers heading out for adventure. Pancakes, eggs, and sourdough toast are standard morning fare, with some places offering **smoked salmon omelets or homemade pastries.** Lunch and dinner menus stick to

ALASKA ACTION PLAN

comfort food—thick chowders, grilled seafood, burgers, and hearty stews that hit the spot after a long day in the tundra. A few bars and roadhouses serve meals with a side of **Alaskan storytelling, where you can hear tales of gold rush prospectors, daring dog mushers, and life on the edge of the Arctic.**

Lodging in Nome is limited but welcoming, with options ranging from small hotels and motels to rustic B&Bs and private guest lodges. Standard hotels offer simple but comfortable rooms, usually with **Wi-Fi, heating, and basic amenities.** Some of the best spots are **locally run B&Bs, where you'll stay in a cozy home, often hosted by longtime Nome residents who know every inch of the town's history.**

If you're looking for something more remote, there are wilderness lodges outside of town catering to adventurers and wildlife watchers. These places offer **guided excursions, fishing trips, and wildlife tours,** but they book up fast during peak seasons. **Summer fills up with birders and gold prospectors, while March sees a rush of visitors arriving for the Iditarod.** If you're visiting during these times, **reserve your stay early—last-minute accommodations in Nome are nearly impossible to find.**

Prices are higher than in larger Alaskan towns due to Nome's isolation, with rooms often costing **$150-$250 per night,** depending on the time of year. Food is also **more expensive than usual, as nearly everything has to be flown in or shipped by barge.** But what Nome lacks in budget-friendly options, it makes up for in warmth and hospitality.

CHAPTER EIGHTEEN
BETHEL AND THE YUKON-KUSKOKWIM DELTA

18.1 Introduction to Bethel

Bethel is the biggest town in the Yukon-Kuskokwim Delta, surrounded by tundra, rivers, and villages with no road connections. You can only get here by plane or boat, and everything—groceries, fuel, supplies—comes in the same way. It's a town of about 6,000 people, but it feels more like a small village where everyone knows each other, and the river is the center of life.

The Yup'ik people have lived here for thousands of years, depending on salmon, moose, and berries for survival. Fishing camps fill the riverbanks in the summer as families catch, dry, and smoke salmon for the winter. Fall and winter are for hunting—moose, seals, birds—whatever the season allows. Even though there are grocery stores, many families still rely on the land for food because it's tradition, it's practical, and it's how life has always been.

Winters are long, dark, and freezing, with temperatures dropping far below zero. You see people traveling on snowmachines and dog sleds, cutting across the frozen river like highways. In summer, the sun barely sets, giving endless daylight for fishing, boating, and berry picking. The tundra turns green, birds from all over the world migrate here, and the river becomes the busiest street in town.

18.2 Getting to Bethel

You can't drive to Bethel. There are no roads connecting it to the rest of the state. You have to fly. The fastest way is a one-hour flight from Anchorage, with Alaska Airlines running multiple flights daily. The Bethel Airport (BET) is small but busy, handling passengers, cargo, and mail for the entire Yukon-Kuskokwim Delta. Most supplies, food, medicine, and everything people need comes in by plane.

Flights get delayed a lot, especially in winter. Snow, wind, and ice make landing difficult, and thick fog can shut everything down for hours or even days. In summer, storms roll in fast, and if you're flying on a smaller plane, expect turbulence. If you're coming here, plan extra time for delays.

When you land, don't expect highways or public transportation. There are some paved roads in town, but they don't go anywhere outside Bethel. People don't rely on cars as much as in other places. Most people use ATVs, snowmachines (snowmobiles), or boats, depending on the season. Taxis are expensive because gas here costs way more than in Anchorage.

If you need to travel beyond Bethel, you have to fly again. Small airlines like Ravn Alaska and Grant Aviation run bush plane flights to surrounding villages. Most of those flights are on small propeller planes, sometimes landing on dirt or ice runways. In summer, you can travel by boat when the Kuskokwim River is open. In winter, people ride snowmachines across frozen tundra and rivers, but that depends on ice conditions.

18.3.1 Cultural Centers

Bethel's cultural centers show you how people have lived here for thousands of years, surviving in the harshest conditions by knowing the land, the water, and the seasons. This isn't just about the past—it's about how traditions are still alive today. When you walk in, you don't just see exhibits, you step into a place where history, storytelling, and real life all mix together.

The Yupiit Piciryarait Cultural Center (YPCC) is the heart of Yup'ik culture in Bethel. It's right downtown, next to the university, and it's more than just a museum. It's a gathering place, a learning center, and a space where people celebrate who they are. Inside, you'll see handmade qaspeqs (traditional hooded parkas), carved ivory figures, woven baskets, fishing tools, and sleds that have been used for generations. These aren't just things to look at—they tell the story of how Yup'ik people survived off the land and the water, fishing, hunting, and traveling across the tundra long before roads or planes existed.

You might see a live dance performance, where the deep beats of a drum guide the dancers as they tell a story without words. Every movement has meaning, every song has been passed down for centuries. This is how history is remembered here—not just written in books, but carried in voices, movements, and traditions.

Sometimes, local artists set up tables and sell handmade crafts. If you're lucky, you'll find walrus ivory carvings, delicate beadwork, and grass baskets woven so tightly they can hold water. These aren't just souvenirs—they're real pieces of Yup'ik tradition, made with skills that have been passed down for generations.

18.3.2 Kuskokwim River

The Kuskokwim River isn't just water—it's the lifeline of Bethel. It's the road, the grocery store, the meeting place, and the connection to everything beyond the town. You don't understand Bethel until you understand the river because it controls how people move, eat, and live every single day.

In the summer, the river is packed with boats. Families head out to set nets for salmon, pulling in their catch to dry, smoke, or freeze for the long winter ahead. People don't fish for fun—they fish to survive. Along the riverbanks, you'll see drying racks lined with strips of bright red fish, smoking slowly in the summer air. Kids play on the shoreline, and boats zip past, loaded with supplies heading to nearby villages that have no roads. The river is the only way to get to many places, and every boat is carrying something important—food, fuel, mail, people.

ALASKA ACTION PLAN

When winter hits, everything changes. The river turns to ice, thick enough to drive on. Locals trade boats for snowmachines and trucks, carving icy paths between villages. It's faster than flying, and for months, the frozen river becomes the most reliable road in the region. It's not unusual to see someone hauling groceries, firewood, or even a couch strapped to the back of a snowmachine, gliding over the ice like it's just another highway.

Then there's the Kuskokwim 300—one of the biggest sled dog races in Alaska. Every January, top mushers from across the state bring their best teams to race across the frozen river. For 300 miles, dog teams push through wind, snow, and brutal cold, battling some of the toughest winter conditions imaginable. The whole town comes out to watch the start and finish, cheering on the mushers and their dogs as they race across the tundra. For Bethel, this isn't just a race—it's tradition, history, and survival all wrapped into one.

18.4.1 Wildlife Viewing

The Yukon-Kuskokwim Delta is one of the wildest places left on Earth, where animals outnumber people and the land stretches for miles without a single road. If you want to see wildlife in its purest form, this is where you go. Moose wade through marshes, caribou cross open tundra, foxes dart between willows, and brown bears roam the riverbanks. The land is alive, constantly moving, constantly changing.

Waterfowl rule this region. Millions of ducks, geese, and swans arrive in the spring, turning the delta into one of the largest nesting grounds in North America. Snow geese, tundra swans, and long-tailed ducks fill the skies. Eagles and hawks circle overhead, scanning for prey. By summer, the air is thick with the sounds of birds calling, wings flapping, and young hatchlings taking their first flights.

Muskoxen graze on the tundra, looking prehistoric with their thick coats and curved horns. They stand their ground against wolves, forming tight defensive circles to protect their young. Wolves are out here too, traveling in packs across the open landscape, hunting caribou and scavenging when food is scarce. Beavers build massive dams along quiet waterways, shaping the flow of the land, while lynx silently stalk through the underbrush, leaving nothing but paw prints in the mud.

Spring and summer are the best times to see wildlife. The long daylight hours mean animals are active at all hours, moving through the wetlands and across the tundra. In fall, caribou migrate, and bears prepare for winter, stuffing themselves with fish and berries. By winter, everything slows down. Snow blankets the land, and many animals disappear into hibernation or move south to escape the brutal cold.

Seeing wildlife here takes patience. The land is massive, the animals move fast, and the weather can turn in an instant. A clear day can suddenly shift into fog, wind, or rain. You need the right gear—layers, waterproof clothing, and binoculars to scan the distance. Most travel is by boat in summer or snowmachine in winter, as there are no roads leading into the wilderness.

18.4.2 Fishing and Boating

The river is the main road, the grocery store, and the workplace. Fishing isn't just something people do—it's how they survive. When the salmon come, the whole town moves. Nets stretch across the water, boats crowd the river, and families work together to catch, clean, and dry fish. Every house smells like smoked salmon, and fish racks line the shore. People fish for king salmon in early summer, then silvers, then chums, filling freezers for the winter. Pike, Arctic char, and whitefish are always an option, even when the river ices over.

Winter doesn't stop fishing. The river turns solid, and ice fishing begins. People cut holes through thick ice, set their lines, and wait.

Some drop nets under the ice, pulling them up later with fish frozen stiff. The river is always moving, whether flowing in summer or freezing into a highway in winter.

Boating isn't a choice—it's a necessity. No roads connect villages, so boats replace cars. People load up with fuel, supplies, and fish, traveling to nearby towns or heading deep into the wilderness. The river changes every year—sandbars shift, logs float down, and currents pull boats off course. You have to know what you're doing. Weather turns fast, and storms can flip a boat in minutes. Life jackets and survival gear aren't optional—they're lifesavers.

18.4.3 Birding in the Delta

This place is like a giant bird airport. Every year, millions of birds fly in from all over the world. They stop here, build nests, and raise their babies before heading south again. The whole sky fills with wings, and the tundra moves like it's alive. You see ducks, geese, cranes, and tiny shorebirds running along the mud. Some birds come from Asia, some from South America, and some fly thousands of miles just to be here for a few months.

Spring and summer are the best times. That's when the birds are everywhere. You see huge flocks of geese and cranes flying over, and sometimes, falcons diving fast to catch them. The water is full of swans, loons, and ducks, all calling out and making noise. If you sit still and watch, you start noticing all kinds of rare birds you don't see anywhere else. Some are bright, some are small, and some have traveled halfway across the world.

But getting close isn't always easy. The land is wet, the mud is deep, and there aren't many trails. You need boots, warm clothes, and a lot of patience. A boat is the best way to explore. You can float through quiet little rivers where the birds don't get scared and fly away.

CHAPTER NINETEEN
THE ARCTIC CIRCLE AND NORTHERN ALASKA

19.1 Utqiagvik (Barrow)

19.1.1 Introduction to Utqiagvik

You are standing at the top of the world, where the land is flat, the ocean stretches endlessly, and the sun behaves in ways that seem unreal. For two months in winter, it never rises. The sky stays dark, the air turns ice-cold, and the wind howls across the frozen tundra. Then, for two months in summer, the sun never sets. It circles above, casting light at midnight, making the ocean shine gold, and turning the land into a never-ending day. Life here is ruled by the Arctic, by long nights, long days, and a sea that freezes solid before breaking open again.

People have lived here for thousands of years. The Iñupiat have always known how to survive in this land, hunting on the ice, following the whales, and reading the sky and ocean like a map. Even today, tradition runs deep. You see families butchering seals on the beach, sled dogs barking in the cold, and elders teaching kids how to navigate by the stars. But modern life is here too—cell phones, four-wheelers, and internet in a place where the nearest road is hundreds of miles away.

It's cold. It's isolated. It's not easy. Planes bring in food and supplies, and when storms roll in, the whole town slows down. But for the people who live here, this is home. The tundra is open, the ocean is full of life, and the past and present exist together. This is the edge of the world, and for those who make it here, it's like nowhere else.

19.1.2 Getting There

The only way to reach Utqiagvik is by air. No roads lead here. No highways connect it to the rest of Alaska. The Arctic Ocean, frozen for much of the year, surrounds it on one side, and endless tundra stretches in every direction. If you want to visit, you fly.

Flights operate daily from Anchorage and Fairbanks. Alaska Airlines is the main carrier, with direct flights from Anchorage taking about **1 hour and 45 minutes** and from Fairbanks **1 hour and 20 minutes.** Some flights stop in other remote villages before reaching Utqiagvik, depending on the day and weather conditions. The Will Rogers–Wiley Post Memorial Airport is small, with a single terminal and basic facilities—no restaurants, no large waiting areas, just a place to land and take off.

Weather delays are common. Arctic storms can roll in fast, bringing strong winds, blizzards, or thick fog that makes flying impossible. If you're planning a trip, build in extra time. A flight scheduled for today might not leave until tomorrow, or even later. In winter, extreme cold can affect aircraft operations, and in summer, dense fog can shut down the runway for hours.

Packing right is key. Utqiagvik can be brutally cold, even in months when other parts of Alaska are warming up. In winter, temperatures can drop to **-40°F (-40°C)** with wind chills even lower. Thick layers, a heavy parka, insulated boots, gloves, and a face covering are necessary. The wind here is no joke—it cuts through light jackets and freezes exposed skin fast. Even in summer, temperatures rarely go above **50°F (10°C),** and the ocean breeze makes it feel colder. A windproof jacket and warm clothing are still a must.

You step off the plane, and the first thing that hits you is the wind. It's strong, sharp, and carries the smell of the sea and tundra. There are no trees, no mountains, nothing to block it. The airport is small, the landscape vast, and the Arctic sky stretches endlessly overhead. You've arrived at the northernmost city in the United States, a place where the world feels bigger, the land wilder, and the air sharper than anywhere else.

19.1.3 Exploring Utqiagvik

Utqiagvik is like nowhere else. The land is flat, open, and stretches endlessly in all directions. The Arctic Ocean meets the shore with waves that freeze in place during the long winter. The air smells of salt, tundra, and sometimes, fresh-hunted seal or whale. Life here follows the seasons—long, dark winters when the sun disappears for **two full months** and endless summer days when it never sets.

You see **snow machines, ATVs, and pickup trucks** moving across town, the main way locals get around. Roads are short, mostly gravel, and icy for much of the year. The cold is sharp, but the people are warm. This is Iñupiat land, where traditions run deep. Subsistence hunting is not just a way of life—it's survival. Families share the meat from **whales, seals, walrus, and caribou,** and nothing goes to waste. You might see people drying fish, cutting blubber, or preparing hides outside their homes. If you visit during a community gathering, you'll hear the steady beat of a drum, the sounds of Iñupiat songs, and stories passed down for generations.

The land is **alive with wildlife.** In summer, you see massive herds of caribou moving across the tundra, and Arctic foxes darting through the brush. The ocean is home to bowhead whales, belugas, and seals. Some days, the ice stretches far into the horizon, other days, it breaks apart, moving with the current. Polar bears sometimes roam the outskirts of town, searching for food. If you're outside, **pay attention,** especially in winter when daylight is short, and the wind hides movement. Locals know how to live with the land, and if you listen, you'll learn.

Walking through town, you feel the **isolation and the resilience.**

This is a place where everything must be flown or barged in. Prices at the store are high. Fresh produce is a luxury. Houses are built to withstand the wind and cold, sitting on stilts to keep the permafrost from shifting beneath them. Despite the extreme conditions, people have lived here for **thousands of years**. They know how to read the ice, track the seasons, and prepare for whatever the Arctic brings.

19.1.4 Arctic Ocean Access

Standing on the edge of the **Arctic Ocean** in Utqiagvik feels like reaching the end of the world. The wind is sharp, the waves are cold, and the horizon stretches endlessly. This is one of the **northernmost places on Earth** where you can walk right up to the Arctic waters, and for some visitors, even stepping into it is an unforgettable challenge.

You can **access the shoreline** near Stevenson Street, not far from town, where the ocean meets the frozen tundra. During summer, the ice melts, revealing dark, frigid waters. Some people dip their hands, feet, or even take a full plunge just to say they've swum in the Arctic. But this isn't like jumping into a cold lake—the **water is dangerously cold year-round**, usually around **28-32°F (-2 to 0°C)**. Even in summer, the wind chills your skin instantly, and the shock can take your breath away. If you go in, **do it fast, get out faster, and have warm clothes ready immediately.**

In winter, the Arctic Ocean **freezes solid,** creating a thick sheet of ice that stretches to the horizon. Locals use it for hunting and travel, but **walking onto the ice is extremely dangerous for visitors.** Cracks, shifting ice, and hidden openings can form suddenly. The safest way to experience the frozen ocean is from the shore, where you can still feel its power without risking your life.

The coastline changes with the seasons. **In late fall and early winter, massive ice chunks crash onto shore, piling up like frozen boulders.** When summer comes, the ice breaks apart, and you might see **floating icebergs drifting past, seals bobbing in the water, or even a bowhead whale surfacing in the distance.** No matter when you visit, the Arctic Ocean is always in motion, shaped by wind, currents, and extreme temperatures.

19.2.1 Oil Fields and Tundra Tours

You can't just show up and explore Prudhoe Bay on your own. **The oil fields are private and heavily restricted, so you need to book a guided tour.** These tours take you **inside the industrial heart of Arctic oil operations**, showing you the massive drilling sites, pipelines, and facilities that keep the industry running in one of the harshest places on Earth. Security is strict, so you **must book at least 24 hours in advance** to get clearance. Most tours last about **1-2 hours** and cost between **$60-$100 per person.**

The moment you step out, **you'll feel the Arctic's power.** Even in summer, **temperatures rarely go above freezing,** and strong winds make it feel even colder. If you visit in winter, you'll be **facing -40°F (-40°C) or worse.** You need **thermal layers, an insulated jacket, gloves, a hat, and boots that can handle ice and snow. Without proper gear, even a short walk outside is brutal.**

The industrial side of Prudhoe Bay is **like a city built for survival.** You'll see **roads on frozen ground, massive storage tanks, drills towering above the tundra, and workers handling extreme conditions year-round.** Pipelines snake across the landscape, carrying crude oil from the Arctic to refineries thousands of miles away. Tour guides explain **how the oil fields function, the dangers of drilling in permafrost, and the challenges of working in complete darkness during** winter.

Step beyond the oil fields, and it's a different world. The **tundra stretches for miles,** an endless expanse of flat, frozen ground. **It looks empty, but it's alive.** In summer, wildflowers bloom, caribou migrate, and **thousands of birds nest in the wetlands.** In winter, the land **turns white and silent,** with nothing but snowdrifts, Arctic fox tracks, and the occasional muskox standing against the wind.

Wildlife is unpredictable. **You might spot a grizzly bear, a snowy owl, or a herd of caribou moving across the ice.** The tundra is one of the last places on Earth where **nature still feels completely untamed.**

Prudhoe Bay is the **end of the Dalton Highway, the furthest north you can drive in the U.S.** Most visitors come for **the Arctic Ocean tour,** where you can **stand on the edge of the continent** and, if you're crazy enough, **take a dip in the freezing water.** If you plan to do this, bring a **towel, warm clothes, and a thick dose of courage.**

19.2.2 Dalton Highway Adventure

The **Dalton Highway** is one of the most dangerous and remote roads you will ever drive, stretching **414 miles from Fairbanks to Deadhorse,** cutting through nothing but tundra, mountains, and endless open space with **no gas stations for 240 miles, no cell service, no emergency help, and some of the worst road conditions you can imagine.** The road was built for the **Trans-Alaska Pipeline,** and truckers own it, driving massive rigs at high speeds, kicking up rocks that will **shatter your windshield in seconds** if you're too close.

The road itself is a mix of **gravel, dirt, and mud,** with some short paved sections, but most of the time you're dodging **deep potholes, sharp rocks, and giant dust clouds in summer or thick ice and blinding snow in winter. Atigun Pass,** the highest point on the road, is steep, narrow, and **has no guardrails,** meaning one wrong move in bad weather can send you sliding off the edge. If you get stuck, you're at the mercy of whoever passes by, because **there are no mechanics, no tow trucks, and no one coming to rescue you.**

If you want to make it, you need to be ready. **You need a 4x4 truck or SUV with off-road tires, two spare tires, extra gas, food, water, warm clothes, and a sleeping bag** because if something happens, you might have to wait hours—or even overnight—for help. Truckers are the kings of this road, so **always move over when they're coming, keep your headlights on, and announce yourself on a CB radio** because cell phones won't work.

The **first stop for gas is Yukon River Camp, 56 miles from Fairbanks**, where you can grab a meal before heading deeper into the wild. If you don't **fill up at Coldfoot, 175 miles in, you won't make it to Deadhorse** because it's the **last fuel stop for 240 miles**. After that, it's nothing but **open tundra, rolling hills, and the steep climb up Atigun Pass, where avalanches can block the road at any time**. When you reach Deadhorse, you're at the **edge of the Arctic Ocean in a frozen, windswept oil camp where everything is built for survival**.

19.2.3 Wildlife Viewing

The Arctic is one of the **last untouched wildernesses**, where animals roam freely across vast, open tundra, moving with the seasons and surviving some of the harshest conditions on Earth. You won't find fences, highways, or crowded tourist areas here—**just endless land, frozen rivers, and the constant presence of wildlife**.

If you're driving the **Dalton Highway**, you have a good chance of seeing **caribou herds migrating across the tundra**. The **Central Arctic Caribou Herd**, one of the largest in Alaska, follows ancient paths across the region, grazing in summer and moving south when winter hits. **Fall is the best time to see them**, when they cross the road in large numbers near Atigun Pass. Keep your distance, **never block their path, and always give them the right of way**—they've been here for thousands of years.

Another iconic Arctic species is the **muskox**, a shaggy, prehistoric-looking animal that looks like a mix between a bison and a goat. These **powerful creatures survive temperatures as low as -50°F** and form tight defensive circles when threatened. They're often seen **near the Sagavanirktok River, north of Coldfoot, and in the open tundra around Deadhorse**. Keep a respectful distance—**muskoxen may look slow, but they can charge fast if they feel cornered**.

Arctic foxes, small and built for the cold, are always hunting for food, darting across the tundra in search of lemmings or scavenging near human settlements. **Winter is the best time to spot them**, when their fur turns pure white, blending with the snow. They're common **near Prudhoe Bay and along the coastal flats**, where they follow polar bears, waiting for scraps.

Birdwatchers will find some of the **most unique species in the world here, especially during summer when millions of migratory birds arrive**. The **tundra swans, snowy owls, and peregrine falcons** nest in these remote areas, while the wetlands near Deadhorse attract **loons, eiders, and Arctic warblers**. If you want the best experience, visit **between June and August**, when the birds are most active.

Bears are a serious safety concern in this region. **Both grizzly bears and polar bears** live in the Arctic, and while grizzlies are seen **inland along the Dalton Highway, polar bears are only found near the coast, particularly around Prudhoe Bay in fall and winter**. If you're traveling near bear country, **carry bear spray, store food properly, and never approach a bear under any circumstances**.

EVERYTHING YOU NEED. NOTHING YOU DON'T

CHAPTER NINETEEN
Practical Travel Tips

20.1 Wildlife Safety

Alaska is full of wild animals, and **you need to know how to stay safe.** You might see **bears, moose, wolves, and other powerful animals** while hiking, driving, or even in town. **They are not afraid of you.** Some might ignore you, some might run away, but some might see you as a threat. **You don't want to be the person who gets too close, does something stupid, or leaves food out and attracts a bear to camp.**

Bears are everywhere. You don't just see them deep in the mountains; they walk through **trails, roads, even backyards.** You might spot a **black bear or a brown bear (grizzly). Black bears are smaller but still dangerous. Grizzlies are much bigger, stronger, and more aggressive.** If you surprise one, it might charge, and **you won't outrun it.** If a bear sees you first, **don't run, don't scream, don't turn your back.** Stay calm, speak firmly, and **back away slowly.** If it follows, **stand your ground and get your bear spray ready.**

If you're hiking, **make noise so you don't surprise a bear.** Talk loud, clap, or wear a bear bell. **Never leave food in your tent.** Lock it in a **bear-proof container or hang it from a tree far from camp.** If a bear starts sniffing around, **don't panic, don't throw food to distract it, don't take selfies.** Use bear spray if it comes too close. **If a grizzly attacks, play dead. If a black bear attacks, fight back.**

Moose are **bigger than a car** and faster than they look. They seem calm, but **they attack more people than bears do.** If a moose **lowers its ears, snorts, or walks toward you,** that's a warning. If it charges, **run.** They don't chase for long, but **they will trample you.** Stay far away, **never walk between a mother and her calf, and never try to feed one.**

Wolves stay away from people, but **they might follow you if they think you're weak or carrying food. Don't run.** Stand tall, wave your arms, and make yourself look big. If you have a dog, **keep it close—wolves will go after pets.**

In the water, **whales, sea lions, and otters look harmless, but they can be unpredictable. Sea lions bite. Whales move fast. Otters defend their space. Stay back. Don't touch. Don't feed them.** It's not safe, and **it's illegal.**

If you're camping, **your food is a bigger danger than you think.** Bears and other animals smell food from miles away. Keep **all food, snacks, and even toothpaste sealed and stored far from where you sleep.** If you leave food out, **you're not just risking your own safety—you're making that bear a problem for everyone else.**

When you see wildlife, **keep your distance.** You're in their space, not the other way around. If you get too close, **you stress them out, you put yourself in danger, and you ruin the experience for others. Use binoculars, stay in your car if you're on the road, and never block their path.** If an animal moves because of you, **you're too close.**

20.2 Health and Safety

Alaska is **big, wild, and unpredictable. The weather changes fast, medical care is far away, and help isn't always available when you need it.** You need to **be prepared, listen to your body, and make smart choices.**

Cold, Wind, and Hypothermia

It doesn't matter if it's **summer or winter—Alaska can be dangerously cold.** Even in July, it can **drop below freezing in the moun-**

tains. The wind makes it worse, and if you get wet, **you can lose body heat fast.** If your body temperature drops too low, **you stop thinking clearly, your body slows down, and you might not even realize you're in danger.**

Early signs of hypothermia: shivering, numb fingers, slurred speech, stumbling. If you or someone with you starts feeling this way, **warm up immediately.** Get into dry clothes, add layers, drink something warm, and find shelter. If shivering stops and the person seems confused or exhausted, **it's an emergency—get help fast.**

Heat and Dehydration

Yes, Alaska can be cold, but **it can also get hot, dry, and exhausting.** If you're hiking or spending long hours outside, **you need to drink more water than you think.** Dehydration sneaks up on you, and if you stop sweating, feel dizzy, or get a headache, **you need water and rest immediately.** Always carry more water than you think you'll need.

Altitude Sickness

If you're traveling to higher elevations, **your body needs time to adjust.** If you get headaches, nausea, dizziness, or shortness of breath, **slow down and drink lots of water.** If it gets worse, **descend to a lower elevation.**

First Aid and Medical Help

Hospitals and clinics are far apart, and cell service is unreliable. If you get hurt, you might be on your own for hours—or days. **Always carry a basic first aid kit with bandages, antiseptic, pain relievers, and any medications you might need.** If you're in the backcountry, **consider carrying a satellite communication device or personal locator beacon.**

Travel Insurance and Evacuation

ALASKA ACTION PLAN

If you get seriously injured or sick, medical evacuation can cost tens of thousands of dollars. Regular travel insurance may not cover it, so make sure you have a policy that includes **air evacuation and emergency rescue.** If you're doing high-risk activities like mountaineering or remote backpacking, **this is not optional—you need coverage.**

Medications and Prescriptions

If you take prescription medication, bring more than you need. Pharmacies are limited, and if you get stuck in bad weather or miss a flight, **you don't want to run out.** Keep medications in their original containers, carry them in your carry-on bag, and **bring a copy of your prescription just in case.**

20.3 Communication and Connectivity

Alaska is **huge, wild, and mostly empty,** which means **cell service is not always there when you need it.** You can't just pull out your phone and expect it to work everywhere because **the further you get from big towns, the less signal you'll have.** If you're traveling in remote areas, **your phone might stop working completely,** and if you don't plan for it, you could find yourself **lost, stuck, or unable to reach help.**

Cell Service and Where It Works

If you stay in **Anchorage, Fairbanks, or Juneau, your phone will work fine,** and you'll get calls, texts, and fast internet. But once you go outside those places—**driving on highways, visiting national parks, or exploring small towns**—you'll start seeing "No Service" pop up on your screen. Even in some places where you see signal bars, **calls may drop, texts might not send, and data could be painfully slow.**

If you're taking a **long road trip or heading into the wilderness,** don't assume your phone's GPS will work. **It needs data or a downloaded map, and without service, you'll have nothing.** The smartest thing to do is **download offline maps before your trip.** If you're using Google Maps, just open it, type in the area you need, and hit the **"Download Offline Map"** button. That way, **even if your phone loses service, you'll still have maps.**

Wi-Fi and Internet Reality

Wi-Fi is available in **hotels, some restaurants, and visitor centers,** but in **small towns and remote lodges, it can be slow, limited, or not free.** Some places charge for Wi-Fi, and others **block video streaming to save bandwidth.** If you need internet for work or keeping in touch, **download what you need before your trip.** Don't assume every café or hotel will have **fast, free Wi-Fi like you're used to.**

Navigation and Battery Life

Your phone is only useful if it has power. If you're driving long distances, **bring a car charger.** If you're hiking or camping, **carry a power bank.** Cold weather **kills phone batteries fast,** so keep your phone warm by **putting it in an inside pocket.** If your phone dies in the middle of nowhere, **and you have no backup, you could be in trouble.**

Always **write down important addresses, phone numbers, and directions on paper.** If your phone dies or stops working, **you'll still have the info you need.**

Satellite Phones and Emergency Devices

If you're going somewhere **super remote, like deep into a national park, hunting, or driving the Dalton Highway,** your phone will be **completely useless.** The only way to stay connected is with a **satellite phone or a personal locator beacon (PLB).**
- **Satellite phones let you call or text from anywhere,** even where there's no cell service.
- **PLBs or satellite messengers (like Garmin inReach or SPOT) let you send SOS signals if you need rescue.**

You can **rent a satellite phone at some outdoor stores, lodges, or airports.** If you're doing anything risky, **this could save your life.**

Plan for No Service

Alaska is **one of the least connected places in the U.S.** If you're traveling here, **expect that your phone won't work all the time.** Before you go anywhere, **download maps, charge your battery, and let someone know your plans.** If you're heading into the wilderness, **get a backup device. Your phone is not enough.**

20.4 Local Customs and Etiquette

When you visit, you're not just passing through; you're stepping into places where people **live, work, and keep traditions alive.** In bigger towns, things might feel more familiar, but in **rural villages and Native communities, life follows different customs.** You need to **respect the way people live, the way they talk, and the way they survive in some of the toughest conditions on Earth.**

People rely on **subsistence hunting, fishing, and gathering** to feed their families, and it's not for fun or sport. If you see someone **butchering a seal, drying salmon, or collecting berries, don't treat it like a tourist attraction.** Don't take pictures, don't interrupt, and don't assume you know what's happening. If you're invited to an event or gathering, **listen more than you talk.** Some ceremonies or traditions are private, and not everything is meant to be shared with outsiders. If you're unsure, **ask respectfully, but don't push.**

People in small towns might **wave or nod as you walk by**—it's polite to do the same. Some people are friendly and talkative, others are private. If you start a conversation, **don't ask personal questions like how much things cost, how people survive the winter, or why they don't move somewhere else.** Instead, ask about **local foods, the best places to see, or how people like to spend their time.** If someone wants to share their story, they will.

Small businesses keep remote towns running. Stores, cafés, and local artists depend on seasonal visitors, so if something seems expensive, **understand that everything here costs more to ship and stock.** If you see handmade Native art, **pay full price—don't haggle.** If a shop or restaurant has a **limited menu, don't complain.** Supplies don't arrive every day, and some places only stock what they can get.

Taking photos? **Not everything is meant to be photographed.** If you see people working, fishing, praying, or hunting, **ask before you take a picture.** Some communities have strict rules about photography, especially for **ceremonies or sacred sites.** Just because you're allowed to be somewhere doesn't mean you should act like a spectator.

20.5 Responsible Travel

Everything you do in Alaska affects the land, water, and wildlife. This place is wild, but it's also fragile. **Once you harm the environment, it takes years, sometimes decades, to recover.** That means you need to travel in a way that doesn't damage what makes this place special.

Leave no trace. Take everything with you. **Food wrappers, plastic bottles, even biodegradable things like orange peels or toilet paper don't belong in nature.** If you're camping or hiking, pack out all trash, bury human waste if needed, and use bear-proof containers for food.

Stay on trails. A single step off the path can kill tundra plants that take decades to regrow. **Don't crush moss, lichen, or wildflowers just for a shortcut.** If you camp, set up on **gravel, rock, or durable surfaces** so you don't destroy the landscape.

Respect wildlife. Never feed animals. If a bear, fox, or moose gets used to human food, it stops fearing people, and that often leads to the animal being killed for safety reasons. **Keep your distance.** Getting too close can stress animals, put you in danger, and even change their natural behavior. **Watch from a distance, use binoculars, and never chase or corner an animal just for a photo.**

Limit waste. Many Alaskan towns don't have big recycling centers, and trash removal is expensive. **Bring a reusable water bottle, avoid plastic bags, and use refillable travel containers.** If you buy something, try to **support local businesses that use sustainable materials** instead of mass-produced souvenirs.

Respect Native lands and local communities. If you visit a historic site, **don't touch, take, or move anything.** That old wooden structure or carved object might have deep cultural significance. If you're unsure whether you're on private property, **ask before walking in.**

Book responsible tours. Some operators respect the environment, while others put profit first. **Choose companies that follow ethical fishing and hunting practices, respect wildlife viewing guidelines, and contribute to conservation efforts.** If you're going on a boat tour, pick one that follows **safe distance rules for marine life and doesn't overcrowd areas with too many boats.**

20.6 Emergency Preparedness

Alaska does not wait for you to be ready. You either prepare or you risk getting stranded, lost, or worse. The weather changes fast, the roads are empty for miles, and if something goes wrong, help is not just a quick phone call away. You need to have a plan before you go anywhere, whether you're driving, flying, or hiking. If you assume everything will go smoothly, you're making a big mistake. Flights get canceled last minute, roads close without warning, and storms come out of nowhere. If you're not ready for that, you can end up in serious trouble.

You need to carry what you need to survive if things don't go as planned. That means food and water for at least a full day longer than your trip. It means real winter gear, even if you think it's warm when you start. If you get wet and the wind picks up, hypothermia can set in fast. If you're hiking, you need fire-starting tools because getting stranded overnight in the cold is dangerous. A fully charged power bank is critical because your phone is useless if it's dead. Even better, you need an offline GPS, a satellite device, or a printed map because most of the state has zero cell service. If you think you'll always have reception, you're wrong.

If you're driving, your car is your lifeline. You need extra fuel because there are stretches of highway with no gas stations for hours. You need a spare tire because tow trucks aren't just waiting on the side of the road to help you. If you break down, you need to be able to stay warm inside your vehicle. That means blankets, extra layers, and an emergency plan. Running out of gas is a better problem than freezing in the middle of nowhere. If you leave your car to find help, you're putting yourself at risk. Most people who die in the cold were found miles from their vehicles because they thought they could walk to safety.

If you're hiking, you need to know exactly where you're going and how long it should take. If the weather changes and you can't see the trail, you stop and wait. You don't keep going in the wrong direction. If you get lost, moving makes it worse. Stay where you are, find shelter, and use bright clothing, a whistle, or a fire to signal for help. If you don't tell someone where you're going before you leave, nobody will know where to start looking. That's how people disappear without a trace.

Wildlife is another serious risk, especially bears. You need to make noise while hiking so you don't surprise one. If you see a bear, you back away slowly and never run. Running triggers an instinct to chase. You should always carry bear spray and know how to use it because if a bear charges, you have seconds to react. Keeping food stored properly is critical because if a bear finds food at your campsite, it's going to come back, and that's when it becomes a real problem. If you're in an area with moose, you need to be just as careful. Moose attack more people than bears do, and they don't bluff. If a moose lowers its head or lays its ears back, it's about to charge, and your best bet is getting behind something solid because they will stomp you.

Flights in Alaska do not operate like flights in big cities. If you're flying into a small town, assume that weather delays will happen. Always have extra food and water in your carry-on in case you get stuck at the airport. If you're heading somewhere remote, make sure someone knows when to expect you. If a storm rolls in, you might be waiting an extra day or two for your flight. If you don't plan ahead, you could run out of supplies before you even make it to your destination.

The biggest mistake people make is thinking they'll figure things out when they get there. Alaska does not work like that. You prepare first, and then you go. If you do it right, you'll have an incredible time. If you don't, you'll learn the hard way that this place does not care about what you expected.

CHAPTER NINETEEN
SAMPLE ITINERARIES

21.1 3-Day Itineraries

21.1.1 Anchorage and Surroundings

Morning: Start your day in downtown Anchorage with breakfast at Snow City Café (1034 W 4th Ave), a popular spot known for its reindeer sausage, stuffed French toast, and giant pancakes. Expect a wait during peak hours, so arrive early or call ahead for pickup. After breakfast, walk a few blocks to the Anchorage Museum (625 C St.), the largest in the state. Plan to spend about two hours exploring exhibits on Alaskan history, Native cultures, and Arctic science.

Midday: From downtown, drive about an hour south along the Seward Highway to Alaska Wildlife Conservation Center (Mile 79, Seward Hwy). This wildlife sanctuary is home to bears, moose, bison, and wolves, offering a chance to see them up close. Admission is $17 per adult, $13 per child (ages 6-18), and free for kids under 5. Plan for 1.5 hours here, walking the trails or driving the loop to view the animals.

Afternoon: On the way back, stop at Beluga Point (Mile 110, Seward Hwy), a popular roadside lookout for seeing beluga whales in July and August. Continue north to Anchorage, then head to 49th State Brewing (717 W 3rd Ave) for an early dinner. Try the bison burger, king crab legs, or locally brewed beer while enjoying a rooftop view of Cook Inlet.

Evening: End your day with a bike ride or a sunset walk along the Tony Knowles Coastal Trail. Rent a bike from Pablo's Bicycle Rentals (436 L St) for $25-$45 per day, or simply stroll along the 11-mile waterfront path. In summer, expect the sun to set late (around 11 PM in June), giving you plenty of daylight. In winter, this is a great spot for northern lights viewing.

Day 2: Scenic Drive to Girdwood and Outdoor Adventure

Morning: Grab a coffee from Dark Horse Coffee (646 F St) and drive 45 minutes south along the scenic Seward Highway to Girdwood, a small ski town surrounded by mountains. Your first stop is Alyeska Resort (1000 Arlberg Ave), where you'll ride the Alyeska Aerial Tram up to 2,300 feet for a panoramic view of the Turnagain Arm and seven glaciers. Tickets cost $35 per adult, $25 per child. Spend about an hour at the top, enjoying the scenery and exploring the short hiking trails.

Midday: Drive 10 minutes south to Winner Creek Trail, an easy 3-mile hike through lush rainforest that leads to a hand-pulled tram over a rushing river. If you don't want to hike, drive to Virgin Creek Falls, a hidden waterfall just a 10-minute walk from the road.

Afternoon: Eat lunch in Girdwood at The Bake Shop (194 Olympic Mountain Loop), famous for its sourdough pancakes and homemade soup. Before heading back, stop at Turnagain Arm Pit BBQ (Mile 90, Seward Hwy) for a quick bite of smoked meats and mac & cheese.

Evening: Drive back to Anchorage and unwind at Crow's Nest (939 W 5th Ave, inside the Hotel Captain Cook) for fine dining with city views, or go casual at Moose's Tooth (3300 Old Seward Hwy), a local favorite for wood-fired pizza and craft beer.

Day 3: Hiking and Glacier Views

Morning: Start your day at Fire Island Rustic Bakeshop (1343 G St.), known for its fresh-baked bread, croissants, and breakfast sandwiches. Then, drive 20 minutes east to Flattop Mountain Trailhead (Glen Alps Parking Lot). The hike to the summit is about 3 miles round-trip, offering 360-degree views of Anchorage, Cook Inlet, and the Chugach Mountains. If hiking sounds too intense, drive to the Glen Alps Overlook for a scenic view without the climb.

Midday: After hiking, drive an hour south to Portage Glacier (Mile 78, Seward Hwy). Stop at the Portage Glacier Visitor Center and then take a 1-hour boat tour across the lake for $45 per adult, $25 per child.

Afternoon: On the way back to Anchorage, grab lunch at The Turnagain Arm Pit BBQ, or stop by Wild Scoops (429 E St) for locally made ice cream, featuring flavors like fireweed honey and birch syrup caramel.

Evening: End your trip at Kincaid Park, one of the best places in the city for wildlife viewing and coastal views. If visiting in winter, this is one of the top spots to see the northern lights.

21.1.2 Juneau Explorer

Day 1: Glaciers, Scenic Views, and Local Flavor

Morning: Start with breakfast at Sandpiper Café (429 W Willoughby Ave), a favorite for crab omelets, blueberry pancakes, and strong coffee. From downtown, take a taxi or the Capital Transit Bus ($2 per ride) to Mendenhall Glacier (about 25 minutes from downtown). Spend 2-3 hours exploring the Mendenhall Glacier Visitor Center ($5 entry), walking the Nugget Falls Trail (easy, 2 miles round-trip), and spotting icebergs in the lake. If you're visiting in summer, you may see salmon spawning and black bears fishing at Steep Creek.

Midday: Head back to downtown Juneau and grab lunch at The Hangar on the Wharf (2 Marine Way). Try the fish & chips, Alaskan king crab, or seafood chowder, all served with waterfront views.

Afternoon: Ride the Mount Roberts Tramway ($50 per adult, $30 per child) up 1,800 feet for stunning views over Juneau and the Gastineau Channel. Explore the short hiking trails at the top, visit the nature center, and watch a Native Tlingit cultural film. If you're up for a longer hike, continue to Father Brown's Cross (2.5 miles round-trip) for even better views.

Evening: For dinner, head to Tracy's King Crab Shack (432 S Franklin St) for massive crab legs, butter-drenched crab bisque, and garlic rolls. This is a casual but must-visit spot—expect a wait during peak hours.

Day 2: Whale Watching and Gold Rush History

Morning: Book a whale-watching tour ($150-$200 per person, 3-4 hours round trip) with a local company like Harv & Marv's or Alaska Tales. Tours depart from Auke Bay Harbor (about 20 minutes from downtown, with shuttles included). Humpback whales are common in summer, and you might see orca pods, sea lions, and bald eagles.

Midday: After whale watching, take a taxi or local bus back to downtown Juneau and stop for lunch at Deckhand Dave's (356 S Franklin St), known for halibut tacos and salmon burgers.

Afternoon: Visit the Alaska State Museum (395 Whittier St, $14 entry), which showcases Alaska Native artifacts, Gold Rush history, and Russian colonial relics. Then, walk a few blocks to the Red Dog Saloon (278 S Franklin St) for a drink in a historic Wild West-style bar. The sawdust-covered floors, swinging doors, and old-time piano music make it feel straight out of the Gold Rush era.

Evening: End the day with a fine dining experience at Salt (200 Seward St), where you can try fresh king salmon, halibut, or Alaskan spot prawns with craft cocktails.

Day 3: Outdoor Adventure and Hidden Gems

Morning: Start with breakfast at Raven Café (222 Seward St) and grab a coffee and fresh pastries. Then, hike the Perseverance Trail (moderate, 4.5 miles round-trip), one of the best trails near downtown. This scenic route follows a river and leads into a deep valley surrounded by waterfalls and old mining tunnels. If you prefer an easier hike, do the Gold Creek Flume Trail instead.

Midday: Have lunch at Twisted Fish Company (550 S Franklin St), known for fresh oysters and halibut burgers.

Afternoon: If you're visiting in summer, take a kayaking tour in Auke Bay ($120-$180 per person, 3 hours) for a chance to paddle alongside seals, sea lions, and eagles. If you'd rather relax, shop for locally made crafts, jewelry, and art in the historic downtown shops.

B: For a casual final meal, eat at The Rookery Café (111 Seward St) for handmade pasta, seafood, and local beer. If you're still up for a drink, head to Amalga Distillery (134 N Franklin St) to try Juneau-made gin cocktails before calling it a night.

21.2 7-Day Itineraries

21.2.1 Southcentral Alaska Highlights

Day 1: Arrive in Anchorage and Explore the City

You land at **Ted Stevens Anchorage International Airport (5000 W International Airport Rd, Anchorage, AK 99502)** and pick up your **rental car at the airport rental center**. If you're relying on public transportation, you take the **People Mover bus route 40 ($2 fare) to downtown Anchorage**. You check in at a **downtown hotel like Hotel Captain Cook (939 W 5th Ave, $250+/night)** or a budget option like Anchorage Downtown Guesthouse ($120+/night).

Start your day with **breakfast at Snow City Café (1034 W 4th Ave, $15–$25 per meal)**, known for **hearty pancakes, smoked salmon eggs benedict, and strong coffee**. Walk to the **Anchorage Museum (625 C St, $20 admission, open 10 AM – 6 PM)** to learn about **Alaska Native culture, Arctic science, and Alaskan history**. Then, head to **Ship Creek (1501 N C St), one of the only places to see salmon swimming in an urban setting**. If it's summer, you'll see locals **fishing right in the city**.

For lunch, you stop at **49th State Brewing (717 W 3rd Ave, $20–$40 per meal)**, where you eat a **reindeer burger with a view of Cook Inlet**. You then **drive or take a rideshare (Uber/Lyft) to Flattop Mountain Trail (Glen Alps Trailhead, 20-min drive from downtown)**. If you want an easy walk, take the **Blueberry Loop Trail**, but if you're up for a challenge, hike the **1.5-mile steep climb to the top of Flattop for sweeping city views**.

For dinner, **Simon & Seafort's (420 L St, $40–$80 per meal) is the go-to spot for fresh seafood like king crab legs and Alaskan halibut**. If you want a budget option, head to **Humpy's Great Alaskan Alehouse (610 W 6th Ave) for fish and chips and local beers**. End the day with a **walk along the Tony Knowles Coastal Trail**, a scenic 11-mile trail right on the water where **moose sightings are common**.

Day 2: Drive to Seward (125 miles, 2.5 hours)

Wake up early and grab coffee at **Black Cup Coffee (341 E Benson Blvd)** before starting the drive south on the **Seward Highway, one of the most scenic roads in the U.S.**. You stop at **Beluga Point (Mile 110 Seward Hwy) to look for beluga whales swimming in Turnagain Arm**. Another quick stop is **Potter Marsh (Mile 117), a great spot to see eagles and waterfowl**.

Around **10 AM, stop in Girdwood (Mile 90)**, a mountain town with an **Alaskan ski-resort feel**. You take the **Alyeska Aerial Tram ($35 round trip, open 10 AM – 6 PM) up to the top for glacier views**. Then, grab lunch at **Jack Sprat (165 Olympic Mountain Loop, $15–$30 per meal), a casual spot with fresh seafood and organic dishes**.

Continue driving south, stopping at the **Alaska Wildlife Conservation Center (Mile 79, $18 entry, open 10 AM – 5 PM)**, where you see **rescued bears, moose, and bison up close**. The last stop before Seward is **Exit Glacier (Mile 3, Herman Leirer Rd), one of the few glaciers you can hike to without a guide**. Walk the **1-mile Edge of the Glacier Trail** for stunning views.

Arriving in **Seward**, you check into **Harbor 360 Hotel (1412 4th Ave, $250+/night) for waterfront views** or a budget lodge like Nauti Otter Inn ($90+/night). Dinner at The Cookery (209 5th Ave, $30–$60 per meal) is a must—try the fresh oysters and seafood chowder.

Day 3: Kenai Fjords National Park – Glacier and Wildlife Boat Tour

After breakfast at **Seasalt Café (1301 4th Ave)**, you take a **Kenai Fjords boat tour (6-8 hours, $180–$250 per person, departs at 8 AM or 11:30 AM)**. This trip takes you past **glaciers crashing into the ocean and offers sightings of whales, sea lions, puffins, and sea otters. Lunch is provided on board**, and you return in the afternoon.

Spend the evening **strolling the small boat harbor** and grabbing dinner at **Ray's Waterfront (1316 4th Ave, $40–$70 per meal), famous for halibut and scallops**.

Day 4: Drive to Homer (170 miles, 4 hours)

After breakfast, you start the **drive to Homer, stopping in Cooper Landing (Mile 50) for a short walk along the turquoise Kenai River**. If you have time, book a **2-hour float trip on the river ($80–$150 per person)**. In **Soldotna (Mile 95)**, grab a quick lunch at The Moose is Loose Bakery (44224 Sterling Hwy, $10–$20 per meal), known for giant cinnamon rolls.

Arriving in **Homer**, you check into **Land's End Resort (4786 Homer Spit Rd, $250+/night)** or budget options like Driftwood Inn ($120+/night). You spend the afternoon exploring the **Homer Spit, a long stretch of land lined with shops and fishing charters. Dinner at Captain Pattie's (4241 Homer Spit Rd, $30–$60 per meal) for fresh halibut.**

Day 5: Homer – Fishing or Bear Viewing

Choose between a **halibut fishing charter ($250 per person) or a bear viewing flight to Katmai ($700+ per person)**. If you stay in town, visit the **Pratt Museum (3779 Bartlett St, $10 entry)** and the **Salty Dawg Saloon**, an iconic bar inside an old lighthouse. **Dinner at The Little Mermaid (4246 Homer Spit Rd) for seafood and wood-fired pizza.**

Day 6: Drive Back North to Girdwood (225 miles, 4.5 hours)

Leaving Homer, you **stop in Ninilchik for photos of the historic Russian Orthodox church**. Lunch in **Cooper Landing at Kingfisher Roadhouse (Mile 47, $15–$40 per meal)**. Arriving in **Girdwood**, check into **Alyeska Resort (1000 Arlberg Ave, $300+/night)** or a budget B&B. Dinner at Seven Glaciers, a fine-dining spot at the top of Alyeska Tram ($75–$150 per person).

Day 7: Return to Anchorage (40 miles, 45 minutes)

Before heading to the airport, **stop at the Alaska Wildlife Conservation Center ($18 per person)** or take one last scenic hike in

Girdwood. Lunch at **Moose's Tooth (3300 Old Seward Hwy, $20–$40 per meal), famous for its reindeer sausage pizza. Drop off your rental car and catch your flight home.**

21.2.2 Inside Passage Adventure

Day 1: Arrive in Juneau and Explore the Capital

You fly into **Juneau International Airport (1873 Shell Simmons Dr, Juneau, AK 99801)** and either pick up a **rental car at the airport or take a taxi ($20 to downtown, 15-minute ride)**. If you're traveling light, you can use **Capital Transit Bus Route 3 ($2 fare, 30-minute ride to downtown)**. You check into a **downtown hotel like Baranof Downtown ($220+/night) or a budget stay like Juneau Hotel ($150+/night)**.

Start with **breakfast at The Rookery Café (111 Seward St, $12–$25 per meal), famous for locally roasted coffee and breakfast burritos**. Walk to the **Alaska State Museum (395 Whittier St, $14 entry, open 9 AM – 5 PM), where you explore exhibits on Indigenous culture, Russian colonial history, and Alaska's natural environment.**

For lunch, **head to Deckhand Dave's (139 S Franklin St, $15–$30 per meal) for the best fish tacos in town**. Then take a **Mount Roberts Tramway ride ($45 round trip, open 9 AM – 9 PM) to see stunning views of the city, followed by a short hike along the Alpine Loop Trail.**

Wrap up your first day with **dinner at Salt (200 Seward St, $35–$70 per meal), where you try fresh seafood like Alaskan king crab legs or halibut.**

Day 2: Mendenhall Glacier and Whale Watching

After breakfast at **Sandpiper Café (429 W Willoughby Ave, $15–$25 per meal)**, take a **shuttle to Mendenhall Glacier Visitor Center ($45 round trip, 30-minute ride, departs from downtown)**. You walk the **Photo Point Trail for the best glacier views or take the 3.5-mile Nugget Falls Trail to see a massive waterfall up close.**

Head back downtown for **lunch at Tracy's King Crab Shack (432

EVERYTHING YOU NEED, NOTHING YOU DON'T

S Franklin St, $40–$80 per meal), where you try award-winning crab bisque and butter-drenched crab legs.

In the afternoon, you **board a whale-watching tour ($150–$180 per person, departs from Auke Bay Harbor, 3–4 hours), where you spot humpback whales, sea lions, and bald eagles**. For dinner, **Twisted Fish Company (550 S Franklin St, $30–$60 per meal)** serves excellent grilled salmon and cocktails.

Day 3: Ferry to Sitka (4.5-hour ride, Alaska Marine Highway System)

You **catch the early morning ferry from Juneau to Sitka ($85 per person, ferry terminal at 6858 Glacier Hwy, check-in at least 1 hour before departure)**. Enjoy the **scenic ride past islands and mountain peaks, with chances to see sea otters and puffins**.

Arriving in Sitka, you check into **Westmark Sitka Hotel (330 Seward St, $200+/night)** or a budget option like Aspen Suites ($160+/night). Lunch at Beak Restaurant (2 Lincoln St, $15–$35 per meal), known for rockfish sandwiches and fresh oysters.

In the afternoon, visit **Sitka National Historical Park (103 Monastery St, free entry), where you walk among towering totem poles and learn about Tlingit and Russian history**. If time allows, explore the **Alaska Raptor Center ($15 entry), where you see bald eagles up close**.

For dinner, **try Ludvig's Bistro (256 Katlian St, $40–$80 per meal)**, a small spot with Mediterranean-inspired seafood dishes.

Day 4: Explore Sitka – Wildlife and Russian Heritage

Breakfast at **Highliner Coffee (327 Seward St, $10–$20 per meal)** before heading to **Fortress of the Bear ($15 entry), a sanctuary where rescued bears roam in a natural environment**. Next, visit **St. Michael's Cathedral (240 Lincoln St, $5 entry), an 1848 Russian Orthodox church**.

For lunch, **The Mean Queen (205 Harbor Dr, $12–$30 per meal)** serves great seafood pizza. Spend the afternoon **kayaking in Sitka**

ALASKA ACTION PLAN

Sound (**$80–$120 per person for a guided tour**) or walking the scenic **Harbor Mountain Trail**.

Dinner at **Halibut Point Crab & Chowder (4513 Halibut Point Rd, $25–$50 per meal) for fresh Dungeness crab**.

Day 5: Ferry to Ketchikan (11-hour overnight ferry ride)

You board the **Alaska Marine Highway System ferry to Ketchikan ($150 per person, departs Sitka in the evening, private cabin option for $100 extra).** You sleep on board as the ferry travels through the Inside Passage.

Day 6: Explore Ketchikan – Totem Poles and Rainforest Walks

Arriving in **Ketchikan in the morning, you check into Cape Fox Lodge (800 Venetia Way, $250+/night) or The Landing Hotel ($180+/night)**.

Breakfast at **Raven's Brew Coffee (1577 Tongass Ave, $5–$15 per meal)** before heading to **Saxman Totem Park ($5 entry, 15-minute bus ride from downtown), where you see the largest collection of standing totem poles in the world**.

For lunch, **The Fish House (5 Creek St, $20–$45 per meal) is a top pick for Alaskan halibut burgers**. Then, explore **Creek Street, a historic boardwalk built over the water, once home to the town's red-light district**.

Afternoon options include **hiking the Rainbird Trail (2-mile round trip, moderate difficulty) or taking a guided boat tour of Misty Fjords National Monument ($220 per person, 4-hour tour)**.

For dinner, **Annabelle's Famous Keg and Chowder House (326 Front St, $30–$60 per meal) is great for king crab legs and Alaskan seafood pasta**.

Day 7: Fly Home from Ketchikan

On your last morning, grab a quick **breakfast at Sweet Mermaids**

(5 Creek St, $10–$25 per meal) before **taking the airport ferry ($6 per person) across the channel to Ketchikan International Airport**.

If you have extra time before your flight, visit **Tongass Historical Museum (629 Dock St, $5 entry) to learn about Ketchikan's logging and fishing history**.

End your trip with memories of glaciers, coastal rainforests, historic towns, and wildlife encounters in the Inside Passage.

CHAPTER TWENTY

FAQ

1. General Questions

Why should I visit Alaska in 2025?

Alaska offers **breathtaking landscapes, abundant wildlife, and unforgettable adventures** in 2025. Whether you want to see **towering glaciers, the northern lights, grizzly bears, or untouched wilderness**, Alaska delivers. The state is perfect for **hiking, wildlife viewing, fishing, and cultural experiences**. The changing climate is making **glaciers and wildlife migrations more dynamic**, meaning now is a great time to experience Alaska's raw beauty.

How do I use this travel guide?

The guide is **structured by cities and regions** so you can easily plan your trip based on where you're going. It includes **key attractions, transportation options, dining recommendations, accommodations, and practical travel tips**. You can **jump to specific chapters** if you're visiting a particular place or follow the **itineraries in Chapter 21** for a ready-made travel plan.

2. Planning Your Trip

What's the best time to visit Alaska?

It depends on what you want to do. **Summer (June–August)** is ideal for **wildlife viewing, hiking, and cruises** with long daylight hours. **Winter (November–March)** is best for **northern lights, dog sledding, and winter sports**. **Spring and fall** offer fewer crowds, cheaper prices, and unique wildlife activity, like bear migrations and birdwatching.

Do I need a passport or visa to visit Alaska?

If you're traveling from **within the U.S., you don't need a passport** but will need a **REAL ID-compliant driver's license or other TSA-approved ID** to fly. If you're coming from **Canada or another country, you need a passport**, and depending on your nationality, a **visa or ESTA (for visa-waiver countries)**.

How much does a trip to Alaska cost?

Alaska can be expensive, but planning helps control costs. **Expect:**
- **Flights:** $300–$800 round trip from the U.S.
- **Lodging:** $100–$400 per night (hotels, lodges, or B&Bs)
- **Food:** $10–$50 per meal (cheaper if you cook or buy from grocery stores)
- **Tours & Activities:** $50–$500+ (depending on the activity, like glacier tours or wildlife excursions)
- **Rental Cars & Transportation:** $50–$150 per day

What should I pack?

Layered clothing is key. **For summer, pack waterproof jackets, hiking shoes, and mosquito repellent. For winter, bring thermal layers, insulated boots, and hand warmers. Year-round essentials include bear spray, a refillable water bottle, a power bank, and a camera.**

3. Transportation in Alaska

What's the best way to get around Alaska?

If you're visiting cities like **Anchorage, Fairbanks, or Juneau**, you can use **public buses, taxis, and walking**. If you want to visit multiple destinations, **rental cars, the Alaska Railroad, and the Alaska Marine Highway ferry system** are the best options. **Flights** are essential for remote areas.

Can I drive in Alaska?

Yes, but roads can be rough in remote areas. **The highways connecting Anchorage, Fairbanks, Denali, and the Kenai Peninsula are paved and well-maintained**. However, if you're driving on **McCarthy Road, Dalton Highway, or Denali Highway**, expect **gravel roads, limited gas stations, and extreme weather conditions**. Always carry **extra fuel, spare tires, and emergency supplies**.

How do I take the Alaska Marine Highway ferry?

The **Alaska Marine Highway System (AMHS) connects coastal towns like Juneau, Sitka, Ketchikan, and Kodiak**. You can **bring a vehicle or travel as a foot passenger**. Book early, especially in summer. **Fares range from $50 to $200 per person, depending on the route**.

4. Wildlife and Safety

Is Alaska safe for travelers?

Yes, but you should **prepare for unpredictable weather, wildlife encounters, and remote conditions**. Always check weather forecasts, inform someone of your travel plans, and carry emergency supplies.
- How do I stay safe around wildlife?
- **Bears:** Make noise while hiking, store food properly, and carry bear spray. Never run from a bear.
- **Moose:** Keep a **safe distance** (at least 50 feet), especially in spring (calving season) and fall (rutting season).
- **Marine life:** Follow guidelines for **safe whale watching and avoid disturbing sea otters, seals, or puffins**.

Can I see the northern lights?

Yes, the **best time is September to March**. The best locations are **Fairbanks, Coldfoot, and Utqiagvik**, where clear skies and low light pollution give you the best chances. **Winter tours with heated cabins** or glass-domed viewing areas** make the experience more comfortable.

5. Destinations & Experiences

What are the top must-visit places in Alaska?

- **Denali National Park:** See **North America's tallest peak, wildlife, and untouched wilderness**.
- **Kenai Fjords National Park: Glaciers, marine life, and boat tours** make it one of the most scenic places.
- **Juneau:** Mendenhall Glacier, whale watching, and historic downtown.
- **Fairbanks:** Best for **northern lights, Chena Hot Springs, and Arctic Circle excursions**.
- **Seward:** A coastal town perfect for **boat tours, hiking, and seafood dining**.
- **Ketchikan:** Known for **totem poles, Misty Fjords National Monument, and salmon fishing**.

What are the best hiking trails in Alaska?

- **Easy:** Exit Glacier Overlook Trail (Seward), Flattop Mountain (Anchorage)
- **Moderate:** Harding Icefield Trail (Seward), Root Glacier Trail (Wrangell-St. Elias)
- **Challenging:** Kesugi Ridge (Denali area), Bonanza Mine Trail (McCarthy)

Where can I go for the best fishing?

- **Homer:** Halibut and salmon charters
- **Kenai River:** Some of the **largest king salmon in the world**
- **Bristol Bay:** Fly fishing paradise, home to the world's largest sockeye salmon runs

6. Practical Tips

Will I have cell service and internet in Alaska?

In major cities like Anchorage, Fairbanks, and Juneau, you'll have good coverage. **In remote areas, expect no signal**—carry a **satellite phone or Garmin InReach if going off-grid**. Many lodges offer **Wi-Fi, but speeds are slow**.

What's the best way to book tours and excursions?

Book in advance, especially for popular activities like **Denali bus tours, glacier hikes, and bear viewing tours**. Many operators require reservations at least 3–6 months ahead for peak season (June–August).

Is tipping expected in Alaska?

Yes, tipping is standard.
- **Restaurants:** 15–20%
- **Tour guides:** $10–$20 per person for day tours
- **Taxi drivers:** 10–15%

What's the best way to budget for an Alaskan trip?

- **Book flights early (3–6 months in advance) for the best prices.**
- **Consider camping, hostels, or vacation rentals instead of hotels.**
- **Use grocery stores instead of eating out every meal.**
- **Take advantage of free attractions like hiking, museums with free days, and scenic drives.**

EVERYTHING YOU NEED, NOTHING YOU DON'T

SOPHIA GLACIAR

CONCLUSION

Alaska is bigger than you imagined, wilder than you expected, and probably nothing like what you saw on social media. You came here looking for something—**adventure, wildlife, open roads, untouched landscapes, small towns, or just a break from the ordinary**—and now you've seen what makes this place so different from anywhere else. The mountains are taller, the glaciers are louder, the animals are bigger, and the distances between places feel endless.

You might have driven **hundreds of miles on the open road**, taken a **ferry through misty fjords**, or flown in a **tiny bush plane over the Arctic tundra**. Maybe you saw a **moose blocking traffic**, watched **bald eagles swoop down for fish**, or stood in front of a **glacier that's been around for thousands of years**. You tasted **fresh salmon straight from the river**, walked through **historic gold rush towns**, or spent the night in a cabin with nothing but the **Northern Lights for company**.

But even after all of that, **you've barely scratched the surface**. No one sees all of Alaska in one trip. It's too big, too wild, too unpredictable. And that's what makes it special. **Every season, every region, every return visit is a new adventure.**

If you came in summer, you haven't seen **the frozen beauty of winter, the dogsled races, or the magic of the Aurora Borealis**. If you explored **Denali and Anchorage**, you still have **Kodiak, the Aleutians, the Arctic, and the Inside Passage waiting for you**. Maybe you didn't try **deep-sea fishing in Homer, kayaking through Kenai Fjords**, or **crossing the Arctic Circle on the Dalton Highway**—but you can next time.

Made in United States
North Haven, CT
06 April 2025

67661385R00143